VISUAL FACTFINDER

NATURAL WORLD

First published in 2004 by Miles Kelly Publishing Ltd
Bardfield Centre, Great Bardfield, Essex, CM7 4SL

Copyright © Miles Kelly Publishing Ltd 2004

This edition printed in 2008

This material also appears in the *1000 Facts* series

4 6 8 10 9 7 5

Editorial Director Belinda Gallagher
Art Director Jo Brewer
Editorial Assistant Bethanie Bourne
Designer Debbie Meekcoms
Design Assistant Louisa Leitao
Indexer Charlotte Marshall
Production Manager Elizabeth Brunwin
Reprographics Anthony Cambray, Mike Coupe, Ian Paulyn

British Library Cataloguing-in-Publication Data
A catalogue record for this book is available from the British Library

ISBN 978-1-84236-380-5

Printed in China

www.mileskelly.net
info@mileskelly.net

www.factsforprojects.com

VISUAL FACTFINDER

NATURAL WORLD

Duncan Brewer John Farndon
Consultants: Jinny Johnson
Steve Parker Peter Riley

Contents

——— ◆ ◆ ◆ ———

Flowers

——— ◆ ◆ ◆ ———

Trees

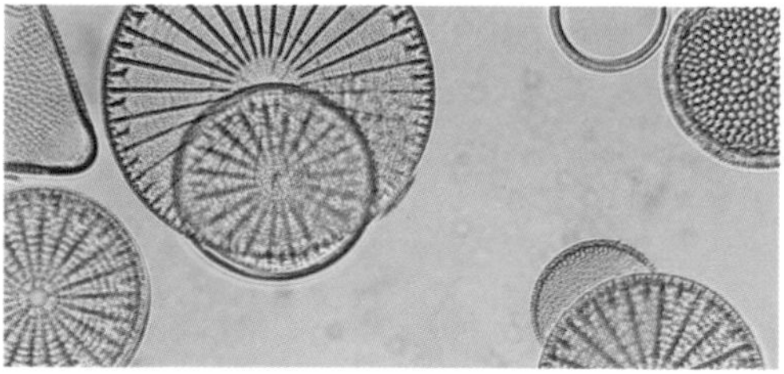

———— ◆ ◆ ◆ ————

Mosses and Fungi

———— ◆ ◆ ◆ ————

Plants and People

— ◆ ◆ ◆ —

How Animals Live

——— ◆ ◆ ◆ ———

Mammals

VISUAL FACTFINDER

NATURAL WORLD

Why are some plants carnivorous?

How do feathers help birds to fly?

Which creature has the biggest eyes?

The answers to these and many other questions can be found
in this amazing book of almost 2500 facts. The book is split
into two parts, each dealing with different aspects of plant
and animal life. The first section takes a close look at the world
of plants. Subjects such as photosynthesis and pollination
are presented alongside information on woodlands,
marine plants and wildflowers.

The second part of the book takes a tour of the animal kingdom.
Hundreds of key facts cover all aspects of animal life including
migration, defence, habitats and reproduction. Throughout,
stunning colour images illustrate the amazing beauty
of the natural world.

Parts of a plant

- **The first plants** to appear on land were simple plants such as liverworts, ferns and horsetails. They grow from tiny cells called spores.

- **Today, most plants** grow not from spores but from seeds. Unlike primitive plants, seed-making plants have stems, leaves and often roots and flowers.

- **The stem of a plant** supports the leaves and flowers. It also carries water, minerals and food up and down between the plant's leaves and roots.

- **A terminal bud** forms the tip of each stem. The plant grows taller here.

- **Lateral buds** grow further back down the stem at places called nodes.

- **Some lateral buds** develop into new branches. Others develop into leaves or flowers.

- **The leaves** are the plant's green surfaces for catching sunlight. They use the sun's energy for joining water with carbon dioxide from the air to make the sugar the plant needs to grow (see photosynthesis).

- **The roots** are the parts of the plant that grow down into soil or water. They anchor the plant in the ground and soak up all the water and minerals it needs to grow.

- **The flowers** are the plant's reproductive organs. In gymnosperms – conifers, cycads and gingkos – the flowers are often small and hidden. In angiosperms (flowering plants) they are usually much more obvious.

> ... FASCINATING FACT ...
> The world's longest plant is the
> rattan vine which can snake
> 150 m through tropical tree tops.

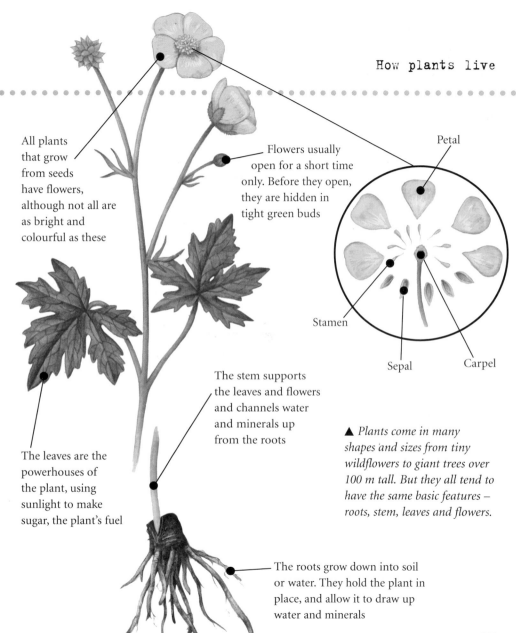

All plants that grow from seeds have flowers, although not all are as bright and colourful as these

Flowers usually open for a short time only. Before they open, they are hidden in tight green buds

Petal

Stamen

Sepal

Carpel

The stem supports the leaves and flowers and channels water and minerals up from the roots

The leaves are the powerhouses of the plant, using sunlight to make sugar, the plant's fuel

▲ Plants come in many shapes and sizes from tiny wildflowers to giant trees over 100 m tall. But they all tend to have the same basic features – roots, stem, leaves and flowers.

The roots grow down into soil or water. They hold the plant in place, and allow it to draw up water and minerals

15

Roots

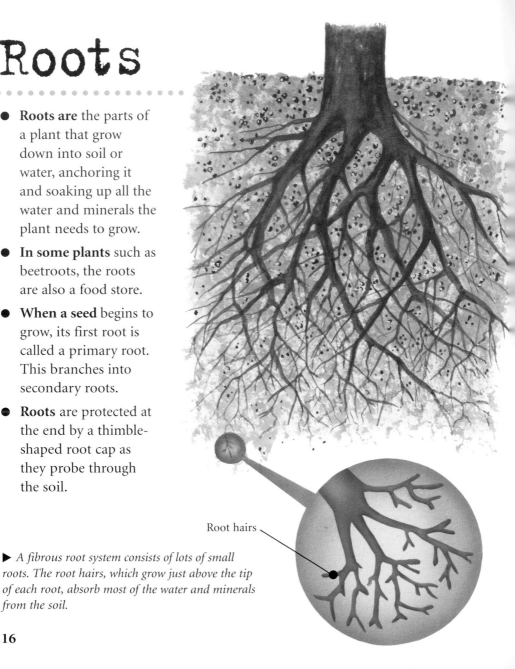

- **Roots are** the parts of a plant that grow down into soil or water, anchoring it and soaking up all the water and minerals the plant needs to grow.

- **In some plants** such as beetroots, the roots are also a food store.

- **When a seed** begins to grow, its first root is called a primary root. This branches into secondary roots.

- **Roots** are protected at the end by a thimble-shaped root cap as they probe through the soil.

Root hairs

▶ *A fibrous root system consists of lots of small roots. The root hairs, which grow just above the tip of each root, absorb most of the water and minerals from the soil.*

16

- **On every root** there are tiny hairs that help it to take up water and minerals.

- **Some plants,** such as carrots, have a single large root, called a taproot, with just a few fine roots branching off.

- **Some plants,** such as grass, have lots of small roots, called fibrous roots, branching off in all directions.

- **Some kinds of orchid** that live on trees have 'aerial' roots that cling to the branches.

- **Mistletoe** has roots that penetrate its host tree.

▲ *The fleshy root of the beetroot is delicious when boiled or pickled.*

...FASCINATING FACT...
The roots of the South African wild fig tree can grow 120 m down into the ground.

17

Plants and water

- **Plants cannot survive** without water. If they are deprived of water, most plants will wilt and die very quickly – although some desert plants manage to get by on very little.

- **Nearly all plants** are almost 70% water, and some algae are 98% water.

- **In plants,** water fills up the tiny cells from which they are made and keeps them rigid, in the same way as air in a balloon.

- **For a plant**, water also serves the same function as blood in the human body. It carries dissolved gases, minerals and nutrients to where they are needed.

- **Some water** oozes from cell to cell through the cell walls in a process called osmosis.

◀ *If a plant isn't watered enough, its leaves will soon start wilting and losing colour. Eventually the leaves will drop off completely and the plant will die.*

- **Some water** is piped through tubes called xylem. These are the fine veins that you can often see on leaves.

- **Water in xylem** is called sap and contains many dissolved substances besides water.

- **Plants lose water** by transpiration. This is evaporation through the leaf pores or stomata.

- **As water evaporates** through the stomata, water is drawn up to replace it through the xylem.

- **If there is too little** water coming up from the roots through the xylem, then the cells collapse and the plant wilts.

▶ *Plants need regular watering to keep them fresh and healthy.*

Epiphytes

- **Epiphytes** are plants that mostly grow above the ground in tropical rainforests, high up on tree branches.

- **Epiphytes** are often known as air plants because they seem to live purely on air, being attached neither to the ground nor to any obvious source of nutrients.

- **Epiphytes** get their water and minerals from rain water, and from debris growing on the branch.

- **Various** orchids, ferns and bromeliads are epiphytes in tropical forests.

- **There are also epiphytes** found in cooler places, including lichens, mosses, liverworts and algae.

- **Pineapples** belong to a big family of plants called the bromeliad family. At least half of them are epiphytes.

- **The pineapple fruit** is the most well-known bromeliad.

▶ *The pineapple plant, a bromeliad epiphyte, grows on the ground and takes its food from the air or from decaying plant matter near its roots.*

▲ *Orchids, such as this cattleya orchid, are amongst the most common epiphytes. They survive best by clinging on to large branches, where their roots can more easily absorb the water and minerals from the tree.*

- **All but one bromeliad** come from America, but they live in a huge range of habitats, living on cacti in deserts to moist forests high up in the mountains.

- **The smallest bromeliads** are moss-like *Tillandsia bryoides*, just a few centimetres long.

- **The biggest bromeliad** is *Puya raimondii*, with a stem up to 4 m long and a flower over 4 m tall.

21

Leaves

- **Leaves** are a plant's powerhouse, using sunlight to join water and carbon dioxide to make sugar, the plant's fuel.
- **Leaves are** broad and flat to catch maximum sunlight.
- **Leaves** are joined to the stem by a stalk called a petiole.
- **The flat part** of the leaf is called the blade.
- **The leaf blade** is like a sandwich with two layers of cells holding a thick filling of green cells.

▲ *If you hold a leaf blade up to the light, you can clearly see the pattern of its veins.*

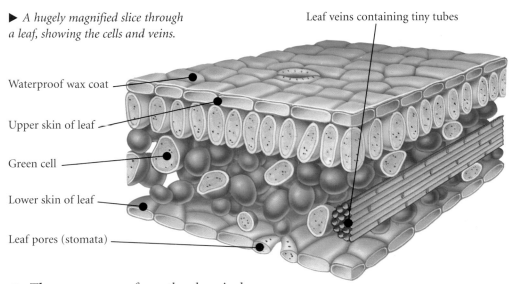

▶ *A hugely magnified slice through a leaf, showing the cells and veins.*

Leaf veins containing tiny tubes

Waterproof wax coat

Upper skin of leaf

Green cell

Lower skin of leaf

Leaf pores (stomata)

- **The green** comes from the chemical chlorophyll. It is this that catches sunlight to make sugar in photosynthesis.

- **Chlorophyll** is held in tiny bags in each cell called chloroplasts.

- **A network** of branching veins (tubes) supplies the leaf with water. It also transports the sugar made there to the rest of the plant.

- **Air containing** carbon dioxide is drawn into the leaf through pores on the underside called stomata. Stomata also let out water in a process called transpiration.

- **To cut down water loss** in dry places, leaves may be rolled-up, long and needle-like, or covered in hairs or wax. Climbing plants, such as peas, have leaf tips that coil into stalks called tendrils to help the plant cling.

Photosynthesis

- **Plants use** sunlight to chemically join carbon dioxide gas from the air with water to make sugary food. The process is called photosynthesis.

- **Photosynthesis** occurs in leaves in two special kinds of cell: palisade and spongy cells.

- **Inside the palisade** and spongy cells are tiny packages called chloroplasts. A chloroplast is like a little bag with a double skin or membrane. Each is filled with a jelly-like substance called the stroma in which float various structures, such as lamellae. The jelly contains a chemical called chlorophyll which makes leaves green.

- **The leaf** draws in air containing the gas carbon dioxide through pores called stomata. It also draws water up from the ground through the stem and veins.

- **When the sun** is shining, the chlorophyll soaks up its energy and uses it to split water into hydrogen and oxygen. The hydrogen released from the water combines with the carbon dioxide to make sugar; the oxygen goes out through the stomata.

- **Sugar is transported** around the plant to where it is needed. Some sugar is burned up at once, leaving behind carbon dioxide and water. This process is called respiration.

- **Some sugar is combined** into large molecules called starches, which are easy for the plant to store. The plant breaks these starches down into sugars again whenever they are needed as fuel.

- **Starch** from plants is the main nutrient we get when we eat food such as bread, rice and potatoes. When we eat fruits, cakes or anything else sweet, the sweetness comes from sugar made by photosynthesis.

- **Together** all the world's plants produce about 150 billion tonnes of sugar each year by photosynthesis.

The leaves take in carbon dioxide
from the air for photosynthesis
and release oxygen

▶ *Every green plant is a
remarkable chemical
factory, taking in energy
from the sun and using it
to split water into
hydrogen and oxygen. It
then combines the
hydrogen with carbon
dioxide from the air to
make sugar, the fuel the
plant needs to grow.*

The minerals are
carried up
through the
plant dissolved
in the water

The plant takes
up water and
minerals from
the soil through
the roots

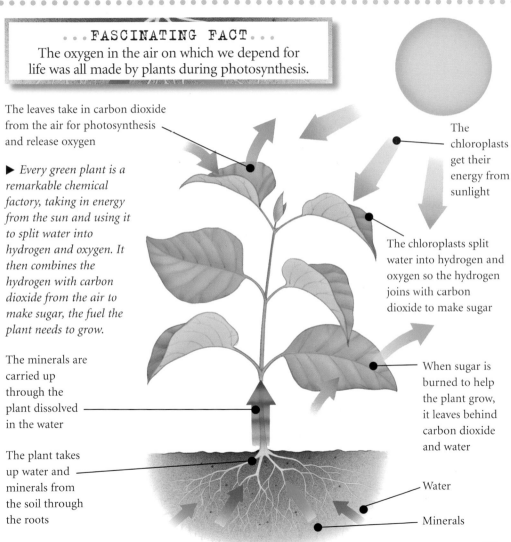

The
chloroplasts
get their
energy from
sunlight

The chloroplasts split
water into hydrogen and
oxygen so the hydrogen
joins with carbon
dioxide to make sugar

When sugar is
burned to help
the plant grow,
it leaves behind
carbon dioxide
and water

Water

Minerals

25

Development of a flower

- **Flowers have both** male parts, called stamens, and female parts, called carpels. Seeds for new plants are made when pollen from the stamens meets the flower's eggs inside the carpels.

- **The carpel** contains the ovaries, where the flower's eggs are made. It is typically a short thick stalk in the centre of the flower.

- **A flower** may have just one carpel or several joined together. When together, they are called the pistil.

- **The stamens** make pollen. Typically they are spindly stalks surrounding the carpels.

▲ *Flowers like this orchid have developed vivid colours to attract pollinating insects.*

- **Pollen is made** in the anthers which are found on top of the stamens.

- **Pollen** is trapped on the top of the ovary by sticky stigma.

- **Pollen** is carried down to the ovary from the stigma via a structure called the style. In the ovary it meets the eggs and fertilizes them to create seeds.

- **Before the flower opens,** the bud is enclosed in a tight green ball called the calyx. This is made up of tiny green flaps called sepals.

- **The colourful part of the flower** is made from groups of petals. The petals make up what is called the corolla. Together the calyx and the corolla comprise the whole flower head, which is known as the perianth. If petals and sepals are the same colour, they are said to be tepals.

3. The sepals open
wider and the petals
grow outwards and
backwards to create
the flower's
beautiful corolla

◄ *At the right time of year,*
buds begin to open to reveal
flowers' blooms so that the
reproductive process can
begin. Some flowers last just a
day or so. Others stay
blooming for months on end
before the eggs are fertilized,
and grow into seeds.

1. The fully
formed flower is
packed away
inside a bud.
Green flaps called
sepals wrap
tightly round it

2. When the
weather is
warm enough,
the bud begins to
open. The sepals curl
back to reveal the
colourful petals

4. The flower
opens fully to
reveal its bright
array of pollen
sacs or anthers

27

Flower facts

- **The world's tallest** flower is the 2.5 m *titan arum* which grows in the tropical jungles of Sumatra.

- **The *titan arum*** is shaped so that flies are trapped in a chamber at the bottom.

- **The world's biggest flower** is rafflesia, which grows in the jungles of Borneo and Sumatra, Indonesia. It is 1 m in diameter and weighs up to 11 kg.

- **Rafflesia** is a parasite and has no leaves, root or stems.

- **Rafflesia and the *titan arum*** both smell like rotting meat in order to attract the insects that   pollinate them.

- **The world's smallest flower** is the Wolffia duckweed of Australia. This is a floating water plant less than 0.6 mm across. It can only be seen clearly when viewed under a magnifying glass.

◀ *The Indonesian name for the* titan arum *is 'Bunga Bangkai', meaning 'corpse flower', due to its repulsive stench.*

- **The biggest flowerhead** is the *puya raimondii* bromeliad of Bolivia which can be up to 2.5 m across and 10 m tall and have 8000 individual blooms.

- **The *Puya raimondii*** takes 150 years to grow its first flower, then dies.

- **Two Australian orchids** actually bloom underground. No-one quite knows how they pollinate.

- **Stapelia flowers** not only smell like rotting meat to attract the flies that pollinate them – they look like it too (all pinky-brown and wrinkled).

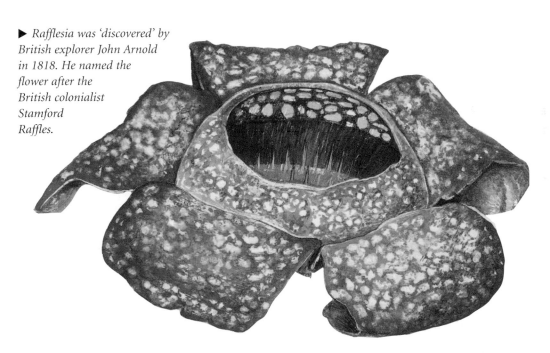

▶ *Rafflesia was 'discovered' by British explorer John Arnold in 1818. He named the flower after the British colonialist Stamford Raffles.*

Pollination

- **For seeds** to develop, pollen from a flower's male anther must get to a female stigma.

- **Some flowers are** self-pollinating and the pollen moves from an anther to a stigma on the same plant.

- **In cross-pollinating** flowers, the pollen from the anthers must be carried to a stigma on a different plant of the same kind.

- **Some pollen** is carried by the wind.

- **Most pollen** is carried on the bodies of insects such as bees or by birds or bats that visit the flower.

◀ *Butterflies, such as this Monarch, feed mainly on nectar and other plant juices, helping plant pollination in the process.*

▶ *Many flowers rely on attracting bees to carry their pollen.*

- **Insect-pollinated flowers** are often brightly coloured and sweet-smelling to attract bees and butterflies.

- **Bees and butterflies** are also drawn by the flower's sweet juice or nectar. As they sip the nectar, they may brush pollen on to the stigma, or take some on their bodies from the anthers to the stigma of other flowers.

- **Bees and butterflies** are drawn to blue, yellow and pink flowers. White flowers draw night-flying moths.

- **Many flowers** have honey guides – markings to guide the bees in. These are often invisible to us and can only be seen in ultraviolet light, which bees and some other insects can see.

- **The cuckoopint** smells like cow-dung to attract the flies that carry its pollen.

Fruit

- **Scientists** say a fruit is the ovary of a plant after the eggs are pollinated and grow into seeds. Corn grains, cucumbers, bean pods and acorns are fruit as well as apples and so on.

- **Some fruits,** such as oranges, are soft and juicy. The hard pips are the seeds.

- **With some fruits,** such as hazelnuts and almonds, the flesh turns to a hard dry shell. These are known as nuts.

- **Fleshy fruits** are either berries like oranges which are all flesh, aggregate fruits like blackberries which are made from lots of berries from a single flower, or multiple fruits like pineapples which are single fruits made from an entire multiple flowerhead.

- **Legumes** such as peas and beans are soft, dry fruits held in a case known as a pod.

- **Berries** and other juicy fruits are called 'true fruits' because they are made from the ovary of the flower alone.

▶ *Almonds grow in a thin, smooth shell. The almond tree produces two different kinds of fruit: sweet, which is edible, and bitter, which is not.*

▼ *There are three kinds of cherries – sweet, sour and 'dukes', which are a sweet-sour cross. We eat mainly sweet cherries like these.*

- **Apples and pears** are called 'false fruits' because they include parts other than the flower's ovary.

- **In an apple** only the core is the ovary.

- **Drupes** are fruit like plums, mangoes and cherries with no pips but just a hard stone in the centre containing the seeds. Aggregate fruits like raspberries are clusters of drupes.

- **Walnuts and dogwood** are actually drupes like cherries.

Spores and seeds

◄ *The giant redwood grows in California and is one of the tallest trees in the world. It grows from a tiny seed to over 100 m tall.*

◀ *Sycamore trees grow from their tiny winged seeds (left). Mushrooms (below right) grow from spores.*

● **Seed plants** are plants that grow from seeds of varying size and shape.

● **Seeds** have a tiny baby plant inside called an embryo from which the plant grows plus a supply of stored food and a protective coating.

● **Spores contain** special cells which grow into new organisms. Green plants like ferns and mosses and fungi such as mushrooms all produce spores.

● **All 250,000 flowering plants** produce 'enclosed' seeds. These are seeds that grow inside sacs called ovaries, which turn into a fruit around the seed.

● **The 800 or so** conifers, cycads and gingkos produce 'naked' seeds, which means there is no fruit around them.

● **Seeds** only develop when a plant is fertilized by pollen.

● **The largest seeds** are those of the double coconut or coco-de-mer of the Seychelles, which can sometimes weigh up to 20 kg.

● **30,000 orchid seeds** weigh barely 1 gm.

● **The world's biggest tree,** the giant redwood, grows from tiny seeds that are less than 2 mm long.

● **Coconut trees** produce only a few big seeds; orchids produce millions, but only a few grow into plants.

Seed dispersal

◄ *Milkweeds have large seed pods which burst open to release their seeds.*

- **After maturing,** seeds go into a state called dormancy. While they are dormant the seeds are scattered and dispersed.

- **Some scattered seeds** fall on barren ground and never grow into plants. Only those seeds that fall in suitable places will begin to grow.

- **Some seeds** are light enough to be blown by the wind. The feathery seed cases of some grasses are so light they can be blown several kilometres.

◀ *Sycamore seeds have wings to help them spin away on the wind.*

▶ *Dandelion seeds have feathery tufts that act like parachutes, whirling them away through the air as they drop to the ground.*

- **Many seeds and fruits** have wings to help them whirl through the air. Maple fruits have wings. So too do the seeds of ashes, elms and sycamores.

- **Seeds** like dandelions, cottonwoods and willows have fluffy coverings, so they drift easily on the wind.

- **Some seeds** are carried by water. Coconut seeds can float on the sea for thousands of kilometres.

- **Many fruits and seeds** are dispersed by animals.

- **Some fruits** are eaten by birds and other animals. The seeds are not digested but passed out in the animal's body waste.

- **Some seeds** stick to animal fur. They have burrs or tiny barbs that hook on to the fur, or even a sticky coating.

- **Some fruits,** like geraniums and lupins, simply explode, showering seeds in all directions.

Growing from seed

- **When seeds mature,** they contain the germ or embryo of a new plant and the food needed to grow it.

- **The seed lies dormant** (inactive) until conditions are right for it to germinate (grow into a plant) – perhaps when the weather begins to warm up in spring.

- **Poppy seeds** can lie buried in soil for years until brought to the surface by ploughing, allowing them to grow.

- **Scientists once grew** plants from lotus seeds that were 10,000 years old.

- **A seed needs** water and warmth to germinate.

- **When a seed germinates,** a root (or radicle) grows down from it and a green shoot (or plumule) grows up.

- **The first leaves** to come up are the seed-leaves or cotyledons, of which there can be one or two. The cotyledons are food stores.

▶ *This illustration shows some of the stages of germination, as a plant grows from a seed – here a bean seed.*

1. The seed lies dormant until conditions are right

2. The seed sends a root down and a shoot up

- **Only certain parts** of a plant, called meristems, can grow. These are usually the tips of shoots and roots.

- **Because** a plant grows at the tips, shoots and roots mainly get longer rather than fatter. This is called primary growth.

- **Later in life** a plant may grow thicker or branch out.

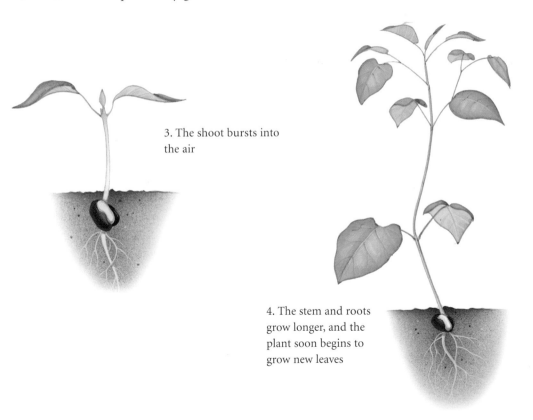

3. The shoot bursts into the air

4. The stem and roots grow longer, and the plant soon begins to grow new leaves

Annuals and biennials

- **Annuals** are plants that grow from seed, flower, disperse their seeds and die in a single season.

- **Some annuals' seeds** lie dormant in the ground before conditions are right for germination.

- **With an annual,** producing flowers, fruits and seeds exhausts the plant's food reserves, so once the seeds are dispersed the green parts of the plant die.

- **Many crops** are annuals, including peas and beans, squashes, and cereals such as maize and wheat.

- **Annual flowers** include petunias, lobelias, buttercups and delphiniums.

▶ *Lobelia, an annual flower, was once used by the Native Americans as the medicine 'Indian bacco'.*

▲ *Foxgloves are typical biennials, flowering in their second summer, then dying back.*

- **Biennials** live for two years.

- **In the first year** the young plant grows a ring of leaves and builds up an underground food store such as a bulb or taproot like beetroots and carrots. The food store sustains the plant through the winter.

- **In the second year** the plant sends up a stem in spring. It flowers in summer.

- **Many vegetables** are biennials, including beetroot, carrots and turnips.

- **Biennial flowers** include wallflowers, carnations, sweet williams and evening primroses.

Perennial flowers

▲ *Chrysanthemums are among the most popular perennials.*

- **Garden perennials** are flowers that live for at least three years.
- **Perennials** may not bloom in the first year, but after that they will bloom every year.
- **Since they bloom** for many years, perennials do not need to produce as many seeds to survive.
- **Some perennials** are herbaceous – that is, they have soft stems. The stems wither at the end of each summer and new stems grow next spring.
- **Woody perennials** have woody stems. Their stems don't wither, but most shed their leaves in autumn.

- **Perennials** from temperate (cool) regions, like asters, irises, lupins, wallflowers, peonies and primroses, need a cold winter to encourage new buds to grow in spring.

- **Tropical perennials,** such as African violets, begonias and gloxinias, cannot survive winters outdoors in temperate climates.

- **Most perennials** spread by sending out shoots from their roots which develop into new stems.

- **Some perennials,** such as columbines and delphiniums, last for only three or four years.

- **Gardeners** make more perennials by taking cuttings – that is, pieces cut from stems or roots.

▶ *Polyanthus are a cross between two perennials, the primrose and cowslip.*

Bulbs and suckers

- **Annuals and biennials** only grow once, from a seed. Many perennials die back and grow again and again from parts of the root or stem. This is called vegetative propagation.

- **Plants such as lupins** grow on the base of an old stem. As the plant ages, the stem widens and the centre dies, leaving a ring of separate plants around the outside.

- **Plants such as irises** sprout from thick stems called rhizomes. These rhizomes grow sideways under the ground.

- **If the end** of a rhizome swells up it forms a lump called a tuber.

- **Potatoes** are the tubers of the potato plant.

▲ *Garlic bulbs are made up of small segments called cloves. According to folklore, garlic is effective at keeping vampires away.*

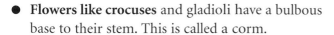

- **Flowers like crocuses** and gladioli have a bulbous base to their stem. This is called a corm.

- **Bulbs like those** of tulips, daffodils and onions look like corms, but they are actually made of leaf parts rather than the stem. This is why they have layers.

- **Garlic bulbs** are separated into four or five segments called cloves.

- **In winter,** rhizomes, tubers, corms and bulbs act as food stores, so that in spring they are able to provide the energy to grow new leaves.

- **Plants can also** propagate (grow new plants) by sending out long stems, called runners, that creep over the ground or suckers, which grow under the ground.

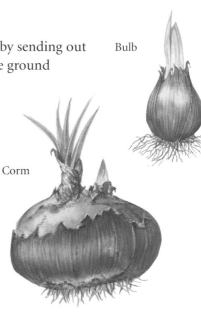

Tuber

Bulb

Corm

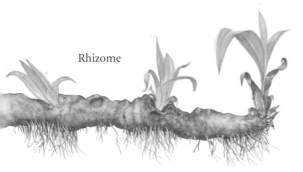

Rhizome

45

Poisonous plants

- **There are thousands** of plants around the world that are poisonous at least in parts.

- **Some parts** of edible plants are poisonous, such as potato leaves and apricot and cherry stones.

- **Some plants** are toxic to eat; some toxic to touch; some create allergic reactions through the air with their pollen.

- **The rosary pea** has pretty red and black seeds often used to make bracelets. But eating just one seed can kill a man.

- **Oleanders** are so poisonous that people have been killed by eating meat roasted on an oleander stick.

▲ *Poison ivy contains an oil that irritates the skin. People can be poisoned simply by walking barefoot through the leaves.*

◄ *The white berries of the mistletoe are poisonous to people. In Germanic mythology, an arrow of mistletoe killed Balder, son of the goddess Frigg.*

46

- **Poison ivy** inflames the skin badly if touched.

- **Hemlock** belongs to the parsley family but is highly poisonous. It was said to be the plant used to kill the Ancient Greek philosopher Socrates.

- **Birthwort** is a poisonous vine, but its name comes from its use in the past to help women through childbirth.

- **Crowfoots,** such as aconite and hellebore, and spurges, such as castor-oil and croton, are all poisonous plants.

- **Many useful drugs** are poisons extracted from plants and given in small doses, including digitalis from foxgloves, morphine from poppies, atropine from deadly nightshade, quinine, aconite, strychnine and cocaine.

◀ *The leaves of certain foxgloves contain a powerful poison used to make the drug* digitalis, *which treats heart disease.*

Carnivorous plants

- **Plants that trap** insects for food are called carnivorous plants. They live in places where they cannot get enough nitrogen from the soil and so the insects provide the nitrogen.

- **There are 550 species** living in places from the high peaks of New Zealand to the swamps of Carolina.

  - **The butterwort** gets its name because its leaves ooze drops that make them glisten like butter. These drops contains the plant's digestive juices.

    - **The sundew** can tell the difference between flesh and other substances and only reacts to flesh.

      - **The sundew's** leaves are covered in tentacles that ooze a sticky substance called mucilage.

      - **The sundew** wraps up its victims in its tentacles and suffocates them in slime in under ten seconds.

    - **A Venus fly-trap's** trap will only shut if touched at least twice in 20 seconds.

      - **Insects** are lured on to many carnivorous plants by sweet-tasting nectar – or the smell of rotting meat.

      - **The juice** of a pitcher plant will dissolve a chunk of steak to nothing in a few days.

      - **The bladders** of bladderworts were once thought to be air sacs to keep the plant afloat. In fact, they are tiny traps for water insects.

◄ Pitchers hang on long tendrils that grow high into the branches of tropical rainforests. Some pitchers are tiny and can trap nothing bigger than an ant. Those of the Nepenthes rajah are big enough to hold a rat.

▶ *Insects are lured into the jaw-like leaf trap of the Venus fly-trap with nectar. Once the insect lands, the jaws clamp shut on the victim in a fraction of a second. At once the plant secretes juices that drown, then dissolve, the insect.*

The fly touches hairs that send an electrical signal to cells on the side of the trap

When triggered, cells on the outside of the trap expand instantly and cells on the inside contract, pulling the trap shut

▼ *When an insect lands on the sticky tentacles of a sundew, it struggles to free itself, but this struggling stimulates the tentacles to tighten their grip. Soon the tentacles exude a digestive juice that dissolves the victim.*

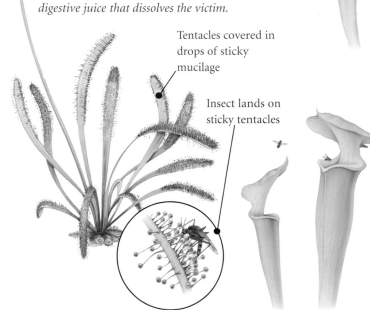

Tentacles covered in drops of sticky mucilage

Insect lands on sticky tentacles

◀ *Like the Venus fly-trap, the Sarracenia is a native of North America. But instead of actively capturing its prey, it provides a deep tube for them to fall into. Insects drawn to the nectar round its rim slide in and are unable to climb out.*

49

Symbiosis

▲ *Leaf-cutter ants line their nests with leaves so that fungi will grow there. They then eat the fungi.*

- **Living things** that feed off other living things are called parasites.

- **Living things** that depend on each other to live are called symbiotic.

- **Many tropical rainforest trees** have a symbiotic relationship with fungi on their roots. The fungi get energy from the trees and in return give the trees phosphorus and other nutrients.

- **A phyte is a plant** that grows on another plant.

- **Epiphytes** are plants that grow high up on other plants, especially in tropical rainforests (see epiphytes).

...FASCINATING FACT...
Many plants rely on bees and butterflies to
spread their pollen. In return, they give nectar.

- **Saprophytes** are plants and fungi that depend on decomposing material, not sunlight, for sustenance.

- **Most orchids** are saprophytic as seedlings.

- **Corsiaceae orchids** of New Guinea, Australia and Chile are saprophytic all their lives.

- **Various ants,** such as leaf-cutter and harvester ants in tropical forests, line their nests with leaves which they cut up. The leaves provide food for fungi which, in turn, provide food for the ants.

51

Parasites

▲ *The parasitic fig tree steals the water supply from the roots of its host tree.*

- **Parasitic plants** are plants that get their food not by using sunlight but from other plants, at the others' expense.

- **In the gloom of** tropical rainforests, where sunlight cannot penetrate, there are many parasitic plants growing on the trees.

- **Lianas** save themselves energy growing a trunk by climbing up other trees, clinging on with little hooks.

- **Rafflesia,** the world's biggest flower, is a parasite that feeds on the roots of the liana.

▶ *Mistletoe, with its distinctive white berries, grows on apple and poplar trees in Eurasia and oaks in America.*

- **Figs** begin growing from seeds left high on branches by birds or fruit bats.

- **Fig roots** grow down to the ground around the roots of the tree, strangling it by taking its water supply. The tree then dies away, leaving the roots of the fig as a hollow 'trunk'.

- **Mistletoes** are semi-parasitic plants that wind round trees. They draw some of their food from the tree and some from sunlight with their own leaves.

- *Viscum album* mistletoe was held sacred by Druids 2000 years ago.

- **The druid** belief in the magic power of mistletoe survives in the tradition of kissing under the mistletoe at Christmas.

- **Broomrapes** grow on sugarcane roots; witchweeds grow on maize and rice roots.

53

Arctic plants

▲ *The dwarf willowherb rarely grows more than 30 cm high – any higher and it will quickly be killed by the icy cold Arctic wind.*

● **The Arctic circle** is icy cold and dark for nine months of the year, but for a few months in summer it is daylight almost all the time.

● **Over 900 species** of plants cope with the Arctic climate.

● **Full-size trees** are rare in the Arctic; but grasses and sedges, mosses and lichens are common.

- **Willow trees** grow in the Arctic, but because of the cold and fierce wind, they grow less than 10 cm tall, spreading out along the ground instead.

- **Many Arctic** plants are evergreen so they are ready to make the most of the brief summer.

- **Many small** flowers are specially adapted to survive Arctic conditions, such as saxifrages, avens, stonecrops, snowbells and willowherbs.

- **The Arctic poppy** is the flower that blooms nearest the North Pole.

- **Butterflies and bees** are rare in the Arctic, so many plants, like mustard, rely on the wind for pollination.

- **The soil is so poor** in the Arctic that seeds make the most of any animal corpse, such as that of a musk ox. Arctic flowers often spring up inside skulls and near bones.

- **Some plants** have dark leaves and stems to soak up the sun's warmth quickly and so melt the snow.

◀ *Some seeds, like those of the arctic lupin, can lie dormant for hundreds of years before they start to grow.*

Tundra

- **Tundras** are regions so cold and with so little rain that tall trees cannot grow.

- **Tundras** are typically covered in snow for at least half the year. Even in summer the soil 1 m or so below the ground may be permanently frozen.

- **The frozen ground** stops water draining away and makes tundras marshy and damp.

- **Winter temperatures** in the tundra can drop to -40°C. Even summer temperatures rarely reach higher than 12°C on average.

- **Mosses and lichens,** grasses and sedges, heathers and low shrubs grow in tundra. Trees only grow in stunted forms such as dwarf willows and ash trees.

- **In spring** tundra plants grow quickly and bright wildflowers spread across the ground.

- **Arctic tundras** occur in places like Siberia and Canada.

- **Alpine tundras** occur high on mountains everywhere.

- **Arctic flowers** include saxifrages, Arctic poppies, fireweeds, cinquefoil, louseworts and stonecrops.

- **Alpine flowers** are often the same as Arctic flowers. They include mountain avens, gentians, saxifrages and snowbells.

▶ *In spring the tundra bursts into glorious colour as flowers bloom to take advantage of the brief warm weather.*

56

Boreal forest

▼ *Boreal forests cover 17% of the Earth's land area. For nine months of the year they are cold and dark, but they spring to life in the three-month summer.*

- **Forests in cool regions** bordering on the Arctic circle, such as the north of Asia, northern Europe and North America, are called boreal forests. The word boreal means 'northern'.

- **Winters** in boreal regions are long and cold. Days are short and snow lies permanently on the ground.

- **In Russia and Siberia** boreal forest is called taiga, which is a Russian word meaning 'little sticks'.

- **Boreal forests** are mostly evergreen conifers such as pine – especially Scots pine – spruce, larch and fir.

- **In Europe** boreal forests include Norway spruce and Sukaczev larch. In Siberia, there are trees such as Siberian larch and fir, chosenia and Siberian stone pine.

- **North American** forests include balsam firs, black spruces, jack pines and lodgepole pines.

- **Boreal forest floors** are covered with carpets of needles. Twinflowers, calypso orchids, lingonberries, baneberries, and coral roots are among the few plants that will grow.

- **Boreal forest trees** are good at recovering after fire. Indeed jack pine and black spruce cones only open to release their seeds after a fire.

- **The Black Dragon Fire** of 1987 in the boreal forests of China and Russia was the biggest fire in history.

. . . FASCINATING FACT . . .
Half the ground under conifers is covered
in moss and lichen.

59

Broad-leaved woodlands

- **Forests** of broad-leaved, deciduous trees grow in temperate regions where there are warm, wet summers and cold winters – in places like North America, western Europe and eastern Asia.

- **Broad-leaved deciduous** woods grow where temperatures average above 10°C for over six months a year, and the average annual rainfall is over 400 mm.

- **If there are** 100 to 200 days a year warm enough for growth, the main trees in broad-leaved deciduous forests are oaks, elms, birches, maples, beeches, aspens, chestnuts and lindens (basswood).

- **In the tropics** where there is plenty of rainfall, broad-leaved evergreens form tropical rainforests.

- **In moist western Europe,** beech trees dominate woods on well-drained, shallow soils, especially chalkland; oak trees prefer deep clay soils. Alders grow in waterlogged places.

- **In drier eastern Europe,** beeches are replaced by durmast oak and hornbeam and in Russia by lindens.

▲ *Broad-leaved trees form shady paths in summer but are light in winter when the trees are bare.*

- **In American woods,** beech and linden are rarer than in Europe, but oaks, hickories and maples are more common.

- **In the Appalachians** buckeye and tulip trees dominate.

- **There is a wide range** of shrubs under the trees including dogwood, holly, magnolia, as well as woodland flowers.

▼ *Plenty of light can filter down through deciduous trees so that all kinds of bushes and flowers grow in the woods, often blooming in spring while the leaves are still thin.*

FASCINATING FACT
Very few woods in Europe are entirely natural; most are 'secondary' woods, growing on land once cleared for farms.

Tropical rainforest

- **Rainforests** are warm and wet, with over 2000 mm of rain a year and average temperatures over 20°C. This is why they are the world's richest plant habitats.

- **Flowering plants** (angiosperms) originated in tropical rainforests. Eleven of the 13 oldest families live here.

- **Most rainforest trees** are broad-leaved and evergreen.

- **Trees** of the Amazon rainforest include rosewood, Brazil nut and rubber, plus myrtle, laurel and palms. Trees in the African rainforest include mahogany, ebony, limba, wenge, agba, iroko and sapele.

- **Many rainforest plants** have big, bright flowers to attract birds and insects in the gloom. Flowers pollinated by birds are often red, those by night-flying moths white or pink and those by day-flying insects yellow or orange.

- **The gloom** means many plants need big seeds to store enough food while they grow. So they grow fragrant fruits that attract animals to eat them and spread the seed in their body waste. Fruit bats are drawn to mangoes. Orang-utans eat durians.

- **Many trees** grow flowers on their trunks to make them easy for animals to reach. This is called cauliflory.

- **Rainforest trees** are covered with epiphytes – plants whose roots never reach the soil but take water from the air.

- **Many plants are parasitic,** which means they feed on other plants. Parasites include mistletoes and rafflesia (see parasites).

> **...FASCINATING FACT...**
> One 23-hectare area of Malaysian rainforest has 375 species of tree with trunks thicker than 91 cm.

▶ *Most tropical rainforests have several layers. Towering above the main forest are isolated emergent trees up to 60 m tall. Below these, 30–50 m above the ground, is a dense canopy of leaves and branches at the top of tall, straight trees. In the gloom beneath is the understorey where young emergents, small conical trees and a huge range of shrubs grow. Clinging lianas wind their way up through the trees and epiphytes grow high on tree branches and trunks where they are able to reach daylight.*

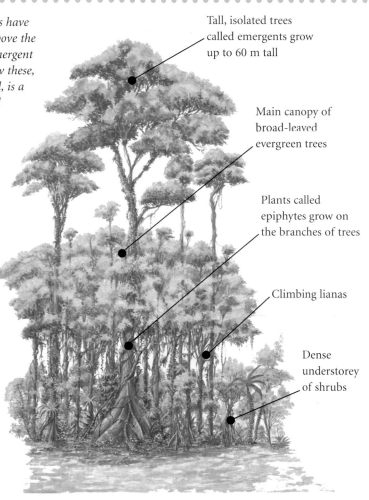

Tall, isolated trees called emergents grow up to 60 m tall

Main canopy of broad-leaved evergreen trees

Plants called epiphytes grow on the branches of trees

Climbing lianas

Dense understorey of shrubs

63

Mountain plants

▲ *As you go higher up a mountain, the trees of the lower slopes thin out. At the top, only mosses and lichens grow.*

- **Conditions get colder,** windier and wetter higher up mountains, so plants get smaller and hardier.

- **On lower slopes** conifers such as pines, firs, spruces and larches often grow.

- **Above a certain height,** called the tree-line, it gets too cold for trees to grow.

- **In Australia,** eucalyptus trees grow near the tree-line. In New Zealand, Chile and Argentina southern beeches grow.

- **Above the tree-line** stunted shrubs, grasses and tiny flowers grow. This is called alpine vegetation.

- **Alpine flowers** like purple and starry saxifrage have tough roots that grow into crevices and split the rocks.

- **There are few insects** high up, so flowers like saxifrage and snow gentian have big blooms to attract them.

- **To make the most** of the short summers, the alpine snowbell grows its flower buds the previous summer, then lets the bud lie dormant through winter under snow.

- **Alpine flowers** such as edelweiss have woolly hairs to keep out the cold. Tasmanian daisies grow in dense cushion-shapes to keep warm.

> **. . . FASCINATING FACT . . .**
> On Mt Kenya in Africa, huge dandelion-like plants
> called giant groundsels grow as big as trees.

Prairie and steppe

- **Grasslands in cool parts** of the world are called prairies or steppes. There is not enough rain all year round for trees to grow.

- **Prairies** are the grasslands of North America. Steppes are the grasslands of Russia. Every region has its own name for grasslands, such as the veld in South Africa and pampas in South America. But now grasslands anywhere with tall grass are usually called prairies and grasslands with shorter grass are usually called steppes.

- **Hundreds of kinds** of grass grow in prairies. In moist areas in North America, there are grasses like switch grass, wild rye, Indian grass and big bluestem. In drier areas, the main grasses are dropseeds, little bluestem, June grass, needlegrass and blue grama. Slough grass grows in marshland. The state of Kentucky is famous for its bluegrass.

- **Meadow grass** is the most common of all grasses, found on grasslands all over the world – and in garden lawns.

- **Shrubs** such as prairie roses often grow amid the grass, while oaks, cottonwoods and willows grow near rivers.

- **The many prairie flowers** include blazing stars, coneflowers, sunflowers, asters and goldenrods.

- **Eurasian grasslands** bloom with vetches, trefoils, worts, orchids and many kinds of herb.

- **Grasslands cover** nearly a quarter of the Earth's land surface.

- **When grasslands** are destroyed by farming, the soil can be blown away by the wind as in the dust bowl of North America in the 1900s.

▼ *When European pioneers first saw the American prairies in the 19th century, they described them as 'a sea of grass, stretching to the horizon'. Now, corn and wheat fields and cattle ranches cover most of them. Wild prairies like this are now very rare.*

...**FASCINATING FACT**...
Prairies and steppes typically have very dark soils such as chernozems. The word *chernozem* is Russian for 'black earth'.

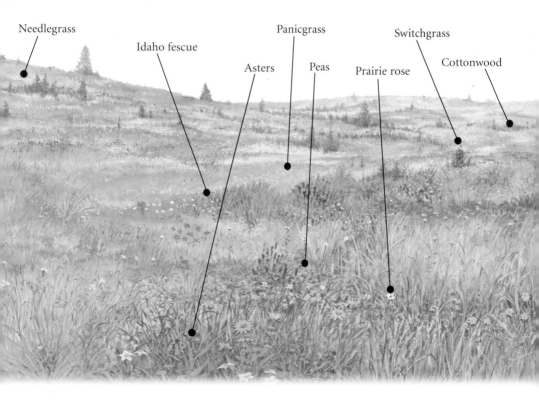

Needlegrass

Idaho fescue

Panicgrass

Switchgrass

Asters

Peas

Prairie rose

Cottonwood

Heathlands

▲ *Heather and other heathland plants are usually pollinated by birds like sunbirds. Few insect species can survive on the tough heathland plants, but those that do, such as wasps and bees, exist in huge numbers and make full use of the heather pollen and nectar.*

- **Heathland** goes under many different names, including scrubland, shrubland and chaparral.

- **Heathlands** occur where the soil is too dry or too poor for trees to grow – typically in Mediterranean regions or areas of sandy soil.

- **Many heathlands** are not natural, but places where human activity has so changed the environment that trees can no longer grow.

- **The most common** heathland shrub is heather. Underneath grasses, sedges and flowers like daisies and orchids grow.

- **Many heathland shrubs** like gorse are thorny to stop animals eating them.

- **The maquis** are the heathlands of the Mediterranean, dominated by tough evergreen shrubs and small trees.

- **Many maquis** plants are aromatic (have a strong scent) – such as mints, laurels and myrtles.

- **Spring blossoms** in the mallee heaths of Australia are so spectacular that they are a tourist attraction.

- **Mallee** is a kind of eucalyptus tree typical of the area.

- **Chaparral** is heathland in California. The climate is Mediterranean, with mild winters and warm summers. The main plants found in this type of heathland are sages and small evergreen oaks.

Tropical grasslands

▲ *In East Africa, the grassland is called savanna, and this name is often used for tropical grassland in other parts of the world.*

- **Tropical grasslands** are regions in the tropics where there is not enough rain half the year for trees to grow.
- **Grasses** in tropical grasslands tend to grow taller and faster than grasses in cooler regions.
- **Grass stalks** may be eaten by grazing animals, burned by bush fires or dry out, but roots survive underground.

- **In Africa** grasses include 3-m-tall elephant grasses. In Australia, they include tall spear grass and shorter kangaroo grass. In South America, there are plants called bunch grasses and species such as briza.

- **Most tropical grasslands** are scattered with bushes, shrubs and trees. In Africa, hardy broad-leaved trees such as curatella and byrsonima are typical.

- **Many grassland trees** are said to be sclerophyllous. This means they have tough leaves and stems to save water.

- **In drier regions** trees such as acacias are armed with spines to protect them against plant-eating animals. The thorns can be up to 50 cm long.

- **In damper places** palm trees often take the place of the thorn trees.

- **Baobab trees** are East African trees with massive trunks up to 9 m across which act as giant water stores.

- **Baobab trees** look so odd that an Arab legend says the devil turned them upside down so their roots stuck up in the air.

▶ *The African baobab has a trunk so wide that 30 people holding hands could just about make a circle around it.*

71

Desert plants

- **Some plants** find water in the dry desert with very long roots. The mesquite has roots that can go down as much as 50 m deep.

- **Most desert plants** have tough waxy leaves to cut down on water loss. They also have very few leaves; cacti have no leaves at all.

- **Pebble plants** avoid the desert heat by growing partly underground.

▲ *Surprisingly, many plants are able to survive the dryness of deserts, including cacti and sagebushes.*

- **Window plants** grow almost entirely underground. A long cigar shape pokes into the ground, with just a small green 'window' on the surface to catch sunlight.

- **Some mosses and lichens** get water by soaking up dew.

- **Resurrection trees** get their name because their leaves look shrivelled, brown and dead most of the time – then suddenly turn green when it rains.

- **The rose of Jericho** is a resurrection plant that forms a dry ball that lasts for years and opens only when damp.

- **Daisies** are found in most deserts.

- **Cacti and ice plants** can store water for many months in special storage organs.

> **...FASCINATING FACT...**
> The quiver tree drops its branches to save
> water in times of drought.

▲ *All cacti produce flowers
which bloom only for a few days
before they lose water and die.*

River plants

- **Some aquatic (water) plants** are rooted in the mud and have their leaves above the surface like water lilies.

- **Some water plants** grow underwater but for their flowers, like water milfoils and some plantains. They may have bladders or air pockets to help keep the stem upright.

- **Tiny plants** called algae grow in red, green or brown films on rivers, lakes and swamps.

▲ Water hyacinths grow so quickly that they may double in number every 10 days.

▼ The Egyptians wrote on papyrus made from the papyrus reeds growing in the Nile.

- **Water hyacinths** are purple American water flowers. They grow very quickly and can sometimes clog up slow-running streams.

- **Giant water lilies** have huge leaves with the edges upturned like a shallow pan to keep them afloat.

- **The leaves** of the royal or Amazon lily can be 2 m across.

- **Papyrus** is a grass-like water plant that grows in the Nile river. Stems were rolled flat by the Ancient Egyptians to write on. The word 'paper' comes from papyrus.

- **Many grass-like** plants grow in water, including reeds, mace, flag and rushes such as bulrushes and cattails.

- **Mangroves, bald cypresses,** cotton gum and other 'hydrophytic' trees are adapted to living in water.

▶ *The papyrus plant still grows in the Nile Valley. It is also found in Syria, Ethopia, southern Italy and Sicily.*

75

Marshes and wetlands

- **There are two kinds of marsh:** freshwater marshes and saltwater marshes.

- **Freshwater marshes** occur in low-lying ground alongside rivers and lakes where the water level is always near the soil surface.

- **Freshwater marshes** are dominated by plants such as rushes, reeds and sedges.

- **Sedges** are like grass but have solid triangular stems. They grow in damp places near the water's edge.

- **Rushes** have long cylindrical leaves and grow in tussocks in damp places along the bank.

- **Reeds** are tall grasses with round stems, flat leaves and purplish flowers. They grow in dense beds in open water.

- **Free-floating** plants like duckweed and frogbit are common in marshes. In rivers they'd be washed away.

- **Water horsetails** are relics of plants that dominated the vast swamps of the Carboniferous Period 300 million years ago.

- **Saltwater marshes** are flooded twice daily by salty seawater. Cordgrasses and salt-meadow grass are common. Reeds and rushes grow where it is least salty.

- **Where mud is firm,** glasswort and seablite take root. Further from the water sea aster and purslane grow. On high banks, sea lavender, sea plantain and thrift bloom.

▼ *Reeds and floating duckweed thrive in open water in marshes.*

Coastal plants

- **Plants** that grow on coasts must be able to cope with exposure to wind and salt spray, and thin, salty soils.

- **Plants** that can tolerate salt are called halophytes.

- **Spray halophytes** can tolerate occasional salt water splashing.

- **True halophytes** can tolerate regular immersion when the tide comes in.

- **The annual seablite** is a true halophyte that lives in between the tides. The word 'blite' comes from an old English word for spinach.

- **The rock samphire's** name comes from St Pierre (St Peter) who was known as 'the rock'. The plant clings to bare rock faces. It was once a popular vegetable and poor people risked their lives to collect it from cliffs.

▲ *The ice plant is native to South Africa but has acclimatized to growing on Cornish cliff tops.*

- **The droppings** of sea birds can fertilize the soil and produce dense growths of algae and weeds such as dock.

- **Lichens** on rock coasts grow in three colour bands in each tidal zone, depending on their exposure to salt.

- **Grey 'sea ivory' lichen** grows above the tide; orange lichens survive constant splashing by waves; black lichens grow down to the low-water mark.

- **On pebble and shingle beaches** salt-tolerant plants like sea holly, sea kale and sea campion can be found.

▶ *Sea pinks are also known as thrift because they 'thrive' all the year round on the most exposed, weather-beaten cliffs.*

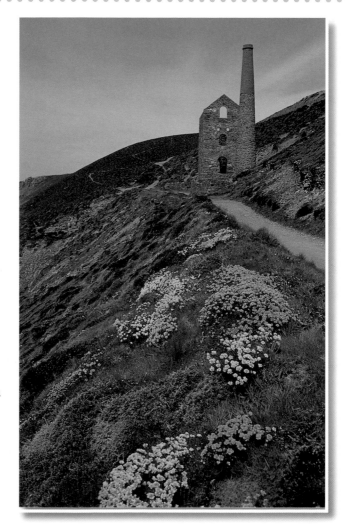

Marine plants

- **Plants in the sea** can only live in the sunlit surface waters of the ocean, called the photic zone.

- **The photic zone** goes down about 100 m.

- **Phytoplankton** are minute, floating, plant-like organisms made from just a single cell.

- **Almost any marine plant** which is big enough to be seen with the naked eye is called seaweed.

- **Seaweeds** are anchored by 'holdfasts' that look like roots but are really suckers for holding on to rocks.

- **Seaweeds** are red, green or brown algae. Red algae are small and fern-like and grow 30–60 m down in tropical seas. Brown algae like giant kelp are big and grow down to about 20 m, mostly in cold water.

▲ *Seaweeds don't have roots, stems, leaves or flowers, but they are plants and make their food from sunlight (see photosynthesis).*

▲ *Kelp is kept afloat by air bladders, and is often used as shelter by lobsters and fish.*

● **Some seaweeds** such as the bladderwrack have gas pockets to help their fronds (leaves) float.

● **The fastest growing** plant in the sea is the giant kelp, which can grow 1 m in a single day. Giant kelp can grow up to 60 m long.

● **The Sargasso Sea** is a vast area of sea covering 5.2 million square kilometres east of the West Indies. Gulfweed floats so densely here that it looks like green meadows.

● **The Sargasso Sea** was discovered by Christopher Columbus in 1492.

Monocotyledons

- **Monocotyledons** are one of the two basic classes of flowering plant. The other is dicotyledons.

- **Monocotyledons** are plants that sprout a single leaf from their seeds.

- **Monocotyledons** are also known as monocots or Liliopsida.

- **There are approximately** 50,000 species of monocots – about a quarter of all flowering plants.

- **Monocots** include grasses, cereals, bamboos, date palms, aloes, snake plants, tulips, orchids and daffodils.

◀ *Palms grow from seeds that have only one cotyledon (seed leaf). They have long, narrow, mature leaves.*

- **Monocots** tend to grow quickly and their stems stay soft and pliable, except for bamboos and palms. Most are herbaceous.

- **The tubes or veins** in monocot leaves run parallel to each other. They also develop a thick tangle of thin roots rather than a single long 'tap' root, like dicots.

- **The flower parts of monocots,** such as petals, tend to be set in threes or multiples of three.

- **Unlike dicots**, monocot stems grow from the inside. Dicots have a cambium, which is the layer of growing cells near the outside of the stem. Monocots rarely have a cambium.

- **Monocots** are thought to have appeared about 90 million years ago, developing from water lily-like dicots that lived in swamps and rivers.

▶ *Daffodils are typical monocots, with long lance-like leaves and petals in threes.*

83

Dicotyledons

▲ *The Japanese maple is typical of the many dicots with its net-veined leaves.*

- **Dicotyledons** are one of two basic classes of flowering plant. The other class is monocotyledons.

- **Dicotyledons** are also known as dicots or Magnoliopsida.

- **Dicots** are plants that sprout two leaves from their seeds.

- **There are about 175,000** dicots – over three-quarters of all flowering plants.

- **Dicots** include most garden plants, shrubs and trees as well as flowers such as magnolias, roses, geraniums and hollyhocks.

- **Dicots** grow slowly and at least 50% have woody stems.

- **The flowers** of dicots have sets of four or five petals.

- **Most dicots** have branching stems and a single main root called a taproot.

- **The leaves of dicots** usually have a network of veins rather than parallel veins.

◀ A dicot begins its life as a pair of leaves growing from a seed.

- **Dicots** usually have a layer of ever-growing cells near the outside of the stem called the cambium.

Wildflowers

- **All flowers** were originally wild. Garden flowers have been bred over the centuries to be very different from their wild originals.

- **Wildflowers** are flowers that have developed naturally.

- **Most wildflowers** are smaller and more delicate than their garden cousins.

- **Each** kind of place has its own special range of wildflowers, although many wildflowers have now been spread to different places by humans.

- **Heathlands** may have purple blooms of heathers, prickly yellow gorse and scarlet pimpernel.

▼ *There are now very few meadows with rich displays of wildflowers like this.*

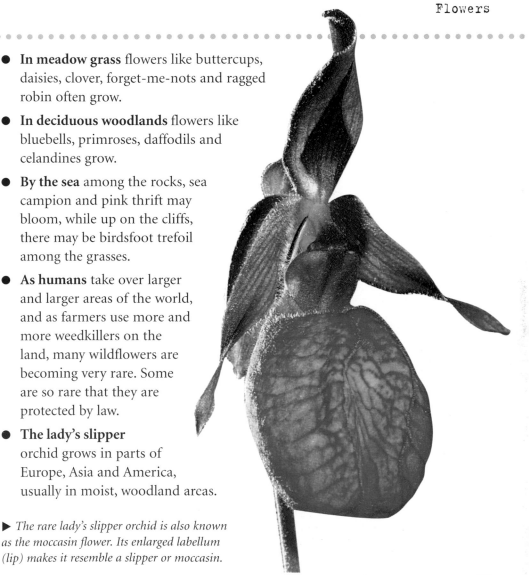

- **In meadow grass** flowers like buttercups, daisies, clover, forget-me-nots and ragged robin often grow.

- **In deciduous woodlands** flowers like bluebells, primroses, daffodils and celandines grow.

- **By the sea** among the rocks, sea campion and pink thrift may bloom, while up on the cliffs, there may be birdsfoot trefoil among the grasses.

- **As humans** take over larger and larger areas of the world, and as farmers use more and more weedkillers on the land, many wildflowers are becoming very rare. Some are so rare that they are protected by law.

- **The lady's slipper** orchid grows in parts of Europe, Asia and America, usually in moist, woodland areas.

▶ *The rare lady's slipper orchid is also known as the moccasin flower. Its enlarged labellum (lip) makes it resemble a slipper or moccasin.*

Dandelions and daisies

- **Dandelions and daisies** are both members of a vast family called *Asteraceae*.

- **All *Asteraceae*** have flower heads with many small flowers called florets, which are surrounded by leaf-like structures called bracts.

- **There are over 20,000** different *Asteraceae*.

- **Garden *Asteraceae*** include asters, dahlias and chrysanthemums.

- **Wild *Asteraceae*** include burdock, butterbur and ragweed, thistles and sagebrush.

▲ *When dandelions mature, they form feathery seeds which are blown away like parachutes by the wind.*

88

- **Lettuces, artichokes** and sunflowers are all varieties of *Asteraceae.*

- **The thistle** is the national emblem of Scotland.

- **Dandelions** are bright yellow flowers that came originally from Europe, and were taken to America by colonists. Unusually, their ovaries form fertile seeds without having to be pollinated, so they spread rapidly.

- **The name dandelion** comes from the French *dent de lion,* which means lion's tooth, because its leaves have edges that look like sharp teeth.

- **The daisy** gets its name from the Old English words 'day's eye' – because like an eye its blooms open in the day and close at night.

▲ *Daisies look like a single bloom, but they actually consist of many small flowers. Those around the edge each have a single petal.*

89

Tulips

- **Tulips** are flowers that bloom in spring from bulbs.

- **Tulips are** monocots and produce one large, bell-shaped bloom at the end of each stem.

- **There are about** 100 species of wild tulip, growing right across Asia to China.

- **Tulips** come in most colours but blue. Reds and yellows are common, but they vary from white to deep purple.

- **There are over 4000** garden varieties.

- **Most tulips** are 'late bloomers' with names like breeders, cottages and parrots.

- **Mid-season bloomers** include tulips such as Mendels and Darwins.

- **Early season** bloomers include single-flowereds and double-flowered earlies.

> **···FASCINATING FACT···**
> The word tulip comes from the Turkish for 'turban', because of their shape.

▶ *Food is stored in the tulip bulb so that, as winter approaches, the bulb remains alive underground while the rest of the plant dies.*

● **Tulips** were introduced to Europe in 1551 by the Viennese ambassador to Turkey, Augier de Busbecq. But Holland became the centre of tulip-growing early in the 1600s, when Europe was gripped by 'tulipmania'. At this time, people would exchange mansions for a single tulip bulb. Holland is still the centre of tulip-growing.

▼ *Huge numbers of tulips are now grown in the fields in Holland. Tulip cultivation is still an important industry there, with Dutch growers producing nearly 2000 varieties.*

Orchids

● **Orchids** are a group of over 20,000 species of flower, growing on every continent but Antarctica.

● **In the moist tropics** many grow on the trunks and branches of trees and so are called epiphytes.

● **A few,** such as the Bird's nest orchid, are saprophytes, living off rotting plants in places where there is no light.

● **Some species** are found throughout the tropics, such as *Ionopsis utricularioides*. Others grow on just a single mountain in the world.

● **Orchids** have a big central petal called the lip or labellum. It is often shaped like a cup, trumpet or bag.

● **The fly orchid** of Ecuador has a lip shaped like a female tachinid fly so as to attract male flies.

▲ *The vanilla orchid produces the flavour vanilla, which is extracted from the fruit, or 'pod'.*

To attract male bees, the bee orchid has a
lip that looks just like a female bee.

- **The flavour vanilla** comes from the vanilla orchid.

- **Ancient Greek** couples expecting a baby often ate the roots of the early
  purple orchid. They believed that if the man ate the flower's large root
  the baby would be a boy. If the woman ate the small root, the baby
  would be a girl.

- **In Shakespeare's** play *Hamlet*,
  the drowned Ophelia is
  covered in flowers,
  including the early
  purple orchid, famous
  as a love potion.
  Hamlet's mother says
  that 'cold maids' call
  the flowers 'dead
  men's fingers'.

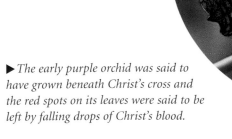

▶ *The early purple orchid was said to
have grown beneath Christ's cross and
the red spots on its leaves were said to be
left by falling drops of Christ's blood.*

93

Lilies

▲ *Hyacinths were so popular in the 18th century that 2000 kinds were cultivated in Holland.*

- **Lilies** are one of the largest and most important flower families, containing about 4000 species.

- **Lilies** are monocots (which means a single leaf grows from their seeds) and give their name to the entire group of monocots – *liliopsidae.*

- **The lily family** includes many flowers called lilies but also other plants such as asparagus and aloes.

- **Hyacinths** belong to the lily family.

▶ *Lilies are a favourite amongst garden flowers and have been cultivated in a wide range of colours.*

● **Lilies** grow from bulbs to produce clusters of bright trumpet-shaped flowers on tall stems. Each flower has six petals.

● **Lily-of-the-valley** has tiny white bell-shaped blooms. According to superstition, anyone who plants it will die within a year.

● **Lilies-of-the-valley** are famous for their fragrance. They are used to scent soaps and perfumes.

● **Easter lilies** are large trumpet-shaped white lilies that have come to symbolize Easter.

● **Leopard lilies** grow in the western coastal states of the United States. They have red-orange flowers spotted with purple.

● **The Madonna lily** is planted in August and lives throughout the winter.

Roses

- **The rose** is one of the most popular of all garden flowers because of its lovely perfume and beautiful blooms.

  - **Wild roses** usually have small flowers and a single layer of five petals. Garden roses usually have big flowers with multiple sets of five petals in two or more layers.

  - **There are 100 species** of wild rose, but all today's garden roses were created by crossing 10 Asian species.

  - **There are now over 13,000** official varieties of garden rose altogether.

  - **Some experts divide garden roses** into groups by when they bloom: old roses bloom once a year in early summer; perpetual roses bloom in early summer, then again in autumn; and everblooming hybrids bloom all summer.

  - **Old roses** include yellow briers, damask roses and many climbing roses.

  - **Perpetuals** include a group of roses called hybrid perpetuals.

  ◀ *Roses often look their best just after they begin to open, when the petals are still in a tight, velvety cluster.*

▲ *The delicately scented dog-rose is one of the most familiar of all wildflowers.*

● **Everblooming hybrids** include floribundas, hybrid teas, gloribundas and polyanthas.

● **Hybrid teas** such as the Peace are the most popular of all roses. They were created by crossing everblooming but fragile tea roses with vigorous hybrid perpetuals.

● **Attar of roses** is a perfume made from roses, especially damask roses.

Magnolias

▲ *Magnolias have a single, large, typically pink or white flower at the end of the stem.*

- **Magnolias** are evergreen shrubs, climbers and trees.
- **Magnolias** are named after the French botanist Pierre Magnol (1638–1715).
- **They produce** beautiful, large, white or pink flowers and are one of the most popular garden plants.
- **Nutmeg trees,** ylang-ylangs and tulip trees are all kinds of magnolia.
- **There are** over 80 different kinds of magnolia.

- **Magnolias may be** the most ancient of all flowering plants. Their fossil remains have been found in rocks 120 million years old – when the dinosaurs lived.

- **A seed 2000 years old,** found by archaeologists (people who study ancient remains) in Japan was planted in 1982. It grew and produced an unusual flower with eight petals.

- **The most popular** garden magnolia was bred in a garden near Paris, France, from a wild Japanese kind (*Magnolia liliiflora*) and a wild Chinese kind (*Magnolia denudata*).

▲ *Nutmeg, a sweet-flavoured spice, comes from the inner part of the seeds produced by the nutmeg tree, a kind of magnolia.*

- **Magnolia trees** have the largest leaves and flowers of any tree outside the tropical forests.

- **The cucumber tree** – a kind of magnolia – is named after its seed clusters, which look like cucumbers.

Rhododendrons

- **Rhododendrons** are a big group of 800 different trees and shrubs which belong to the heath family.

- **The word 'rhododendron'** means 'rose tree'.

- **Most rhododendrons** originally came from the Himalayas and the mountains of Malaysia where they form dense thickets.

- **Many rhododendrons** are now widely cultivated for their big red or white blooms and evergreen leaves.

- **There are over 6000** different cultivated varieties of rhododendron.

- **The spectacular June blooming** of the   catawba rhododendron or mountain rosebay in the Great Smoky Mountains, USA, is now a tourist attraction.

- **The Dahurian** is a famous purply-pink rhododendron originally from Siberia and Mongolia.

- **The Smirnow** was discovered in the 1880s high up in the Caucasus Mountains on the Georgian–Turkish border.

- **Smirnows** have been bred with other rhododendrons in order to make them very hardy.

- **Azaleas** were once considered a separate group of plants, but they are now classified with rhododendrons.

▼ *Rhododendrons generally grow in cool, mountainous regions. Some magnificent species can be found in Nepal.*

Cacti

- **Cacti** are American plants that are covered in sharp spines, have thick, bulbous green stems and no leaves.

- **Most cacti** grow in hot, dry regions but a few grow in rainforests and in cold places such as mountain tops.

- **Cacti** in deserts have a thick, waxy skin so as to cut water loss to the bare minimum.

- **The fat stems** of cacti hold a lot of water so that they can survive in hot, dry deserts.

▶ *The huge saguaro cactus grows only in the dry foothills and deserts of southern Arizona, southeast California and northwest Mexico.*

- **Because of their moist stems,** cacti
  are called succulents.

- **Cacti have spines** to protect
  themselves from animals which will
  eat any kind of moist vegetation.

- **Cacti** have to pollinate just like
  every flowering plant. So
  every few years, many
  produce big colourful
  blooms to attract
  insects quickly.

- **Most cacti** have very
  long roots to collect
  water from a large area.
  The roots grow near the
  surface to collect as much
  rainwater as possible.

- **The biggest cactus** is the
  saguaro, which can grow up to
  20 m tall and 1 m thick.

▲ *After rain, cactus flowers bloom briefly, adding
splashes of colour to the barren desert.*

103

Bamboo

▲ *Pandas have an extra 'thumb' which helps them to grasp the bamboo between their paws.*

- **Bamboos** are giant, fast-growing grasses with woody stems.

- **Most bamboos** grow in east and southeast Asia and on islands in the Indian and Pacific oceans.

- **Bamboo stems** are called culms. They often form dense thickets that exclude every other plant.

- **Bamboo culms** can reach up to 40 m and grow very fast. Some bamboos grow 1 m every three days.

- **Most bamboos** only flower every 12 years or so. Some flower only 30–60 years. Phyllostachys bambusoides flowers only after 120 years.

- **Pandas** depend on the Phyllostachys bamboo, and after it flowers they lose their source of food.

- **The flowering** of the muli bamboo around the Bay of Bengal every 30–35 years brings disaster as rats multiply to take advantage of the abundance of fruit.

- **The Chinese** have used the hollow stems of bamboo to make flutes since before the Stone Age. The Australian aboriginals use them to make droning pipes called didgeridoos.

- **Bamboo** is an incredibly light, strong material, and between 1904 and 1957 athletes used it for pole-vaulting. American Cornelius Warmerdam vaulted 4.77 m with a bamboo pole.

- **Bamboo** has long been used to make paper. *The Bamboo Annals*, written on bamboo, are the oldest written Chinese records, dating from the 8th century BC.

▲ *Bamboo is a grass distantly related to wheat, oats and barley, but it grows to a giant size.*

105

Parts of a tree

- **Trees** have one tall, thick, woody stem called a trunk which is at least 10 cm thick, allowing the tree to stand up by itself.

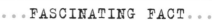

...FASCINATING FACT...
The world's fastest-growing tree is the tropical pea tree *Albizia falcata*, which can grow 10 m a year.

- **The branches** and leaves together are called the crown. The trunk supports the crown and holds it up to the sun.

- **The trunks of conifers** typically grow right to the top of the tree. The lower branches are longer because they have been growing longest. The upper branches are short because they are new. So the tree has a conical shape.

- **Trees with wide flat leaves** are called broad-leaved trees. They usually have crowns with a rounded shape.

- **The trunk and branches** have five layers from the centre out: heartwood, sapwood, cambium, phloem and bark.

- **If a tree** is sawn across, you can see the annual growth rings that show how the tree has grown each year. The edge of each ring marks where growth ceased in winter. Counting the rings gives the age of the tree.

- **Heartwood** is the dark, dead wood in the centre of the trunk. Sapwood is pale living wood, where tiny pipes called xylem carry sap from the roots to the leaves.

- **The cambium** is the thin layer where the sapwood is actually growing; the phloem is the thin food-conducting layer.

- **The bark** is the tree's protective skin made of hard dead tissue. Bark takes many different forms and often cracks as the tree grows, but it is always made from cork.

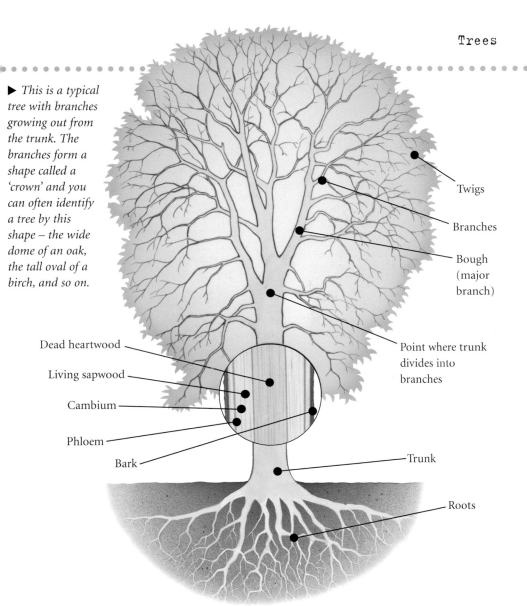

▶ *This is a typical tree with branches growing out from the trunk. The branches form a shape called a 'crown' and you can often identify a tree by this shape – the wide dome of an oak, the tall oval of a birch, and so on.*

Twigs

Branches

Bough (major branch)

Point where trunk divides into branches

Dead heartwood

Living sapwood

Cambium

Phloem

Bark

Trunk

Roots

Conifers

- **Conifers** are trees with needle-like, typically evergreen leaves that make their seeds not in flowers but in cones.

- **With gingkos and cycads** they make up the group of plants called gymnosperms, all of which make their seeds in cones.

- **The world's tallest tree,** the redwood, is a conifer.

- **The world's most massive tree,** the giant sequoia, is a conifer.

- **One of the world's oldest trees** is the bristlecone pine of California and Nevada, almost 5000 years old.

▶ *The gnarled bristlecone pine appears dead, but can survive with just a few of its branches and roots left.*

108

- **The world's smallest trees** are probably conifers including natural bonsai cypresses and shore pines which reach barely 20 cm when fully grown.

- **Many conifers** are cone-shaped, which helps them shed snow from their branches in winter.

- **The needle-like shape** and waxy coating of the leaves helps the conifer to save water.

- **The needles of some pines** can grow up to 30 cm long. But the biggest needles ever were those of the extinct Cordaites, over 1 m long and 15 cm wide.

- **Conifers** grow over most of the world, but the biggest conifer forests are in places with cold winters, such as north Siberia, northern North America and on mountain slopes almost everywhere.

▲ *Most conifers are instantly recognizable from their conical shapes, their evergreen, needle-like leaves and their dark brown cones.*

109

Cones

▲ *These Scots pine cones are brown and were fertilized about three years ago.*

- **Cones** are the tough little clusters of scales that coniferous trees carry their seeds in.

- **The scales** on a cone are called bracts. The seeds are held between the bracts. Bracts are thin and papery in spruces and thick and woody in silver firs.

- **Pine cone bracts** have a lump called an umbo.

- **All cones** are green and quite soft when they first form, then turn brown and hard as they ripen.

- **Cones stand upright** on the branch until they are ripe and ready to shed their seeds.

- **Most cones** turn over when ripe to hang downwards so that the seeds fall out.

- **The cones of cedars** and silver firs stay upright and the bracts drop away to release the seeds.

- **Long, hanging cones** like those of the pine and spruce hang throughout winter then release seeds in spring.

- **The monkey puzzle** tree has a unique, pineapple-shaped cone with golden spines and edible seeds.

▶ *The monkey puzzle tree is native to Chile and Argentina. It is so called because the first settlers puzzled at how monkeys could reach the seeds on the prickly maze of branches. They failed to realize that there were no monkeys there at all!*

111

Tree leaves

- **Trees** can be divided into two groups according to their leaves: broad-leaved trees and conifers with needle-like leaves.

- **The leaves** of broad-leaved trees are all wide and flat to catch the sun, but they vary widely in shape.

- **You can identify** trees by their leaves. Features to look for are not only the overall shape, but also: the number of leaflets on the same stalk, whether leaflets are paired or offset and if there are teeth round the edges of the leaves.

- **Trees such as birches** and poplars have small triangular or 'deltoid' leaves; aspens and alders have round leaves.

- **Limes** and Indian bean trees have heart-shaped or 'cordate' leaves.

- **Maples** and sycamores have leaves shaped a bit like hands, which is why they are called 'palmate'.

- **Ash and walnut trees** both have lots of leaflets on the same stalk, which gives them a feathery or 'pinnate' look.

Hand-shaped leaf of a horse chestnut

Lobed leaves of the English oak

- **Oaks and whitebeams** have leaves indented with lobes round the edge.

- **Many shrubs,** like magnolias and buddleias, and trees like willows, cherries, sweet chestnuts and cork oaks, have long narrow leaves.

- **Elms, beeches,** pears, alders and many others all have oval leaves.

Long, narrow willow leaves

Pinnate or feather-shaped walnut leaves

▲ *Trees can be identified by their leaves, some varieties of which are shown here.*

113

Tree flowers

- **All trees have flowers,** but the flowers of conifers are usually tiny compared with those of broad-leaved trees.

- **Flowers** are the reproductive organs of the tree.

- **Some flowers are male** and some are female.

- **Sometimes the male** and female flowers are on separate trees. Sometimes, as in willows and some conifers, they are on the same tree.

- **'Perfect' flowers** like those of cherry and maple trees have both male and female parts.

- **Pollen** is carried from male flowers by insects or the wind to fertilize female flowers.

- **A blossom** can be any flower, but often refers especially to the beautiful flowers of fruit trees such as cherries and apples that bloom in spring.

▲ *Japanese cherry trees are especially noted for their attractive, delicate blossoms.*

▲ *Apple blossoms are usually pink. They bloom quite late in spring, after both peach and cherry blossoms.*

● **Many blossoms** are pink and get their colour from what are called anthocyanin pigment, which are the same chemical colours that turn leaves red in autumn.

● **Washington DC** is famous for its Cherry Blossom Festival each spring.

● **Omiya** in Japan is famous for its park full of cherry trees which blossom in spring.

115

Seeds and nuts

- **Seeds are the tiny** hard capsules from which most new plants grow.

- **Seeds** develop from the plant's egg once it is fertilized by pollen.

- **Each seed** contains the new plant in embryo form plus a store of food to feed it until it grows leaves.

- **The seed** is wrapped in a hard shell known as a testa.

- **Some fruit** contain many seeds; nuts are fruit with a single seed in which the outside has gone hard.

▶ *Neither Brazil nuts nor coconuts are true nuts. Coconuts (right) are the stones of drupes, while Brazil nuts (left) are just large seeds.*

116

- **Acorns and hazelnuts** are true nuts.

- **Cola drinks** get their name from the African kola nut, but there are no nuts in them. The flavour is artificial.

- **Some nuts,** such as almonds and walnuts, are not true nuts but the hard stones of drupes (fruit like plums).

- **Brazil nuts** and shelled peanuts are not true nuts but just large seeds.

- **Nuts are** a concentrated, nutritious food – about 50% fat and 10–20% protein. Peanuts contain more food energy than sugar and more protein, minerals and vitamins than liver.

▶ *Almonds come from trees native to southwest Asia but are now grown all over the world.*

117

Evergreen trees

- **An evergreen** is a plant that keeps its leaves in winter.

- **Many tropical broad-leaved trees** are evergreen.

- **In cool temperate regions** and the Arctic, most evergreen trees are conifers such as pines and firs. They have needle-like leaves.

- **Old needles** do turn yellow and drop, but they are replaced by new needles (unless the tree is unhealthy).

- **Evergreens** may suffer from sunscald – too much sun – in dry, sunny spots, especially in early spring.

▲ *In cool northern climates where the summers are brief, conifers stay evergreen to make the most of the available sunshine.*

- **Five coniferous groups,** including larches and cypresses, are not evergreen.

- **Many evergreens** were sacred to ancient cultures. The laurel or bay was sacred to the Greek god Apollo and was used by the Romans as a symbol of high achievement.

- **Yews are grown** in many European churchyards – perhaps because the trees were planted on the sites by pagans in the days before Christianity. But the bark of the yew tree and its seeds are poisonous.

- **The sakaki** is sacred to the Japanese Shinto religion, and trees are uprooted to appear in processions.

◀ *The leaves of the conifer may be scale-like, as they are here, or needle-like. The scale-like leaves cling to the stem.*

119

Pine trees

- **Pine trees** are evergreen conifers with long needle-like leaves. They grow mostly in sandy or rocky soils in cool places.

- **Pine trees** belong to the largest family of conifers.

- **There 90–100 species of pine** – most of them coming originally from northern Eurasia and North America.

- **Pines grow** fast and straight, reaching their full height in less than 20 years – which is why they provide 75% of the world's timber.

- **Some pines** produce a liquid called resin which is used to make substances such as turpentine, paint and soap.

- **Soft or white pines**, such as sugar pines and piñons, have soft wood. They grow needles in bundles of five and have little resin.

▼ *Like all conifers, Corsican pines produce cones. The cones look very different from flowers but serve the same purpose – making the seeds from which new trees grow.*

- **Hard or yellow pines**, such as Scots, Corsican and loblolly pines, have harder wood. They grow needles in bundles of two or three and make lots of resin.

- **Eurasian pines** include the Scots pine, Corsican pine, black pine, pinaster and stone pine.

- **North American pines** include the eastern white pine, sugar pine, stone pines, piñons, Ponderosa pine, and Monterey pine.

- **The sugar pine** is the biggest of all pines, often growing to 70 m tall and 3.5 m thick. The eastern white pine has valuable fine white wood.

▲ *Resin comes from several varieties of pine tree. It is used in the preparation of paints, varnishes and glues.*

Deciduous trees

- **Deciduous trees** lose their leaves once a year.

- **In cool places,** deciduous trees lose their leaves in autumn to cut their need for water in winter when water may be frozen.

- **In the tropics** deciduous trees lose their leaves at the start of the dry season.

- **Leaves fall** because a layer of cork grows across the leaf stalk, gradually cutting off its water supply.

- **Eventually the leaf** is only hanging on by its veins, and is easily blown off by the wind.

- **Leaves go brown** and other colours in autumn because their green chlorophyll breaks down, letting other pigments shine through instead.

- **Among the most spectacular** autumn colours are those of the sweet gum tree, which was brought to Europe from Mexico c.1570.

- **The main deciduous trees** found in cool climates are oaks, beeches, birches, chestnuts, aspens, elms, maples and lindens.

- **Most deciduous trees** are broad-leaved, but five conifer groups including larches are deciduous.

- **Some tropical evergreen trees** are deciduous in regions where there is a marked dry season.

▶ *In autumn, the leaves of deciduous trees turn glorious colours.*

Oak trees

- **Oaks** are a group of over 450 different trees. Most belong to a family with the Latin name *Quercus.*

- ***Quercus* oaks** grow in the northern half of the world in temperate regions or high up in the tropics.

- **Southern oaks,** such as the Australian and Tasmanian oaks, don't actually belong to the *Quercus* family.

- **Most oaks** from warmer places, such as the holm oak, are evergreen.

- **When a nail** is driven into freshly cut oak, it creates a blue stain as tannin in the wood reacts with the iron.

- **Tannin from oak bark** has been used for curing leather for as long ago as the days of ancient Greece.

▶ *Oaks have leaves with four or five pairs of lobes. They grow fruits called acorns in a little cup.*

124

- **Oak trees** can live a thousand years or more and grow up to 40 m. In Europe, oaks are the oldest of all trees.

- **Oak wood** is very strong and durable and so was the main building wood for centuries – used for timber frames in houses and for building ships.

- **Oak trees** are divided into white oaks such as the English oak and red oaks like the North American pine oak. The colour refers to the colour of their wood.

▶ *Cork is made from the bark of cork oaks. It serves a number of different uses, including bottle stoppers (below), floor coverings and shoe soles.*

125

Ash trees

- **Ash trees** are 70 species of deciduous trees that grow through much of northern Eurasia and North America.

- **Ash trees** are among the most beautiful of all trees and are prized for their wood. It was once used to make oars and handles for axes and tennis rackets and for skis.

- **The tallest of all flowering plants** is the Australian mountain ash which grows over 100 m tall.

1   2   3   4   5

▲ *The Australian mountain ash (4) is the fourth highest tree ever recorded, measuring 114 m. The tallest ever measured is the Australian eucalyptus (1) at 132.6 m, followed by two douglas firs (2 and 3.) The fifth highest is the coast redwood, standing at 112 m.*

- **Ash trees** are part of the olive family.

- **The Vikings** worshipped the ash as a sacred tree. Yggdrasil, the Tree of the World, was a giant ash whose roots reached into hell but whose crown reached heaven.

- **In Viking myth** Odin, the greatest of the gods, created the first man out of a piece of ash wood.

- **The manna ash** got its name because it was thought that its sugary gum was manna. Manna was the miraculous food that fell from heaven to feed the biblical Children of Israel in the desert as they fled from Egypt.

- **The mountain ash** is also known as the rowan or quickbeam. In America it is known as dogberry. It is not related to other ash trees.

- **Rowan trees** were once linked to witchcraft. The name may come from the Viking word runa, meaning charm. Rowan trees were planted in churchyards, and the berries were hung over doors on May Day, to ward off evil.

- **Rowans** grow higher up mountains than any other tree.

▲ *The leaves of the ash grow opposite each other in groups of five to nine and have tooth edges. The clusters of flowers are small and often showy.*

127

Maple trees

- **Maples** are a huge group of trees that belong to the Acer family.

- **Maples grow** all over the temperate regions of the northern hemisphere, especially in China.

- **Many maple tree leaves** turn brilliant shades of red in autumn.

- **Several North American maple** trees, including the sugar maple and the black maple, produce maple syrup.

- **Maple syrup** is 'sweet-water' sap. This is different from ordinary sap and flows from wounds during times of thaws when the tree is not growing. Syrup is collected between mid January and mid April.

- **Maple syrup** was used by the Native Americans of the Great Lakes and St Lawrence River regions long before Europeans arrived in North America.

- **About 30 litres** of sap give 1 litre of maple syrup.

Samara

▶ *All maple trees have winged seeds called samaras or keys. Many also have three-lobed leaves, like these of the sugar maple.*

Maple leaf

128

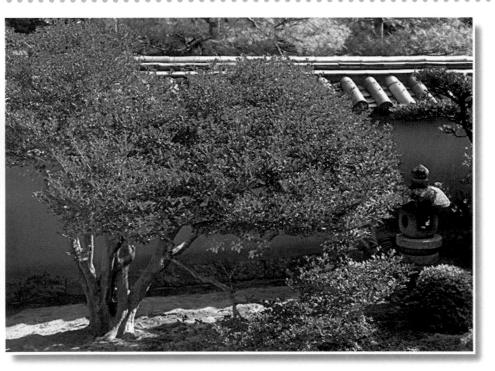

▲ *The fiery red leaves of the Japanese maple make it a popular ornamental tree for small gardens.*

● **The leaf of the sugar maple tree** is Canada's national symbol.

● **Many small maples** are grown as garden plants. Japanese maples have been carefully bred over the centuries to give all kinds of varieties with different leaf shapes and colours.

● **The red maple** is planted in many North American cities for its brilliant red autumn leaves.

129

Cycads and gingkos

- **Cycadophytes and gingkophytes** were the first seed plants to appear on land. The cycads and gingkos of today are their direct descendants.

- **Like conifers,** cycads and gingkos are gymnosperms. This means their seeds do not develop inside a fruit like those of flowering plants or angiosperms.

- **Cycads** are mostly short, stubby, palm-like trees. Some are hundreds of thousands of years old.

▶ *Cycads first grew on earth over 225 million years ago. They probably provided an important source of food for some dinosaurs.*

- **Cycads have** fern-like leaves growing in a circle round the end of the stem. New leaves sprout each year and last for several years.

- **The gingko** is a tall tree that comes from China.

- **The gingko** is the only living gingkophyte.

- **The gingko** is the world's oldest living seed-plant.

- **Fossil leaves** identical to today's gingko have been found all over the world in rocks formed in the Jurassic period, 208–144 million years ago.

- **Scientifically,** the gingko is called *Gingko Biloba*. It is also called the maidenhair tree.

- **All today's** gingkos may be descended from trees first cultivated in Chinese temple gardens 3000 years ago.

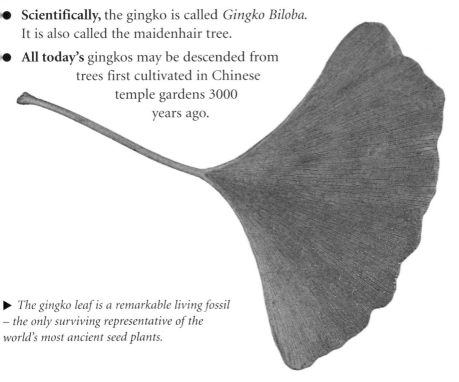

▶ *The gingko leaf is a remarkable living fossil – the only surviving representative of the world's most ancient seed plants.*

Palm trees

- **Palms** are a group of 2780 species of tropical trees and shrubs.

- **Palms** have a few very large leaves called fronds.

- **The fronds** grow from the main bud at the top of a tall thin trunk.

- **If the main bud** at the top of the trunk is damaged, the tree will stop growing and die.

- **Palm trunks** do not get thicker like other trees; they simply grow taller.

- **Some palms** have trunks no bigger than a pencil; others are 60 m high and 1 m across.

- **Palm fruits** vary enormously. Some are no bigger than a pea. The fruit of the coco-de-mer coconut palm is the biggest seed in the world, growing over 60 cm across.

▲ *The coconut is the fruit of the coconut palm. Its hollow centre contains a sweet liquid called coconut milk.*

... FASCINATING FACT ...
The world's largest leaves are those of the Raffia palm, which grow up to 20 m long.

- **Palm trees** are a very ancient group of plants, and fossil palms have been found dating back 100 million years to the time of the dinosaurs.

- **Date palms** have been cultivated in the hottest parts of North Africa and the Middle East for at least 5000 years. Muslims regard it as the tree of life.

▼ *Date palms produce several clusters of 600–1700 dates towards the end of the year, each year, for about 60 years.*

Date

Palm tree

Raffia Palm

133

Eucalyptus trees

▲ *Eucalyptus leaves provide the koala with its staple food, but can be harmful to other animals.*

- **Eucalyptus trees** make up a group of over 400 species of Australian trees. They grow fast and straight, and often reach tremendous heights.

- **Eucalyptus trees** grow best in warm places that have alternate wet and dry seasons, such as Australia and the southern United States.

134

- **In winter** eucalyptus trees simply stop growing and produce no new buds.

- **Eucalyptus trees** that grow in California originally come from seeds brought over from Tasmania.

- **Australians** often call eucalyptus trees gum trees or just gums.

- **Eucalyptus leaves** produce eucalyptus oil, which is used as a vapour rub for treating colds.

- **The most important** tree grown for oil is the blue mallee or blue gum. Blue gum trees are the most widespread in North America.

- **Some eucalyptus trees** give Botany Bay kino, a resin used to protect ships against worms and other animals that make holes in their hulls.

- **The jarrah** is an Australian eucalyptus that gives a red wood rather like mahogany. Other eucalyptus woods are used to make everything from boats to telegraph poles.

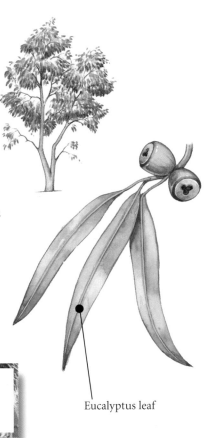

▼ *Eucalyptus trees have long, narrow, leathery leaves which are cut, pressed and then steamed to make eucalyptus oil.*

Eucalyptus leaf

... FASCINATING FACT ...
Eucalyptus trees can grow to over 90 m tall – taller than any trees but Californian redwoods.

135

Tropical trees

- **Nearly all tropical trees** are broad-leaved trees.

- **Most tropical trees** are evergreen. Only where there is a marked dry season in 'monsoon' regions do some trees loose their leaves to save water.

- **Most tropical trees** are slow-growing hardwoods such as teak and mahogany. Once cut down, they take many years to replace.

- **Mahogany** is a tall evergreen tree with beautiful hard wood that turns red when it matures after a century or so.

- **Most mahogany** wood comes from trees such as the African *Khaya* or the *Shorea* from the Philippines.

- **The best mahogany** is from the tropical American *Swietenia macrophylla*.

- **Balsa** is so light and such a good insulator that it is used to make passenger compartments in aircraft.

- **Teak** is a deciduous tree that comes from India. It is one of the toughest of all woods and has been used to construct ships and buildings for more than 2000 years.

- **Chicle** is a gum drained from the Central American sapota tree in the rainy season. It is the main ingredient in chewing-gum. The best quality chicle comes from Guatemala.

. . . FASCINATING FACT . . .
Balsa wood from Central America is the
lightest and softest wood of all.

▶ *Mangrove trees are famous for their dangling pods which can drop like a sword on passersby.*

Trees

Forestry

- **Forests** provide fuel, timber, paper, resins, varnishes, dyes, rubber, kapok and much more besides.
- **Softwood** is timber that comes from coniferous trees such as pine, larch, fir and spruce. 75–80% of the natural forests of northern Asia, Europe and the USA are softwood.
- **In vast plantations** fast-growing conifers are set in straight rows so they are easy to cut down.

▼ *A tropical rainforest has more kinds of trees than any other area in the world.*

▶ *The signs of pollarding are easy to see in these trees in winter when the leaves are gone.*

- **Hardwood** is timber from broad-leaved trees such as oak. Most hardwood forests are in the tropics.

- **Hardwood trees** take over a century to reach maturity.

- **Tropical hardwoods** such as mahogany are becoming rare as more hardwood is cut for timber.

- **Pollarding** is cutting the topmost branches of a tree so new shoots grow from the trunk to the same length.

- **Coppicing** is cutting tree stems at ground level to encourage several stems to grow from the same root.

- **Half the world's remaining** rainforests will be gone by 2020 if they are cut down at the current rate.

. . . **FASCINATING FACT** . . .
Every year the world uses 3 billion cubic metres of wood – a pile as big as a football stadium and as high as Mt Everest.

Rotting trees

▲ *Rotting trees provide a home for many kinds of plants, such as this spruce growing on an old stump.*

- **Trees** are dying in forests all the time.

- **In the past** foresters used to clear away dead trees or chop down those that were dying, but it has now become clear that they play a vital part in the woodland ecosystem.

- **When a tree falls** it crashes down through the leaves and opens up a patch of woodland, called a glade, to the sky.

- **In the glade,** saplings (new young trees) are able to sprout and flourish in the sunlight.

- **Many other woodland plants** flourish in the sunshine of a glade.

- **Flowers** such as foxgloves and rosebay willowherbs often spring up in a glade.

- **Bracken and shrubs** such as brambles grow quickly in a glade.

- **The rotting tree trunk** provides food for fungi such as green-staining and candle-snuff fungus.

- **Many insects** such as beetles find a home in the rotting wood.

- **As the rotting tree is broken down** it not only provides food for plants, insects and bacteria; it enriches the soil too.

▶ *The candle-snuff fungus gets its name from the tips which look like snuffed-out candle*

Tree facts

- **The biggest tree** ever known was the Lindsey Creek Tree, a massive redwood which blew over in 1905. It weighed over 3300 tonnes.

- **The tallest living tree** is the 112-m high Mendocino redwood tree, which is growing in the Montgomery State Reserve, California, United States.

- **The tallest tree** ever known was a Eucalyptus on Watts River, Victoria, Australia, which was measured at over 150 m in 1872.

- **The great banyan** tree in the Indian Botanical Garden, Calcutta, has a canopy that covers 1.2 hectares.

▲ *The banyan tree or Indian fig tree has wide-spreading branches that send down hundreds of hanging roots. These take hold of the soil and act as supports for the branches.*

Banyan trees grow trunk-like roots from their branches.

● **A European chestnut** known as the Tree of the Hundred Horses on Mt Etna in Sicily had a girth (the distance round the trunk) of 57.9 m during the 1790s.

▲ *General Sherman in California is the biggest living tree. It is a giant sequoia over 83 m tall and with a trunk 11 m across.*

A Moctezuma baldcypress near Oaxaca in Mexico has a trunk measuring over 12 m in diameter.

The world's oldest plant is the King's Holly in southwestern Tasmania, thought to be 43,000 years old.

● **The ombu tree** of Argentina is the world's toughest tree, able to survive axes, fire, storms and insect attacks.

··· **FASCINATING FACT** ···
The 'Eternal God' redwood tree in Prairie Creek, California is 12,000 years old.

Algae

- **Algae** are simple organisms that live in oceans, lakes, rivers and damp mud.

- **Some algae** live inside small transparent animals.

- **Algae vary** from single-celled microscopic organisms to huge fronds of seaweed (brown algae) over 60 m long.

- **The smallest** float freely, but others, such as seaweeds, need a place to grow like a plant.

- **Algae** are so varied and often live very differently from plants, so scientists put them not in the plant kingdom but in a separate kingdom called the Proctista, along with slime moulds.

- **The most ancient** algae are called blue-green algae or cyanobacteria and are put in the same kingdom as bacteria. They appeared on the Earth 3 billion years ago.

- **Some algae** can multiply very quickly in polluted lakes and rivers. The thick layers can often upset the water's natural balance and deprive it of oxygen.

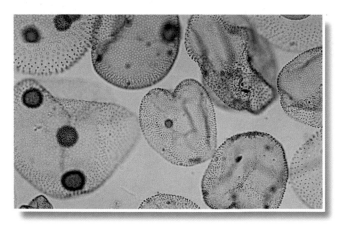

◀ *Volvox are green algae that live in colonies about the size of a pinhead, containing as many as 60,000 cells.*

▲ *Algae may be tiny but they are a vital food source for creatures from shrimps to whales.*

- **Green algae** are found mostly in freshwater. The green is the chlorophyll that enables plants to get their energy from sunlight.

- **Green algae** called Spirogyra form long threads.

- **Red or brown algae** are found in warm seas. Their chlorophyll is masked by other pigments.

145

Plankton

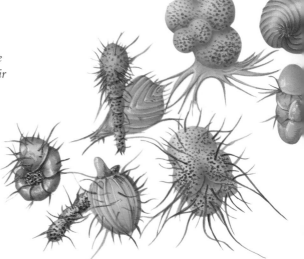

▶ *Single-celled predators such as these heliozoans and foraminiferans use their long tentacles to catch microscopic plankton (phytoplankton).*

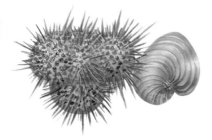

- **Plankton** are tiny floating organisms (living things) that are found in both the sea and ponds and lakes.

- **The word 'plankton'** comes from a Greek word meaning 'wandering'.

- **Plankton** is a general term that includes every marine organism too small and weak to swim for itself.

- **The smallest algae** are called plankton, but large floating algae (seaweeds) are not called plankton.

- **Plankton** can be divided into phytoplankton, which are tiny plants, and zooplankton, which are tiny animals, but the division is blurred.

146

- **Most phytoplankton** are very tiny indeed and so called nannoplankton and microplankton. Zooplankton are generally bigger and called macroplankton.

- **Green algae** that give many ponds a bright green floating carpet are kinds of plankton.

- **Phytoplankton** get their energy by photosynthesis just like other plants.

- **Countless puffs** of oxygen given out by plankton early in Earth's history gave the air its vital oxygen.

- **Plankton** is the basic food of all large ocean animals.

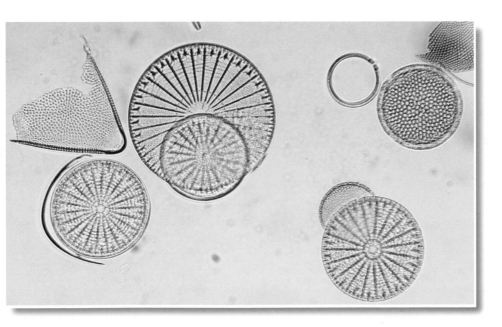

▲ *Diatoms are at the start of the ocean food chain. They use the Sun's light energy for growth.*

Fungi

- **Fungi** are a huge group of 50,000 species. They include mushrooms, toadstools, mould, mildew and yeast.

- **Fungi** are not plants, because they have no chlorophyll to make their food. So scientists put them in a group or kingdom of their own.

- **Because fungi** cannot make their own food, they must live off other plants and animals – sometimes as partners, sometimes as parasites.

- **Parasitic fungi** feed off living organisms; fungi that live off dead plants and animals are called saprophytic.

- **Fungi** feed by releasing chemicals called enzymes to break down chemicals in their host. The fungi then use the chemicals as food.

- **Cheeses** like Camembert, Rocquefort, Stilton and Danish Blue get their distinctive flavours from chemicals made by moulds added to them to help them ripen. The blue streaks in some cheeses are actually moulds.

The chanterelle is a sweet-smelling, edible amber-coloured mushroom. But it looks very like the poisonous jack o'lantern

▶ *These are some of the tens of thousands of different fungi, which are found growing everywhere, from on rotting tree stumps to inside your body.*

Fly agaric is a toadstool – that is, a poisonous mushroom. It is easy to recognize from its spotted red cap

The destroying angel is the most poisonous of all fungi, and usually kills anyone who eats one

Many mould fungi are the source of life-saving antibiotic drugs such as penicillin.

Fungi can grow in all kinds of shapes, earning them names like this orange peel fungi

- **Fungi are made** of countless cotton-like threads called hyphae which absorb the chemicals they feed on. Hyphae are usually spread out in a tangled mass. But they can bundle together to form fruiting bodies like mushrooms.

- **Some fungi** grow by spreading their hyphae in a mat or mycelium; others scatter their spores. Those that grow from spores go through the same two stages as mosses.

- **Truffles** are fungi that grow near oak and hazel roots. They are prized for their flavour and sniffed out by dogs or pigs. The best come from Perigord in France.

The field mushroom, which grows wild and is cultivated, is the most widely eaten mushroom

Honey mushrooms belong to the Armillaria genus of fungi, which includes the world's largest and oldest living organisms

Puffballs have big round fruiting bodies that dry out and puff out their spores in all directions when burst

The water-measure earthstar grows in soil or on rotting wood in grassy areas or woods

149

Mushrooms

- **Mushrooms** are umbrella-shaped fungi, many of which are edible.

- **Mushrooms** feed off either living or decaying plants.

- **Poisonous mushrooms** are called toadstools.

- **The umbrella-shaped** part of the mushroom is called the fruiting body. Under the surface is a mass of fine stalk threads called the mycelium.

- **The threads** making up the mycelium are called hyphae (said 'hi-fi'). These absorb food.

- **The fruiting body** grows overnight after rain and lasts just a few days. The mycelium may survive underground for many years.

- **The fruiting body** is covered by a protective cap. On the underside of this cap are lots of thin sheets called gills. These gills are covered in spores.

- **A mushroom's** gills can produce 16 billion spores in its brief lifetime.

- **The biggest mushrooms** have caps up to 50 cm across and grow up to 40 cm tall.

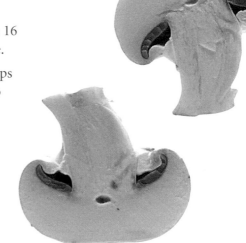

▶ *The ubiquitous button mushroom forms part of many international dishes, from Italian risotto to the classic English fry-up.*

● **Fairy rings** are rings of bright green grass once said to have been made by fairies dancing. They are actually made by a mushroom as its hyphae spread outwards. Chemicals they release make grass grow greener. Gradually the mycelium at the centre dies while outer edges grow and the ring gets bigger.

◄ *Like other fungi, mushrooms cannot make their own food and feed off hosts such as trees.*

151

Poisonous fungi

▲ *The most deadly fungus is the death cap* Amanita phalloides. *It can kill in just six hours.*

- **Many fungi** produce poisons. Scientists call poisons 'toxins' and poisons made by fungi 'mycotoxins'.

- **Some poisonous fungi** are very small microfungi which often form moulds or mildew. Many are either 'sac' fungi (*Ascomycetes*) or 'imperfect' fungi (*Deuteromycetes*).

- **Ergot** is a disease of cereals, especially rye, caused by the sac fungus *Claviceps purpurea*. If humans eat ergot-infected rye, they may suffer an illness called St Anthony's Fire. Ergot is also the source of the drug LSD.

152

- *Aspergillus* is an imperfect fungus that may cause liver damage or even cancer in humans.

- **False morel** is a poisonous sac fungus as big as a mushroom. True morels are harmless.

- **About 75 kinds** of mushroom are toxic to humans and so called toadstools. Most belong to the *Amanita* family, including destroying angels, death caps and fly agarics.

- **Death caps** contain deadly phalline toxins that kill most people who eat the fungus.

- **Fly agaric** was once used as a poison for flies.

- **Fly agaric** and the *Psilocybe mexicana* mushroom were eaten by Latin American Indians because they gave hallucinations.

▲ *Fly agaric contains a poison called muscarine. It rarely kills but makes you feel sick and agitated.*

. . . FASCINATING FACT . . .
Athlete's foot is a nasty foot condition caused by a fungus.

Lichen

- **Lichens** are a remarkable partnership between algae and fungi.

- **The algae** in lichen are tiny green balls which make the food from sunlight to feed the fungi.

- **The fungi make a protective** layer around the algae and hold water.

- **There are 20,000** species of lichen. Some grow on soil, but most grow on rocks or tree bark.

- **Fruticose lichens** are shrub-like, foliose lichens look like leaves, and crustose lichens look like crusts.

- **Lichens only grow** when moistened by rain.

- **Lichens can survive** in many places where other plants would die, such as the Arctic, in deserts and on mountain tops.

- **Some Arctic lichens** are over 4000 years old.

◀ *Crustose rock lichens form dense crusts which attach themselves to the rocks by their whole undersurface.*

▲ *Lichens are tiny and slow-growing – some growing only a fraction of a millimetre a year. But they are usually long-lived.*

- **Lichens are very sensitive** to air pollution, especially sulphur dioxide, and are used by scientists to indicate air pollution.

- **The oakmoss lichen** from Europe and North Africa is added to most perfumes and after-shaves to prevent flower scents from fading. Scandinavian reindeer moss is a lichen that is eaten by reindeer. It is exported to Germany for use as decorations.

155

Mosses

- **Mosses** are tiny, green, non-flowering plants found throughout the world. They form cushions just a few millimetres thick on walls, rocks and logs.

- **Unlike other plants** they have no true roots. Instead, they take in moisture from the air through their stems and tiny, root-like threads called rhizoids.

- **Mosses reproduce** from minute spores in two stages.

- **First** tadpole-like male sex cells are made on bag-like stems called antheridae and swim to join the female eggs on cup-like stems called archegonia.

  - **Then** a stalk called a sporophyte grows from the ova. On top is a capsule holding thousands of spores.

    - **When the time** is right, the sporophyte capsule bursts, ejecting spores. If spores land in a suitable place, male and female stems grow and the process begins again.

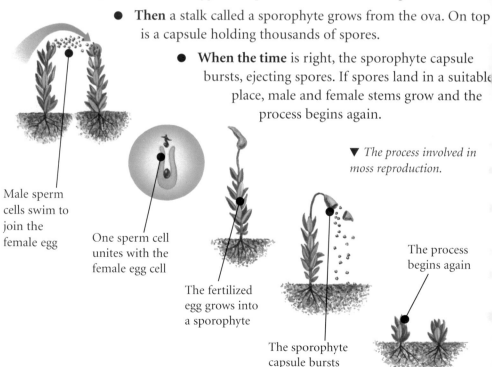

▼ *The process involved in moss reproduction.*

Male sperm cells swim to join the female egg

One sperm cell unites with the female egg cell

The fertilized egg grows into a sporophyte

The sporophyte capsule bursts

The process begins again

▲ *Mosses grow in damp places everywhere. They need to be wet in order to reproduce.*

Mosses can survive for weeks without water, then soak it up like a sponge when it rains.

The sphagnum or peat moss can soak up 25 times its own weight of water.

Male cells can only swim to female cells if the moss is partly under water. So mosses often grow near streams where they get splashed with water.

Spanish moss was often used as a filler in packing cases and to pad upholstery.

157

Ferns

- **Ferns** belong to a group of plants called featherplants or pteridophytes, along with club mosses and horsetails.

- **Featherplants** are among the world's most ancient plants, found as fossils in rocks 400 million years old.

- **Coal is made** largely of fossilized featherplants of the Carboniferous Period 360 – 286 million years ago.

- **There are now** 10,000 species of fern living in damp, shady places around the world.

- **Some ferns** are tiny, with mossy leaves just 1 cm long.

- **Rare tropical tree ferns** can grow up to 25m tall.

- **Fern leaves** are called fronds. When new they are curled up like a shepherd's crook, but they gradually uncurl over time.

▲ *Most ferns grow on the ground in damp, shady places, but some grow on the leaves or stems of other plants.*

Ferns grow into new plants not from seeds but from spores in two stages.

First spores are made in sacs called sporangia. These are the brown spots on the underside of the fronds. From these spores spread out. Some settle in suitable places.

Second spores develop into a tiny heart-shaped plant called a prothallus that makes male and female cells. When bathed in rain, the male cells swim to the female cells, fertilizing them. A new root and stem then grow into a proper fern frond and the tiny prothallus dies.

◄ *Coal is made from dead plants such as ferns. Over 200 million years ago, the ferns would have become buried underground and very gradually turned to coal under the immense pressure of the Earth.*

Gardens

- **The ancient Chinese and Greeks** grew fruit trees, vegetables and herbs in gardens for food and for medicines.
- **In the 1500s** there were five famous botanical gardens in Europe designed to study and grow herbs for medicine.
- **The first botanical gardens** were at Pisa (1543) and Padua (1545) in Italy.

▼ *Kew Gardens was once owned by the Royal Family, but since 1841 has been open to the public.*

- **Carolus Clusius** set up a famous flower garden in Leiden in Holland in the late 1500s. Here the first tulips from China were grown and the Dutch bulb industry began.

- **The most famous gardener** of the 17th century was John Evelyn who set up a beautiful garden at Sayes Court in Deptford near London.

- **The Royal Botanic Gardens** at Kew near London were made famous by Sir Joseph Banks in the late 1700s for their extensive collection of plants from around the world.

- **Today Kew Gardens** has 33,400 classes of living plants and a herbarium of dried plants with 7 million species – that's 98% of the world's plants.

- **Plants** such as rubber plants, pineapples, bananas, tea and coffee were spread around the world from Kew.

▲ *Gardening has become one of the most popular of all pastimes.*

- **Lancelot 'Capability' Brown** (1716-83) was a famous English landscape gardener. He got his nickname by telling clients that their gardens had excellent 'capabilities'.

- **Ornamental gardens** are ordinary flower gardens in which a variety of flowers are laid out in patterns that are pleasing to the eye.

161

Garden flowers

- **All garden flowers** are descended from plants that were once wild, but they have been bred over the centuries to produce flowers quite unlike their wild relatives.

- **Garden flowers** like tea roses, created by cross-breeding two different species, are called hybrids.

- **Garden flowers** tend to have bigger blooms and last for longer than their wild cousins.

- **By hybridization** gardeners have created colours that are impossible naturally, such as black roses.

- **Ornamentals** are flowers cultivated just for show.

▶ *Gardeners try to mix flowers that bloom at different times so the garden is always full of colour.*

162

Botanical gardens such as those at Kew, London, display collections of flowers from many parts of the world.

18th-century botanist Carl Linnaeus made a clock by planting flowers that bloomed at different times of day.

The earliest flowerbeds were the borders of flower tufts Ancient Persians grew along pathways.

A herbaceous border is a traditional flowerbed that is planted with herbaceous perennial flowers such as delphiniums, chrysanthemums and primroses. It flowers year after year.

◀ *Most gardens now have a mix of trees and shrubs, mixed beds of herbaceous flowers and early-flowering bulbs such as crocuses.*

163

Cut flowers

- **Cut flowers** are flowers that are sold by the bunch in florists.

- **The cut flower** trade began in the Netherlands with tulips in the 1600s.

- **In 1995** 60% of the world's cut flowers were grown in Holland.

- **Latin American countries** like Colombia, Ecuador, Guatemala and Costa Rica are now major flower-growers. So too are African countries like Kenya, Zimbabwe, South Africa, Zambia and Tanzania.

- **In China** the growing popularity of St Valentine's day has meant huge areas of China are now planted with flowers.

- **After cutting,** flowers are sent by air to places like Europe and North America. During the journey they are chilled so they will arrive fresh.

- **Most of the world's** cut flowers are sold through the huge flower market in Rotterdam in Holland.

◀ *Garden flowers, when cut and put into water, are ideal for adding a touch of colour and freshness to people's homes.*

- **By encouraging** certain flowers, flower-growers have made cut flowers last longer in the vase – but they have lost the rich scents they once had. Scientists are now trying to reintroduce scent genes to flowers.

- **A corsage** is a small bouquet women began to wear on their bodices in the 18th century.

- **A nosegay** was a small bouquet Victorian ladies carried in their hands. If a man gave a lady a red tulip it meant he loved her. If she gave him back a sprig of dogwood it mean she didn't care. Various pink flowers meant 'no'.

Holland is still famous for its flower markets.

165

The first crops

- **The first crops** were probably root crops like turnips. Grains and green vegetables were probably first grown as crops later.

- **Einkorn and emmer wheat** and wild barley may have been cultivated by Natufians (stone-age people) around 7000BC at Ali Kosh on the border of Iran and Iraq.

▲ *Pumpkins are grown on bushes or on vines like these throughout Europe and North America.*

▶ *Flax was the most important vegetable fibre in Europe before cotton. It is still used to make linen.*

- **Pumpkins** and beans were cultivated in Mexico c.7000BC.

- **People** in the Amazon have grown manioc to make a flat bread called cazabi for thousands of years.

- **Corn** was probably first grown about 9000 years ago from the teosinte plant of the Mexican highlands.

- **Russian botanist** N. I. Vavilov worked out that wheat and rye came from the wild grasses of central Asia, millet and barley from highland China and rice from India.

- **Millet** was grown in China from c.4500BC.

- **In northern Europe** the first grains were those now called fat hen, gold of pleasure and curl-topped lady's thumb.

- **Sumerian** farmers in the Middle East c.3000BC grew barley, wheat, flax, dates, plums and grapes.

...**FASCINATING FACT**...
Beans, bottle gourds and water chestnuts were grown at Spirit Cave in Thailand 11,000 years ago.

167

The farming year

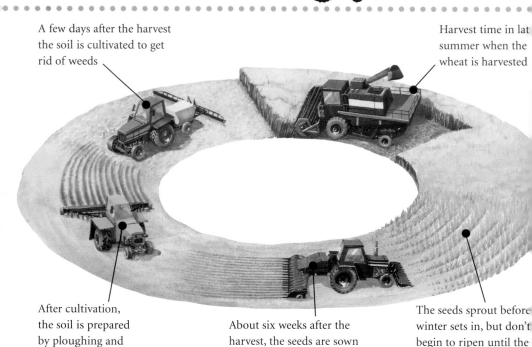

A few days after the harvest the soil is cultivated to get rid of weeds

Harvest time in late summer when the wheat is harvested

After cultivation, the soil is prepared by ploughing and harrowing

About six weeks after the harvest, the seeds are sown in the prepared soil

The seeds sprout before winter sets in, but don't begin to ripen until the following spring

▲ *This illustration shows the typical sequence of events in a grain farmer's year, from ploughing and sowing the seed right through to the harvest the following autumn.*

- **The farming year** varies considerably around the world, and farmers do different tasks at different times of year in different places.

- **In temperate regions** the crop farmer's year starts in autumn after the harvest. Once the straw has been baled and the surplus burned, the race starts to prepare the soil for next year's crops before snow and frost set in.

- **A tractor** drags a cultivator (like a large rake) across the field in order to make weeds 'chit' (germinate). A few days later the soil is cultivated again to uproot the seedlings.

- **Next the soil** is ploughed to break up the soil ready for the seed to be sown, then harrowed to smooth out the furrows made by the plough.

- **Within six weeks** of the harvest if the weather holds,

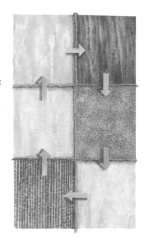

▶ *Without artificial fertilizers, the soil is quickly exhausted if grain crops are planted year after year. So in the past, farmers rotated fields with different crops to allow the soil to rest. Rotation systems varied, but usually included grain, green plants, and 'rest' crops. The earliest systems had just two alternating fields. Medieval farmers used three fields. From the 1700s, rotations became more complex.*

winter wheat or barley seed is sown, fertilizer is applied and the seed soon sprouts like a carpet of grass.

- In winter, the farmer turns to tasks like hedge-cutting, ditching and fencing.

- **In spring** potatoes, oats and spring wheat and barley are planted, and winter crops treated with nitrogen fertilizer. In spring and summer, many farmers treat crops with 30 or more pesticides and weedkillers.

- **As the summer wears on** the wheat turns gold and is ready for harvesting when the electronic moisture metre shows it contains less than 18% moisture.

- **If the summer** is damp, the grain's moisture content may not go down below 25%, making harvesting difficult. But warm sun can quickly rectify the situation.

- **The farming year** ends with the harvest. In the past this used to be separated into various stages – harvesting, threshing, winnowing and baling. Now combine harvesters allow the farmer to complete them all at one go.

Fertilizers

▼ *Once the soil is broken up by ploughing, fertilizers are applied to prepare the soil for planting.*

- **Fertilizers** are natural or artificial substances added to soil to make crops and garden plants grow better.

- **Natural fertilizers** such as manure and compost have been used since the earliest days of farming.

- **Manure** comes mostly from farm animals, though in some countries human waste is used.

- **Manure** contains the chemicals nitrogen, phosphorus and potassium plants need for growth. It is also rich in humus, organic matter that helps keep water in the soil.

- **Artificial fertilizers** are usually liquid or powdered chemicals (or occasionally gas), containing a mix of nitrogen, phosphorus or potassium. They also have traces of sulphur, magnesium and calcium.

- **Nitrogen fertilizer**, also called nitrate fertilizer, is made from ammonia, which is made from natural gas.

- **The first fertilizer** factory was set up by Sir John Lawes in Britain in 1843. He made superphosphate by dissolving bones in acid. Phosphates now come from bones or rocks.

- **Potassium fertilizers** come from potash dug up in mines.

- **The use of artificial** fertilizers has increased in the last 40 years, especially throughout the developed world.

- **Environmentalists** worry about the effects of nitrate fertilizers entering water supplies, and the huge amount of energy that is needed to make, transport and apply them.

Cereals

- **Cereals** such as wheat, maize, rice, barley, sorghum, oats, rye and millet are the world's major sources of food.

- **Cereals are grasses** and we eat their seeds or grain.

- **The leaves and stalks** are usually left to rot into animal feed called silage.

- **Some grains** such as rice are simply cooked and eaten. Most are milled and processed into foods such as flour, oils and syrups.

- **In the developed world** – that is, places like North America and Europe – wheat is the most important food crop. But for half the world's population, including most people in Southeast Asia and China rice is the staple food.

- **Many grains** are used to make alcoholic drinks such as whisky. A fermentation process turns the starch in the grains to alcohol. Special processing of barley creates a food called malt, which is used by brewers to make beer and lager.

- **Oats** have a higher food value than any other grain.

- **Rye** makes heavy, black bread. The bread is heavy because rye does not contain much gluten which yeast needs to make bread rise.

- **Russia** grows more oats and rye than any other country.

- **Millet** produces tiny seeds and is grown widely in dry regions of Africa and Asia. It was the main crop all over Europe, Asia and Africa in ancient and medieval times.

▶ *Harvesting wheat and using it to make flour is a surprisingly complex process. The process is still done with simple tools in some parts of the world. But in the developed world, the entire process is largely mechanized.*

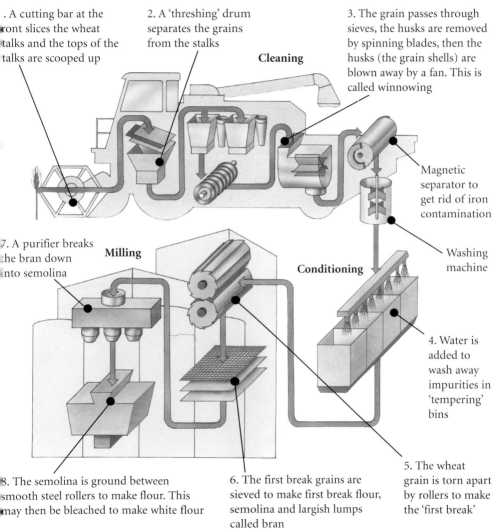

. A cutting bar at the ront slices the wheat talks and the tops of the talks are scooped up

2. A 'threshing' drum separates the grains from the stalks

Cleaning

3. The grain passes through sieves, the husks are removed by spinning blades, then the husks (the grain shells) are blown away by a fan. This is called winnowing

Magnetic separator to get rid of iron contamination

Washing machine

7. A purifier breaks the bran down into semolina

Milling

Conditioning

4. Water is added to wash away impurities in 'tempering' bins

8. The semolina is ground between smooth steel rollers to make flour. This may then be bleached to make white flour

6. The first break grains are sieved to make first break flour, semolina and largish lumps called bran

5. The wheat grain is torn apart by rollers to make the 'first break'

173

Wheat

- **Wheat grows** over more farmland than any other crop and is the basic food for 35% of the world's population.

- **Wheat was** one of the first crops ever grown. It was planted by the first farmers some 11,000 years ago.

- **Today** there are over 30 varieties. Among the oldest are emmer and einkorn.

- **Spring wheat** is planted in spring and then harvested in early autumn.

- **Winter wheat** is planted in autumn and harvested the following summer.

▲ Bread can be moulded into many different shapes and sizes, such as this plaited loaf.

◄ An ear of wheat with the seeds which are stripped of their shells or husks before being ground to make flour.

Wheat is a kind of grass, as are other cereals.

Young wheat plants are short and green and look like ordinary grass, but as they ripen they turn golden and grow up to 1.5 m.

Branching from the main stem are stalks called tillers. Wrapped round them is the base or sheath of the leaves. The flat top of the leaf is called the blade.

The head of the corn where the seeds or grain grow is called the ear or spike. We eat the seed's kernels (core), ground into flour to make bread, pasta and other things.

Pasta is made from durum (hard-grain) wheat. Italians have been using it in their cooking since the 13th century, but now pasta dishes are popular worldwide.

Harvesting grain

- **When grain** is ripe it is cut from its stalks. This is called reaping.

- **After reaping** the grain must be separated from the stalks and chaff (waste). This is called threshing.

- **After threshing** the grain must be cleaned and separated from the husks. This is called winnowing.

- **In some places** grain is still reaped in the ancient way with a long curved blade called a sickle.

- **In most developed countries** wheat and other cereals are usually harvested with a combine harvester.

- **A combine harvester** is a machine that reaps the grain, threshes it, cleans it and then pours it into bags or reservoirs.

- **The first horse-drawn** combine was used in Michigan in 1836, but modern self-propelled harvesters only came into use in the 1940s.

- **If the grain is damp** it must be dried immediately after harvesting so it does not rot. This is always true of rice.

▲ *Some grains are eaten simply after being cooked. But most are further processed into foods such as flour, meal, syrup or oil.*

▲ *The combine harvester's full name is combined harvester–thresher, as it both reaps and threshes.*

● **If the grain is too damp** to harvest, a machine called a windrower may cut the stalks and lay them in rows to dry in the wind. They will then be threshed and cleaned.

● **A successful harvest** is traditionally celebrated with a harvest festival. The cailleac or last sheaf of corn is said to be the spirit of the field. It is made into a harvest doll, drenched with water and saved for the spring planting.

177

Maize or corn

- **Maize or corn** is the USA's most important crop, and the second most important crop around the world after wheat. Rice is the third.

- **Corn,** like all cereals, is a kind of grass.

- **Corn** was first grown by the Indians of Mexico over 7000 years ago and so came to be called Indian corn by Europeans like Columbus.

- **In the USA** only varieties that give multi-coloured ears are now known as Indian corn.

◄ *Popcorn is a popula* *snack food. When heated in a saucepan, the kernels make a lou* *'popping' noise and literally jump out of th* *pan. The 'popped' popcorn can then be eaten straight away, with salt or sugar for extra taste.*

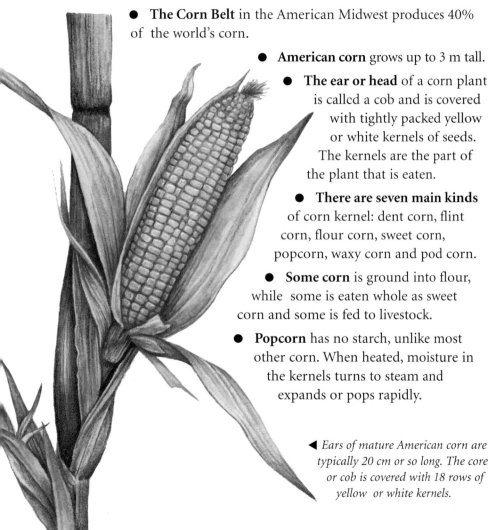

● **The Corn Belt** in the American Midwest produces 40% of the world's corn.

● **American corn** grows up to 3 m tall.

● **The ear or head** of a corn plant is called a cob and is covered with tightly packed yellow or white kernels of seeds. The kernels are the part of the plant that is eaten.

● **There are seven main kinds** of corn kernel: dent corn, flint corn, flour corn, sweet corn, popcorn, waxy corn and pod corn.

● **Some corn** is ground into flour, while some is eaten whole as sweet corn and some is fed to livestock.

● **Popcorn** has no starch, unlike most other corn. When heated, moisture in the kernels turns to steam and expands or pops rapidly.

◄ *Ears of mature American corn are typically 20 cm or so long. The core or cob is covered with 18 rows of yellow or white kernels.*

179

Rice

▲ *Rice appears in many different kinds of foods, such as breakfast cereals, soups and snacks.*

- **Rice** is a cereal grain that is the basic food of half the world's population. It is especially important in Southeast Asia.
- **The wild rice** or Indian rice collected by Native Americans for thousands of years is not related to rice.
- **Like other cereals,** rice is a grass, but it grows best in shallow water in tropical areas.
- **Rice growers** usually flood their fields to keep them wet. The flooded fields are called paddies.

...FASCINATING FACT...
A lot of wheat is fed to livestock, but 95%
of all rice is eaten by people.

- **The rice seeds** are sown in soil, then when the seedlings are 25–50 days old they are transplanted to the paddy field under 5–10 cm of water.

- **Brown rice** is rice grain with the husk ground away. White rice is rice grain with the inner bran layer ground away as well, and is far less nutritious.

- **Rice-growing** probably began in India about 3000BC.

- **In 1962** researchers in the Philippines experimented with hybrids of 10,000 strains of rice. They made a rice called 'IR-8' by crossing a tall, vigorous rice from Indonesia and a dwarf rice from Taiwan.

- **IR-8** sometimes gave double yields, and was called 'miracle rice', but it did not grow well in poor soils.

▲ *To keep paddies flooded, fields on hillsides are banked in terraces.*

Green vegetables

- **Green vegetables** are the edible green parts of plants, including the leaves of plants such as cabbages and lettuces, and the soft stems of plants like asparagus.

- **Cabbages** are a large group of green vegetables called the brassicas.

- **Cabbages were** originally developed from the sea cabbage (Brassica oleracea) which grew wild near sea coasts around Europe.

- **Kale and collard** are types of cabbage with loose, open leaves.

- **Common and savoy** cabbages are cabbages with leaves folded into a tight ball. Brussels sprouts are cabbages with lots of compact heads.

- **Cauliflower and broccoli** are cabbages with thick flowers. Kohlrabi is a cabbage with a bulbous stem.

▶ *The edible young stems of the asparagus are called spears. If the spears are not harvested they grow into tall, feathery plants.*

● **The leaves of green vegetables** are rich in many essential vitamins including vitamin A, vitamin E and folic acid (one of the B vitamins).

● **Spinach** looks a little like kale, but it is actually a member of the goosefoot family, rich in vitamins A and C, and also in iron. The discovery of the iron content made spinach into the superfood of the cartoon hero Popeye, who would eat it to give himself strength.

● **Asparagus** belongs to the lily family. Garden asparagus has been prized since Roman times.

● **In Argenteuil** in France, asparagus is grown underground to keep it white. White asparagus is especially tender and has the best flavour.

▲ *Fresh spinach can be steamed or boiled, or used in salads, soups and pies. Sometimes it is sold frozen or tinned.*

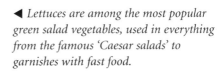

◀ *Lettuces are among the most popular green salad vegetables, used in everything from the famous 'Caesar salads' to garnishes with fast food.*

183

Root vegetables

▲ *Turnip roots are most commonly cooked in stews and casseroles, or used as animal feed.*

- **Vegetables** are basically any parts of a plant, except for the fruit, that are eaten, cooked or raw.

- **Root vegetables** are parts of a plant that grow underground in the soil.

- **Turnips, rutabaga,** beets, carrots, parsnips and sweet potatoes are the actual roots of the plant.

- **Potatoes and cassava** are tubers or storage stems.

- **Potatoes** were grown in South America at least 1800 years ago. They were brought to Europe by the Spanish in the 16th century.

● **Poor Irish** farmers came to depend on the potato, and when blight ruined the crop in the 1840s, many starved.

● **Yams are tropical roots** similar to sweet potatoes. They are an important food in West Africa. A single yam can weigh 45 kg or more.

● **Mangel-wurzels** are beet plants grown mainly to feed to farm animals.

● **Tapioca** is a starchy food made from cassava. It makes a popular pudding.

● **Carrots came** originally from Afghanistan, but were spread around the Mediterranean 4000 years ago. They reached China by the 13th century AD.

▼▶ *Potatoes and carrots are important root vegetables. Carrots are a source of vitamin A, potatoes are a source of many vitamins, such as C.*

Sugar

- **Sugars** are sweet-tasting natural substances made by plants and animals. All green plants make sugar.

- **Fruit and honey** contain a sugar called fructose. Milk contains the sugar named lactose.

- **The most common sugar** is called sucrose, or just sugar – like the sugar you sprinkle on cereal.

▼ *Sugar cane was first grown by South Pacific islanders more than 8000 years ago.*

- **Sugar is made** from sugar cane and sugar beet.

- **Sugar cane** is a tropical grass with woody stems 2–5 m tall. It grows in places like India and Brazil.

- **Sugar juice is made** from cane by shredding and crushing the stems and soaking them in hot water to dissolve the sugar.

- **Sugar beet** is a turnip-like plant that grows in temperate countries.

- **Sugar juice is made** from beet by soaking thin slices of the root in hot water to dissolve the sugar.

- **Sugar juice** is warmed to evaporate water so crystals form.

- **White sugar** is sugar made from sugar beet, or by refining (purifying) cane-sugar. Brown sugars such as muscovado and demerara are unrefined cane-sugar. Molasses and black treacle are by-products of cane-sugar refining.

Crystals of demerara sugar are made from the ugary juice from the stems of the tropical sugar cane.

Citrus fruit

▲ *Orange trees are planted in groves. The fruit are green when they first appear, but turn orange as they ripen.*

- **Citrus fruits** are a group of juicy soft fruits covered with a very thick, waxy, evenly coloured skin in yellow, orange or green.
- **Citrus** fruits include lemons, limes, oranges, grapefruits and shaddocks.
- **Inside the skin,** the flesh of a citrus fruit is divided into clear segments, each usually containing one or several seeds or pips.

Citrus fruits grow in warm Mediterranean climates, and they are very vulnerable to frost.

Some citrus fruit-growers warm the trees with special burners in winter to avoid frost-damage.

The sharp tang of citrus fruits comes from citric acid.

Lemons were spread through Europe by the crusaders who found them growing in Palestine.

Columbus took limes to the Americas in 1493.

Scottish physician James Lind (1716–1794) helped eradicate the disease scurvy from the British navy by recommending that sailors eat oranges and lemons.

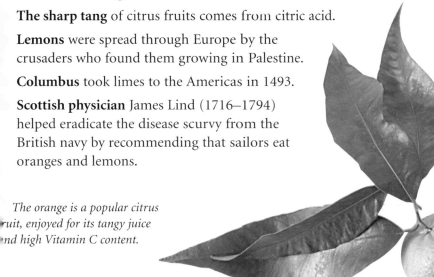

The orange is a popular citrus fruit, enjoyed for its tangy juice and high Vitamin C content.

...FASCINATING FACT...
Citrus fruits are richer in Vitamin C than any other fruit or vegetable.

189

Temperate fruit

- **Fruits of temperate regions** must have a cool winter to grow properly.

- **The main temperate fruits** are apples, pears, plums, apricots, peaches, grapes and cherries.

- **Apples were eaten** by the earliest Europeans hundreds of thousands of years ago. They were spread through the USA by Indians, trappers and travellers like Johnny 'Appleseed' Chapman.

▲ *Cherries grow on trees that do not thrive well in extreme temperatures.*

- **The world** picks 32 million tonnes of apples a year, half are eaten fresh and a quarter are made into the alcoholic drink cider. The USA is the world's leading producer of cider apples.

- **The world's most** popular pear is the Williams' Bon Chrétien or Bartlett. The best is said to to be the Doyenne du Comice, first grown in France in 1849.

▶ *Plums are a kind of fruit called a drupe. This means the seed is contained inside a hard stone in the middle of the fruit.*

◀ *Pears are the second most important temperate fruit after apples. The leading producer is China.*

▶ *Apricots are smaller than peaches with smoother skin. They are eaten fresh, dried, or in jams or puddings.*

◀ *Peaches are native to China but are now widely grown in southern Europe. Their sweet, fragrant flesh makes them a popular delicacy.*

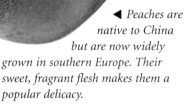

● **New pear trees** are grown not from seeds but by grafting branches on to roots such as those of quinces.

● **Plums** came originally from the Caucasus Mountains in Turkey and Turkey is still the world's major plum grower. The damson plum came from Damascus.

● **Plums** are dried to make prunes.

● **The peach** is 87% water and has far fewer calories than fruit like apples and pears.

● **Grapes are grown** in vineyards to make wine. Grape-growing or viticulture is described in detail in Ancient Egyptian hieroglyphs of 2400BC.

191

Tropical fruit

- **Tropical fruits** grow mainly in the tropics where it is warm because they canno survive even a light frost.

- **The best-known tropical fruits** are bananas and pineapples. Others include guavas, breadfruit, lychees, melons, mangoes and papayas.

- **Banana plants** are gigantic herbs with trunks that grow 3–6 m high.

- **Alexander the Great** saw bananas in India in 326BC. Bananas were taken to the Caribbean from the Canaries in about 550. They are now one of the main Caribbean crops.

▲ *Bananas are picked green and unripe, shipped in refrigerated ships, then artificially ripened with 'ethylene' gas to turn them yellow.*

There are hundreds of varieties of banana. Most widely used is the Gros Michel. Plantains are cooking bananas.

Pineapples come from Central America, and would have been seen by Christopher Columbus and Sir Walter Raleigh.

The Portuguese took pineapples to India about 1550. Thailand is now the world's leading producer.

Mangoes grow on evergreen trees of the cashew family in Burma and India.

The mango is sacred to Buddhists because the mango groves provided welcome shade for Buddha.

Melons are a huge group of big, round fruit with soft, juicy flesh, including canteloupes. They grow on trailing vines. Watermelons are not in fact true melons.

Tropical fruits come in a variety of weird and wonderful shapes, colours and sizes.

Berries

- **Berries** are fleshy fruit which contain lots of seeds. The bright colours attract birds which eat the flesh. The seeds pass out in the birds' droppings and so spread.

- **Bananas,** tomatoes and cranberries are all berries.

- **Strawberries,** raspberries and blackberries are not true berries. They are called 'aggregate' fruits because each is made from groups of tiny fruit with one seed.

- **Gean,** damson and blackthorn berries contain a single seed. Holly berries and elderberries contain many.

- **Cloudberries are aggregate fruits like raspberries.** The tiny amber berries grow close to the ground in the far north, and are collected by Inuits and Sami people in autumn to freeze for winter food.

▲ *Many berries are bright red and shiny to attract birds.*

- **Cloudberries** are also known as salmonberries, bakeberries, malka and baked appleberries.

- **Cranberries** grow wild on small trailing plants in marshes, but are now cultivated extensively in the USA in places such as Massachusetts.

- **Wild huckleberries** are the American version of the European bilberry. But the evergreen huckleberry sold in florists is actually a blueberry.

- **The strawberry tree's** Latin name is *unedo*, which means 'I eat one'. The red berries are not as tasty as they look.

- **According to Greek mythology,** the wine-red mulberry was once white but was stained red by the blood of the tragic lovers Pyramus and Thisbe, whose story is retold in Shakespeare's *Midsummer Night's Dream.*

Surprisingly, bananas are berries, as they are soft, fleshy and contain seeds.

Grapes

▲ *The vineyards of Provence, like every region in France, produce wine with its own distinct flavour.*

- **Grapes** are juicy, smooth-skinned berries that grow in tight clusters on woody plants called vines.

- **Grapes** can be black, blue, green, purple, golden or white, depending on what kind they are.

- **Some grapes** are eaten fresh and some dried as raisins, but 80% are crushed to make wine.

- **Grapes** are grown all round the world in places where there are warm summers and mild winters, especially in France, Italy, Spain, Australia, Chile, Romania, Georgia, South Africa and California.

196

- **Among the best wine grapes** are the Cabernet Sauvignon and Chardonnay for white wine and the Pinot Noir for red wine.

- **The Ancient Egyptians** made wine from grapes around 5000 years ago.

- **Grapes are made** into wine by a process called fermentation.

- **Grapes** for eating fresh are called table grapes and are bigger and sweeter than wine grapes. Varieties include Emperor, red Tokay, green Perlette and black Ribier.

- **Grapes grown** for raisins are seedless. The best known is Thompson's seedless, sometimes called the sultana.

- **Grapevines** are grown from cuttings. They start to give fruit after three or four years and may bear fruit for a century. Each vine usually gives 10–35 kg of grapes.

▲ *Grapes have been cultivated since the earliest times. Purple grapes like these will be used to make red wine.*

197

Cocoa

- **Cocoa beans** are the fruit of the cacao tree.

- **Cocoa beans** are called cocoa beans and not cacao beans due to a spelling mistake made by English importers in the 18th century when chocolate first became popular.

- **Cocoa beans** are the seeds inside melon-shaped pods about 30 cm long.

- **Cacao trees** came originally from Central America. Now they are grown in the West Indies and West Africa too.

- **Chocolate** is made by grinding the kernels of cocoa beans to a paste called chocolate liquor. The liquor is hardened in moulds to make chocolate.

- **Cooking chocolate** is bitter. Eating chocolate has sugar and, often, milk added.

- **Cocoa powder** is made by squeezing the cocoa butter (fat) from chocolate liquor and then pulverizing it.

- **When Spanish explorer** Hernán Cortés reached the court of Moctezuma (Aztec ruler of Mexico in 1519) he was served a bitter drink called xocoatl. The people of Central America had regarded xocoatl as a sacred drink since the time of the Mayans.

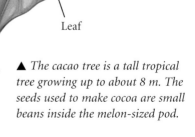

Cacao tree

Pod

Leaf

▲ *The cacao tree is a tall tropical tree growing up to about 8 m. The seeds used to make cocoa are small beans inside the melon-sized pod.*

Belgian chocolates are renowned for their excellent quality. Many Belgian chocolate makers like to keep their recipes secret so they can't be copied.

- **In the 1600s,** Europeans began to open fashionable chocolate houses to serve xocoatl as hot chocolate sweetened with sugar. In the 1700s, the English began adding milk to improve the flavour.

- **'Cacao'** is a Mayan word for 'bitter juice'; the word 'chocolate' comes from the Mayan for 'sour water'.

Coffee and tea

- **Coffee** comes from the glossy, evergreen Coffee arabica shrub, which originally grew wild in Ethiopia. Coffee is now grown in tropical countries around the world.

- **The coffee plant** is a mountain plant and grows best from about 1000 to 2500 m up.

▼ *Workers called 'tea pluckers' pick leaves from mature tea plants by hand. The leaves are then taken to a nearby factory to be dried, crushed and treated.*

- **Coffee beans** are not actually beans at all; they are the seeds inside the red coffee berries.

- **Coffee plants** can grow to over 6 m tall, but they are usually pruned to under 4 m to make picking easier.

- **A coffee plant** yields only enough berries to make about 0.7 kg of coffee each year.

- **Coffee berries** are picked by hand then pulped to remove the flesh and finally roasted.

▲ *Coffee berries appear green at first, then turn yellow and eventually bright red as they ripen.*

Tea is the leaves of the evergreen tea plant that grows in the tropics, mostly at an altitude of between 1000 and 2000 m.

Tea plants have small, white, scented flowers and nuts that look like hazelnuts.

Tea plants grow 9 m tall but they are pruned to 3 m.

... FASCINATING FACT ...
Legend says Ethiopian goatherds discovered coffee when they saw their goats staying awake all night after eating the berries of the coffee plant.

201

Herbs

- **Herbs** are small plants used as medicines or to flavour food.

- **Most herbs** are perennial and have soft stems which die back in winter.

- **With some herbs** such as rosemary, only the leaves are used. With others, such as garlic, the bulb is used. Fennel is used for its seeds as well as its bulb and leaves. Coriander is used for its leaves and seeds.

- **Basil** gets its name from the Greek *basilikon* or 'kingly', because it was so highly valued around the Mediterranean for its strong flavour. In the Middle Ages, judges and officials used to carry it in posies in order to ward off unpleasant smells.

- **Rosemary** is a coastal plant and gets its name from the Latin *ros marinus*, meaning 'sea dew'. People who study herbs – herbalists – once thought it improved memory.

- **Bay leaves** are the leaves of an evergreen laurel tree. They were used to make crowns for athletes, heroes and poets in Ancient Rome. It is said that a bay tree planted by your house protects it from lightning.

- **Oregano** or marjoram is a Mediterranean herb used in Italian cooking. The plant gave its name to the American state of Oregon where it is now commonly used.

- **Sage** is a herb thought by herbalists of old to have special healing qualities. Its scientific name *Salvia* comes from the Latin word *salvere*, 'to save'.

- **St John's wort** is a perennial herb with yellow flowers which was said to have healing qualities given by St John the Baptist. The red juice of its leaves represented his blood. Now many people use it to treat depression.

▼ *These are some of the more common herbs used in cooking, either fresh or dried. The flavour comes from what are called 'essential oils' in the leaves. Parsley, thyme and a bay leaf may be tied up in a piece of muslin cloth to make what is called a bouquet garni. This is hung in soups and stews while cooking to give them extra flavour, but is not actually eaten.*

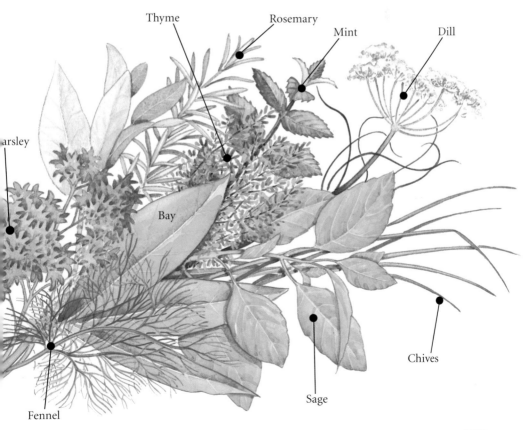

Thyme

Rosemary

Mint

Dill

Parsley

Bay

Chives

Sage

Fennel

203

Spices

● **The Phoenicians** traded in spices 2500 years ago.

● **The great voyages** of exploration of the 1400s, like those of Columbus, were mainly to find ways to reach sources of spices in Southeast Asia.

● **The Molucca Islands** in Indonesia were known as the Spice Islands because they were the main source of cloves, nutmeg and mace.

● **Sesame** was used by the Ancient Chinese for ink and by the Romans as sandwich spread. Arabs thought it had magical powers. In *Ali Baba and the 40 Thieves*, Ali says, 'open sesame' to magically open a door.

● **Cinnamon** is the inner bark of a laurel tree native to Sri Lanka. It was once more valuable than gold.

▼ *The yellow stigmas of the purple saffron crocus make the valuable spice, saffron.*

Spices made from fragrant tropical plants have long been used to flavour food.

Allspice is the berries of a myrtle tree native to the West Indies. It gets its name because it tastes like a mixture of cloves, cinnamon and nutmeg.

In Ancient Greece and Rome people often paid their taxes in peppercorns.

Cloves are the dried buds of a large evergreen tree that grows in the Moluccas.

From 200 BC Chinese courtiers sucked cloves to make their breath smell sweet for the Emperor.

Saffron is the yellow stigmas of the purple saffron crocus, used as a dye by Buddhist priests. It is the most costly of all spices. It takes 170,000 flowers to make just 1 kg.

Medicinal plants

- **Prehistoric neanderthal people** probably used plants as medicines at least 50,000 years ago.

- **Until quite recently** herbaceous plants were our main source of medicines. Plants used as medicines were listed in books called herbals.

- **An ancient Chinese** list of 1892 herbal remedies that was drawn up over 3000 years ago is still used today.

- **The famous illustrated herbal** of Greek physician Dioscorides was made in the 1st century BC.

▶ *The bitter-tasting Centaury herb was once used to combat fevers and treat digestive disorders.*

▲ *Henbane is a pungent, poisonous herb. It produces a drug called hyoscyamine, used to dilate the pupils of the eyes.*

Vincristine is a drug made from the Madagascar periwinkle that helps children fight cancer.

The most famous English herbalist was Nicholas Culpeper, who wrote *A Physical Directory* in 1649.

Most medicines, except antibiotics, come from flowering plants or were first found in flowering plants.

Powerful painkilling drugs come from the seeds of the opium poppy.

Digitalis is a heart drug that came from foxgloves. It is poisonous if taken in large doses.

Garlic is thought to protect the body against heart disease – and vampires!

The bark of the willow tree was originally used to make aspirin, the painkiller most widely used today.

Cotton

▲ *Mechanical cotton-pickers pull cotton from the bolls and blow it into a steel basket behind.*

- **Cotton** is a fibre that comes from the cotton plant.
- **The cotton plant** is a small shrub that grows in the tropics and subtropics.
- **Cotton plants** are annuals and are planted fresh each spring.

*The bolls picked for cotton develop from the seed
?d left when the petals of the cotton flower drop
f in summer.*

Cotton plants grow seed pods
called bolls, containing 20–40
seeds – each covered with soft,
downy hairs or fibres.

As bolls ripen they burst open
to reveal the mass of fluffy
fibres inside.

When separated from the
seeds, the fluff is known as
cotton lint.

Cotton seeds are processed to
make products such as oil, cattle
cake and fertilizer.

There are 39 species of cotton
plant, but only four are cultivated: the
upland, Pima, tree and Levant.

Upland plants produce about 90% of the
world's cotton.

Upland and Pima both came from the Americas, unlike tree and Levant, which
are from the Middle East and Africa.

Timber

- **Timber** is useful wood. Lumber is a North American term for timber once it is sawn or split.

- **Lumberjacks** are people who cut down trees using power saws or chainsaws.

- **Round timbers** are basically tree trunks that have been stripped of their bark and branches and cut into logs.

- **Round timbers** are used for fencing and telegraph poles or driven into the ground as 'piles' to support buildings and quays.

▲ *After the timber is sawn and trimmed, it is stacked in the timberyard to dry.*

- **Lumber** is boards and planks sawn from logs at sawmills. At least half of lumber is used for building.

- **Before lumber** can be used, it must usually be seasoned (dried) or it will shrink or twist. Sometimes it is dried in the open air, but more often it is warmed in a kiln or treated with chemicals.

- **Sometimes** planks are cut into thin slices called veneers.

- **Plywood** is three or more veneers glued together to make cheap, strong wood. Chipboard is wood chippings and sawdust mixed with glue and then pressed into sheets.

- **Softwood lumbers** come from trees such as pines, larches, firs, hemlocks, redwoods and cedars.

- **MDF** or medium density fibreboard is made from wood fibres glued together.

▶ *Tree surgeons stripping branches from a felled tree with chainsaws.*

The Green Revolution

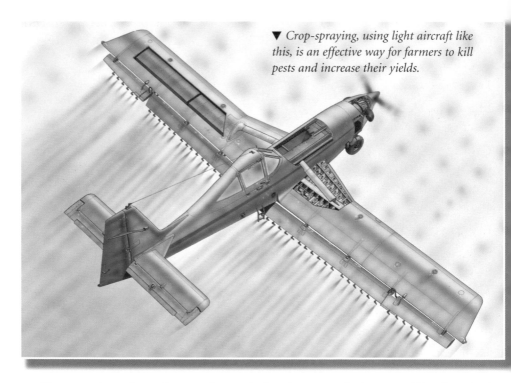

▼ *Crop-spraying, using light aircraft like this, is an effective way for farmers to kill pests and increase their yields.*

- **Since ancient times** farmers have tried to improve their crops. They brushed pollen from one species on to another to combine desirable qualities.

- **In 1876** Charles Darwin discovered that inbreeding – pollinating with almost identical plants – made plants less vigorous. Cross-breeding between different strains produced healthier plants.

● **In the early 1900s** American scientists found that they could improve the protein content of corn by inbreeding – but the yield was poor.

● **In 1917** Donald Jones discovered the 'double-cross', by combining four strains (not the normal two) to create a hybrid corn which gave high yield and high protein.

● **Hybrid corn** changed US farming, raising yields from 2000 litres per hectare in 1933 to 7220 in 1980.

● **In the 1960s** US farmers began growing wheat crosses such as Gaines, developed by Norman Borlaug from Japanese dwarf wheats.

● **Gaines and Nugaines** are short-stemmed wheats that grow fast and give huge yields – but they need masses of artificial fertilizers and pesticides.

● **In India and Asia** new dwarf wheats and rices created a 'Green Revolution', doubling yields in the 1960s and 1970s.

● **The Green Revolution** means farmers now use ten times as much nitrogen fertilizer as they did in 1960.

● **The huge cost** of special seeds, fertilizers and pesticides has often meant that only big agribusinesses can keep up, forcing small farmers out of business.

► *Forty years ago, many farmers abandoned traditional wheat seeds (below right) and began planting big 'superwheat' seeds (top right.)*

Evolution

- **Charles Darwin's** Theory of Evolution, first published in 1859, showed how all species of plant and animal adapt and develop over millions of years.

- **Darwin's theory** depended on the fact that no two living things are alike.

- **Some animals** start life with characteristics that give them a better chance of surviving to pass the characteristics on to their offspring.

- **Other animals' characteristics** mean that they are less likely to survive.

- **Over many generations** and thousands of years, better-adapted animals and plants survive and flourish, while others die out or find a new home.

- **Fossil discoveries** since Darwin's time have supported his theory, and lines of evolution can be traced for thousands of species.

- **Fossils** also show that evolution is not always as slow and steady as Darwin thought. Some scientists believe change comes in rapid bursts, separated by long slow periods when little changes. Other scientists believe that bursts of rapid change interrupt periods of long steady change.

▼ *One of the horse's earliest ancestors,* Hyracotherium, *appeared about 45 mya. It was a small woodland creature which browsed on leaves. When the woods began to disappear and grasslands became more widespread, it paid to be faster to escape predators. The modern horse,* Equus, *is the latest result of this evolutionary adaptation.*

Hyracotherium

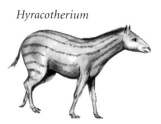

Mesohippus

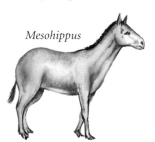

Parahippus

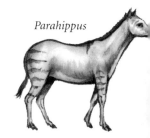

For the first 3 billion years of Earth's history, the only life forms were microscopic, single-celled, marine (sea) organisms such as bacteria and amoeba. Sponges and jellyfish, the first multi-celled creatures, appeared by 700 million years ago (mya).

About 600 mya, evolution speeded up dramatically in what is called the Precambrian explosion. Thousands of different organisms appeared within a very short period of time, including the first proper animals with bones and shells.

After the Precambrian era, life evolved rapidly. Fish developed, then insects and then, about 380 mya, amphibians, which were the first large creatures to crawl on land. About 340 mya, reptiles evolved – the first large creatures to live entirely on land.

Dinosaurs developed from these early reptiles about 220 mya and dominated the Earth for 160 million years. Birds also evolved from the reptiles, and cynodonts furry, mammal-like creatures.

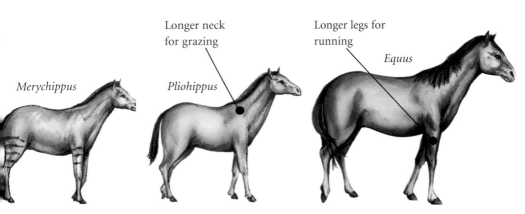

Merychippus

Pliohippus

Longer neck for grazing

Longer legs for running

Equus

Animal senses

- **Animals** sense the world in a variety of ways, including by sight, hearing, touch, smell and taste. Many animals have senses that humans do not have.

- **Sea creatures** rely on their senses of smell and taste, detecting tiny particles drifting in the water. For balance they often rely on simple balance organs called statocysts.

- **Sharks** have a better sense of smell than any other kind of fish. They can detect one part of animal blood in 100 million parts of water.

- **For land animals**, sight is usually the most important sense. Hunting animals often have very sharp eyesight. Eagles, for instance, can see a rabbit moving from as far as 5 km away.

◀ *Hares, like rabbits, have long ears (up to 20 cm long). These are ideal for picking up the faint sounds from approaching predators.*

The slow loris is nocturnal, and its enormous eyes help it jump safely through forests in the darkness.

- **Owls** can hear sounds ten times softer than any human can.

- **Male gypsy moths** can smell a mate from a distance of over 11 km.

- **Pit vipers** have special sensory pits (holes) on their heads which can pinpoint heat. This lets them track warm-blooded prey such as mice in pitch darkness.

- **The forked tongues** of snakes and lizards are used to taste the air and detect prey.

- **Cats' eyes** absorb 50% more light than human eyes, so they can see very well in the dark.

... **FASCINATING FACT** ...
Many butterflies can smell with special sense organs in their feet.

217

Eating food

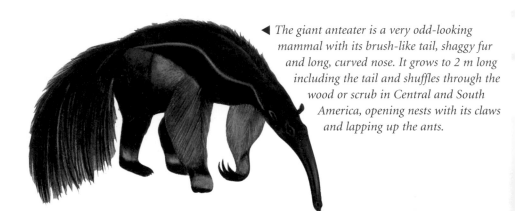

◀ *The giant anteater is a very odd-looking mammal with its brush-like tail, shaggy fur and long, curved nose. It grows to 2 m long including the tail and shuffles through the wood or scrub in Central and South America, opening nests with its claws and lapping up the ants.*

- **Herbivores** are animals that usually eat only plants.
- **Carnivores** are animals that eat animal flesh (meat).
- **Omnivores** eat plants and animals. Many primates such as monkeys, apes and humans are omnivorous.
- **Insectivores** eat insects. Some, such as bats and shrews, have teeth for breaking through insects' shells. Others, such as anteaters, have long, sticky tongues for licking up ants and termites, but few or no teeth.
- **Herbivores** such as cattle, elephants and horses either graze (eat grass) or browse (eat mainly leaves, bark and the buds of bushes and trees).
- **Herbivores** have tough, crowned teeth to cope with their plant food.
- **Carnivores** have pointed canine teeth for tearing meat.
- **Some carnivores,** such as hyenas, do not hunt and instead feed on carrion (the remains of dead animals).

Herbivores eat for much of the time. However, because meat is very nourishing, carnivores eat only occasionally and tend to rest after each meal.

Every living thing is part of the food chain. It feeds on the living thing that comes before it in the chain and is in turn eaten by the living thing that comes after it in the chain.

▲ *Bears are omnivores, eating fish and other meat, although they will eat berries, leaves and almost anything when hungry.*

219

Defence

- **Animals** have different ways of escaping predators – most mammals run away, while birds take to the air.

- **Some animals** use camouflage to hide (see colours and markings). Many small animals hide in burrows.

- **Turtles and tortoises** hide inside their hard shells.

- **Armadillos** curl up inside their bendy body armour.

- **The spiky-skinned** armadillo lizard of South Africa curls up and stuffs its tail in its mouth.

- **Hedgehogs,** porcupines and echidnas are protected by sharp quills (spines).

- **Skunks** and the stinkpot turtle give off foul smells when they are threatened.

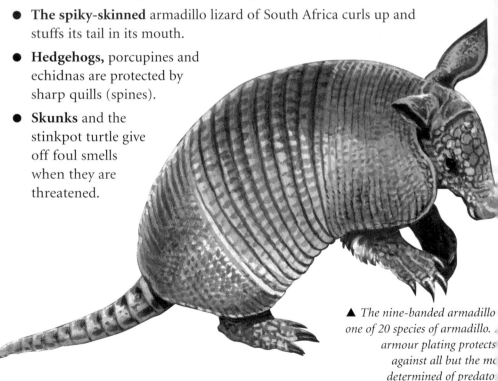

▲ *The nine-banded armadillo one of 20 species of armadillo. armour plating protects against all but the mo determined of predato*

220

▲ *Meerkats stand on their hind legs and give a shrill call to alert other meerkats to danger.*

The plover, a type of bird, pretends to be injured in order to lure hunters away from its young.

Many animals defend themselves by frightening their enemies. Some, such as peacock butterflies, flash big eye-markings. Others, such as porcupine fish and great horned owls, blow themselves up much bigger.

Other animals send out warning signals. Kangaroo rats and rabbits thump their feet. Birds shriek.

> ...FASCINATING FACT...
> The hognosed snake rolls over and plays dead to escape predators. It even smells dead.

Colours and markings

▼ *This red checked nightjar blends superbly with the fallen leaves on which it nests.*

- **Protective colouring** helps an animal hide from its enemies or warns them away.

- **Camouflage** is when an animal is coloured to blend in with its surroundings, making it hard to see.

- **Ground-nesting birds** like the nightjar are mottled brown, making them hard to spot among fallen leaves.

- **The fur of wild pig** and tapir babies is striped and spotted to make them hard to see in dappled jungle light.

- **Squid** can change their colour to blend in with new surroundings.

- **Disruptive colouring** distorts an animal's body so that its real shape is disguised.

- **Bright colours** often warn predators that an animal is poisonous or tastes bad. For example, ladybirds are bright red and the cinnabar moth's caterpillars are black and yellow because they taste nasty.

Some creatures mimic the colours of poisonous ones to warn predators off. Harmless hoverflies, for instance, look just like wasps.

Some animals frighten off predators with colouring that makes them look much bigger. Peacock butterflies have big eyespots on their wings.

Courting animals, especially male birds like the peacock, are often brightly coloured to attract mates.

A zebra's stripes may seem to make it easy to see, but when it
moving they actually blur its outline and confuse predators.

The mating game

- **In some species** of Australian marsupial mouse, the male dies after a two-week mating period.

- **A beaver stays with its mate** for many years, producing a new litter each year.

- **A male hedgehog** courts a female by circling her, sometimes wearing a deep groove in the soil, until she accepts him.

- **Male Californian sea-lions** bark to guard their mating territory. Underwater, the barks produce bursts of bubbles.

- **The hooded seal** impresses females by inflating a nostril lining into a red balloon.

▲ *The mandrill's facial markings and reddish-blue rump signify to females his suitability as a mate.*

- **The red markings** on a male mandrill's blue and red face become brighter during the mating season.

- **To attract potential mates**, orang-utan males emit a series of loud roars that tail off into groans.

- **White rhino males** have strict territorial boundaries. They try to keep receptive females within the territory, but if a female strays outside, he will not follow her.

- **Hippos** prefer to mate in the water, with the female often completely submerged, and having to raise her head to breathe every so often.

▼ *A male narwhal's tusk can be up to 3 m long, and is actually one of its only two teeth.*

...FASCINATING FACT...
Narwhal males compete for mates by 'fencing' with their long, spiral tusks.

Life on the seashore

- **Seashores** contain a huge variety of creatures which can adapt to the constant change from wet to dry as the tide rolls in and out.

- **Crabs, shellfish** and other creatures of rocky shores have tough shells to protect them from pounding waves and the sun's drying heat.

- **Anemones, starfish** and shellfish such as barnacles have powerful suckers for holding on to rocks.

- **Limpets** are the best rock clingers and can only be prised off if caught by surprise

- **Anemones** may live on a hermit crab's shell, feeding on its leftovers but protecting it with their stinging tentacles.

- **Rock pools** are pools of water left among the rocks when the tide goes out.

- **Rock pool creatures** include shrimps, hermit crabs, anemones and fish such as blennies and gobies.

- **Sandy shores** are home to burrowing creatures such as crabs, razor clams, lugworms, sea cucumbers and burrowing anemones.

- **Sandhoppers** are tiny shelled creatures that live along the tide line, feeding on seaweed.

- **Beadlet anemones** look like blobs of jelly on rocks when the tide is out. But when the water returns, they open a ring of flower-like tentacles to feed.

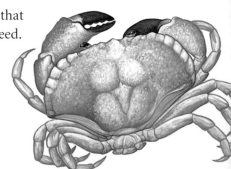

▶ *The edible crab, like all crabs, has five pairs of legs. The front pair have pincers.*

▼ *Crabs, lugworms, sandhoppers, shellfish and many other creatures live on seashores. Many birds come to feed on them.*

Life in the oceans

- **Oceans** cover 70% of the Earth and they are the largest single animal habitat.

- **Scientists divide the ocean** into two main environments – the pelagic (which is the water itself), and the benthic (which is the seabed).

- **Most benthic animals** live in shallow waters around the continents. They include worms, clams, crabs and lobsters, as well as bottom-feeding fish.

- **Scientists call the sunny surface waters** the euphotic zone. This extends down 150 m and it is where billions of plankton (microscopic animals and plants) live.

- **Green plant plankton** (algae) in the oceans produce 30% of the world's vegetable matter each year.

- **Animal plankton** include shrimps and jellyfish.

- **The surface waters** are also home to squid, fish and mammals such as whales.

- **Below the surface zone,** down to about 2,000 m, is the twilight bathyal zone. Here there is too little light for plants to grow, but many hunting fish and squid live.

- **Below 2,000 m** is the dark abyssal zone, where only weird fish like gulper eels and anglerfish live (see strange sea creatures).

- **The Sargasso** is a vast area in the western Atlantic where seaweed grows thick. It is a rich home for barnacles and other sea creatures.

▶ *The tassel-finned anglerfish is hardly larger than your thumb. The fleshy tassels on its chin resemble seaweed.*

▼ *Many kinds of fish and other sea creatures live in the sunlit zone near the surface of the oceans.*

Life in rivers and lakes

- **Rivers, lakes** and other freshwater habitats are home to all sorts of fish, including bream and trout.

- **Fast-flowing streams** are preferred by fish such as trout and grayling. Slow-flowing rivers and lakes are home to tench, rudd and carp.

- **Some fish feed** on floating plant matter, while others take insects from the surface of the water.

- **Common bream and barbel** hunt on the riverbed, eating insect larvae, worms and molluscs.

- **Perch and pike** are predators of lakes and slow-flowing rivers.

- **Pike** are the sharks of the river – deadly hunters that lurk among weeds waiting for fish, or even rats and birds. Pike can weigh up to 30 kg.

▶ *Upland lakes like these are home to many fish, including char, powan and bullhead. Fish such as brown trout swim in the streams that tumble down into the lake.*

● **Mammals of rivers and lakes** include voles, water rats and otters.

● **Birds of rivers and lakes** include birds that dive for fish (such as kingfishers), small wading birds (such as redshanks, avocets and curlews), large wading birds (such as herons, storks and flamingos), and waterfowl (such as ducks, swans and geese).

● **Insects** include dragonflies and water boatmen.

Amphibians include frogs and newts.

➤ *The grayling looks like a small trout, about 45 cm long, but with a larger sail-shaped back or dorsal fin. Like most members of the salmon family it has little, sharp teeth.*

Life on the grasslands

- **Grasslands** form in temperate (moderate temperature) regions where there is too little rainfall for forests, but enough to allow grass to grow.

- **Temperate grasslands** include the prairies of North America, the pampas of South America, the veld of South Africa, and the vast steppes of Eurasia.

- **There is little cover** on grasslands, so many grassland animals have very good eyesight and large ears to detect predators from afar.

- **Some grassland animals escape** from predators by speed. These include jack rabbits, deer, pronghorn antelopes, wild asses and flightless birds like emus.

- **Some animals,** such as mice and prairie dogs, escape by hiding underground in burrows.

- **Some birds hide** by building their nests in bushes. These include meadowlarks, quails and blackbirds.

- **The main predators** are dogs like the coyote and fox.

- **The North American prairies** have a small wild cat called the bobcat.

▲ *Coyotes eat a vast range of prey from beetles to deer as well as fruits.*

- **Prairie dogs** live in huge underground colonies called towns. One contained 400 million animals and covered over 60,000 square kilometres.

- **When they meet,** prairie dogs kiss each other to find out whether they are from the same group.

▲*Until they were wiped out by European settlers, vast herds of bison (buffalo) roamed the North American prairies.*

Life in woodlands

▲ *On a walk through a deciduous wood, you may be lucky enough to catch a glimpse of a shy young red deer as it crosses a clearing.*

- **Woodlands** in temperate zones between the tropics and the poles are home to many creatures.

- **Deciduous trees** lose their leaves in autumn. Evergreens keep theirs through cold winters.

- **In the leaf litter** under the trees live tiny creatures such as worms, millipedes, and ants and other insects.

- **Spiders, shrews, salamanders and mice** feed on the small creatures living in the leaf litter.

● **Some birds**, such as woodcocks, nest on the woodland floor and have mottled plumage to hide themselves.

Birds such as owls, nuthatches, treecreepers, tits, woodpeckers and warblers live on and in trees, as well as insects such as beetles, moths and butterflies, and small mammals such as squirrels and raccoons.

Other woodland mammals include badgers, chipmunks, opossums, stoats, weasels, polecats, pine martens and foxes.

Beavers, frogs, muskrats and otters live near woodland streams.

● **The few large woodland mammals** include bears, deer, wolves and wild boar. Many of these have become rare because woods have been cleared away.

● **In winter,** many birds of deciduous woods migrate south, while small mammals like dormice hibernate.

The long flight feathers of an owl's wings are tipped with down which muffles the noise of the wing beats. Silent flying allows the owl much better chance of catching prey.

235

Life in tropical rainforests

- **Tropical rainforests** are the richest and most diverse of all animal habitats.

- **Most animals** in tropical rainforests live in the canopy (treetops), and are either agile climbers or can fly.

- **Canopy animals** include flying creatures such as bats, birds and insects, and climbers such as monkeys, sloths, lizards and snakes.

- **Many rainforest creatures** can glide through the treetops – these include gliding geckos and other lizards, flying squirrels and even flying frogs.

▶ *Year-round rainfall and warm temperatures make rainforests incredibly lush, with a rich variety of plant life.*

236

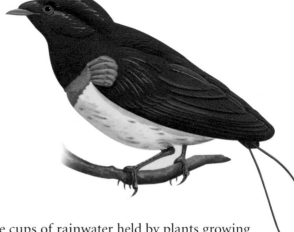

Like the other 41 species in the bird of paradise group, the ...ing bird lives in rainforests. In ...ourtship the male vibrates his ...ings for display.

Some tree frogs live in the cups of rainwater held by plants growing high up in trees.

Antelopes, deer, hogs, tapir and many different kinds of rodent roam the forest floor, hunting for seeds, roots, leaves and fruit.

Beside rivers in Southeast Asian rainforests, there may be rhinoceroses, crocodiles and even elephants.

Millions of insect species live in rainforests, including butterflies, moths, bees, termites and ants. There are also many spiders.

Rainforest butterflies and moths are often big or vividly coloured, including the shimmering blue morpho of Brazil and the birdwing butterflies.

Rainforest birds can be vividly coloured too, and include parrots, toucans and birds of paradise.

Life in tropical grasslands

▲ *With their long necks, giraffes can feed on the high branches of the thorn trees that dot the savannah grasslands of Africa.*

- **Tropical grasslands** are home to vast herds of grazing animals such as antelope and buffalo – and to the lions, cheetahs and other big cats that prey on them.

- **There are few places to hide** on the grasslands, so most grassland animals are fast runners with long legs.

- **Pronghorn** can manage 67 km/h for 16 km.

- **There are more than 60 species** of antelope on the grasslands of Africa and southern Asia.

- **A century ago in South Africa,** herds of small antelopes called springboks could be as large as 10 million strong and hundreds of kilometres long.

▼ *The white rhino can weigh over 3.5 tonnes. The 'white' does not refer to the colour, which is pale grey. It means 'wide' from the broad snout.*

● **The springbok** gets its name from its habit of springing 3 m straight up in the air.

● **Grazing animals** are divided into artiodactyls and perrisodactyls, according to how many toes they have.

● **Artiodactyls** have an even number of toes on each foot. They include camels buffalo, deer, antelope and cattle.

● **Perrisodactyls** have an odd number of toes. They include horses, rhinos and tapirs.

...**FASCINATING FACT**...
Cheetahs are the fastest runners in the world, reaching 110 km/h in short bursts.

Life in the desert

- **In the Sahara desert,** a large antelope called the addax survives without waterholes because it gets all its water from its food.

- **Many small animals** cope with the desert heat by resting in burrows or sheltering under stones during the day. They come out to feed only at night.

- **Desert animals** include many insects, spiders, scorpions, lizards and snakes.

- **The dwarf puff adder** hides from the sun by burying itself in the sand until only its eyes show.

- **The fennec fox** and the antelope jack rabbit both lose heat through their ears. This way they keep cool.

- **The kangaroo rats** of California's Death Valley save water by eating their own droppings.

- **The Mojave squirrel** survives through long periods of drought by sleeping for five o six days a week.

- **Swarms of desert locusts** car cover an area as big as 5,000 square kilometres.

- **Sand grouse** fly hundreds of kilometres every night to reach watering holes.

◀ *The fennec fox lives in the Sahara Desert region where feeds mainly on ants, termit and other tiny prey.*

▼ *Deserts like this are among the world's toughest environments for animals to survive.*

... **FASCINATING FACT** ...
The African fringe-toed lizard dances to keep cool, lifting each foot in turn off the hot sand.

Life in the mountains

- **Mountains** are cold, windy places where only certain animals can survive – including agile hunters such as pumas and snow leopards, and nimble grazers such as mountain goats, yaks, ibex and chamois.

  - **The world's highest-living** mammal is the yak, a type of wild cattle which can survive more than 6,000 m up in the Himalayas of Tibet.

    - **Mountain goats** have hooves with sharp edges that dig into cracks in the rock, and hollow soles that act like suction pads.

◄ *Sheep like these dall shee are well equipped for life in th mountains, with their thic woolly coats and nimble fee*

In winter, the mountain goat's pelage (coat) turns white, making it hard to spot against the snow.

The Himalayan snowcock nests higher than almost any other bird – often above 4,000 m in the Himalayas.

The Alpine chough has been seen flying at 8,200 m up on Everest.

Lammergeiers are the vultures of the African and southern European mountains. They break tough bones by dropping them from a great height onto stones and then eating the marrow.

The Andean condor of the South American Andes is a gigantic scavenger which can carry off deer and sheep. It is said to dive from the skies like a fighter plane (see also vultures).

The puma, or mountain lion, can jump well over 5 m up onto a rock ledge – that is like you jumping into an upstairs window.

The snow leopard of the Himalayan mountains is now one of the rarest of all the big cats, because it has been hunted almost to extinction for its beautiful fur coat.

The puma ranges from southern canada rough North and central America to Patagonia South America. It has a muscular build and uses the alk-and-pounce method to catch prey.

Life in cold regions

- **The world's coldest places** are at the Poles in the Arctic and Antarctic, and high up mountains.

- **Only small animals** such as ice worms and insects can stand the extreme polar cold all year round.

- **Insects** like springtails can live in temperatures as low as -38°C in Antarctica, because their body fluids contain substances that do not freeze easily.

- **Birds** such as penguins, snow petrels and skuas live in Antarctica. So do the leopard seals that eat penguins.

- **Polar seas** are home to whales, fish and shrimp-like krill.

- **Fish of cold seas** have body fluids that act like car anti-freeze to stop them freezing.

- **Mammals such as polar bears**, sea lions and walruses are so well insulated against the cold with their fur and fat that they can live on the Arctic ice much of the year.

- **Many animals** live on the icy tundra land in the far north of America and Asia. They include caribou, Arctic foxes and hares, and birds such as ptarmigans and snowy owls.

- **Arctic foxes and hares**, ermines and ptarmigans turn white in winter to camouflage them against the snow.

◀ *The leopard seal is so-called because of its spotted grey coat. Its diet includes fish, squid and other seals. It lives on the pack ice around Antarctica.*

▲ *Other animals are the only substantial food in the Arctic wastes,
so polar bears have to be carnivorous.*

...FASCINATING FACT...
Ptarmigans can survive through the
bitter Arctic winter by eating twigs.

Baby animals

- **All baby mammals** except monotremes (see strange mammals) are born from their mother's body, but most other creatures hatch from eggs.

- **Most creatures** hatch long after their parents have disappeared. Birds and mammals, though, usually look after their young.

- **Most birds** feed their hungry nestlings until they are big enough to find food for themselves.

- **Some small birds** may make 10,000 trips to the nest to feed their young.

- **Cuckoos** lay their egg in the nest of another, smaller bird. The foster parents hatch it and look after it as it grows. It then pushes its smaller, foster brothers and sisters out of the nest.

▶ *Lion cubs are looked after by several females until they are big enough to fend for themselves. Like many babies they have big paws, head and ears for their body.*

Mammals nurse their young (they feed them on the mother's milk). The nursing period varies. It tends to be just a few weeks in small animals like mice, but several years in large animals like elephants.

Many animals play when they are young. Playing helps them develop strength and co-ordination, and practise tasks they will have to do for real when adults.

When they are young, baby opossums cling all over their mother as she moves around.

Some baby animals, including baby shrews and elephants, go around in a long line behind the mother, clinging to the tail of the brother or sister in front.

A baby elephant is fed by its mother for two years. By the time it is fully grown it will be eating about 150 kg of food each day – the weight of two people!

Communication

- **Crows** use at least 300 different croaks to communicate with each other. But crows from one area cannot understand crows from another one.

- **When two howler monkey troops** meet, the males scream at each other until one troop gives way.

- **The male orang-utan** burps to warn other males to keep away.

- **Dogs** communicate through barks, yelps, whines, growls and howls.

- **Many types of insect communicate** through the smell of chemicals called pheromones, which are released into the air from special glands.

- **Tropical tree ant species** use ten different pheromones, combining them with different movements to send 50 different kinds of message.

◀ *Orang-utans are shy and seldom seen. However, they may be heard occasionally – making burping noises to scare off other males*

Lone wolves often howl at dusk or in the night to signal their ownership of a particular territory and to warn off rival wolves.

A gorilla named Coco was trained to use over 1,000 different signs to communicate, each sign meaning a different word. She called her pet cat 'Soft good cat cat', and referred to herself as 'Fine animal gorilla'.

Female glow worms communicate with males by making a series of flashes.

Many birds are mimics and can imitate a whole variety of different sounds, including the human voice and machines like telephones.

> **. . . FASCINATING FACT . . .**
> Using sign language, Coco the gorilla took an IQ test and got a score of 95.

Surviving the winter

- **Some animals** cope with the cold and lack of food in winter by going into a kind of deep sleep called hibernation.

- **During hibernation**, an animal's body temperature drops and its heart rate and breathing slow, so it needs little energy to survive.

- **Small mammals** such as bats, squirrels, hamsters, hedgehogs and chipmunks hibernate. So do birds such as nighthawks and swifts.

- **Reptiles** such as lizards and snakes go into torpor whenever the temperature gets too low. This is a similar state to hibernation.

- **Butterflies and other insects** go into a kind of suspended animation called diapause in winter.

- **The pika** (a small lagomorph) makes haystacks from grass in summer to provide food for the winter.

▼ *With its bright fur and neat ear tufts, the red squirrel very distinctive. It sometim buries seeds and nuts, ar sniffs them out later in th year from deep in the so*

Many mammals survive cold winters by hibernating. Some, like this Arctic fox, will sleep for a few days at a time when there is little food to be found.

Beavers collect branches in autumn and store them next to their lodges so that they can feed on the bark during the winter months.

Bears go to sleep during winter, but not all scientists agree that they go into true hibernation.

Squirrels bury stores of nuts in autumn to feed on during winter. They seem to have remarkable memories, as they can find most stores when they need them.

. . . **FASCINATING FACT** . . .
Macaque monkeys in Japan keep warm in winter by bathing in hot volcanic springs.

251

Migration

- **Migration** is when animals move from one place to another to avoid the cold or to find food and water.

- **Some migrations** are daily, some are seasonal, and some are permanent.

- **Starlings** migrate every day from the country to their roosts in towns and cities.

- **Many birds, whales seals and bats** migrate closer to the tropics in the autumn to escape the winter cold.

▲ *No other creature migrates so far every year as the Arctic tern. It breeds in the short Arctic summer, then flies halfway around the world to spend another summer in Antarctica.*

- **One knot** (a kind of small bird) took just 8 days to fly 5,600 km, from Britain to West Africa.

- **Barheaded geese** migrate right over the top of the Himalayan mountains, flying as high as 8,000 m.

- **Migrating birds** are often brilliant navigators. Bristle-thighed curlews find the way from Alaska to tiny islands in the Pacific 9,000 km away.

- **Shearwaters,** sparrows and homing pigeons are able to fly home when released by scientists in strange places, thousands of kilometres away.

- **The Arctic tern** is the greatest migrator, flying 30,000 km from the Arctic to the Antarctic and back again each year.

- **Monarch butterflies** migrate 4,000 km every year, from North America to small clumps of trees in Mexico. Remarkably, the migrating butterflies have never made the journey before.

▼ *In summer, moose spend most of the time alone. But in winter they gather and trample areas of snow (called yards) to help each other get at the grass beneath.*

What are insects?

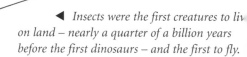

◀ *Insects were the first creatures to liv on land – nearly a quarter of a billion years before the first dinosaurs – and the first to fly.*

- **Insects** may be tiny, but there are more of them than all the other animals put together – over 1 million known species.

- **They range** from tiny flies to huge beetles, and they are found everywhere there is land.

- **Insects** have six legs and a body that is divided into three sections – which is why they are called insects ('in sections'). The sections are the head, thorax (middle and abdomen.

- **An insect's body** is encased in such a tough shell (its exoskeleton) that there is no need for bones.

- **Insects grow** by getting rid of their old exoskeleton and replacing it with a bigger one. This is called moulting.

- **Insects change** dramatically as they grow. Butterflies, moths, and beetles undergo metamorphosis (see butterflies). Grasshoppers and mayflies begin as wingless nymphs, then gradually grow wings with each moult. Silverfish and springtails simply get bigger with each moult.

- **Insects' eyes** are called compound because they are made up of many lenses – from six (worker ants) to more than 30,000 (dragonflies).

- **Insects have** two antennae (feelers) on their heads.

Insects do not have lungs. Instead, they breathe through holes in their sides called spiracles, linked to their body through tubes called tracheae.

The world's longest insect is the giant stick insect of Indonesia, which can grow to 33 cm long.

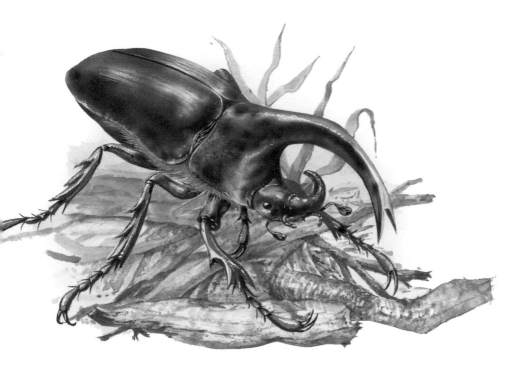

▲ The rhinoceros beetle shown here can push an object 850 times its own weight, which is equivalent to a person pushing a 50-tonne army tank!

255

Worms

- **Worms** are long, wriggling, tube-like animals. Annelids are worms such as the earthworm whose bodies are divided into segments.

- **There are 15,000 species** of annelid. Most live underground in tunnels, or in the sea.

- **The world's largest earthworm** is the giant earthworm of South Africa, which can grow to as long as 6.5 m when fully extended.

- **Earthworms** spend their lives burrowing through soil. Soil goes in the mouth end, passes through the gut and comes out at the tail end.

- **An earthworm** is both male and female (hermaphrodite), and after two earthworms mate, both develop eggs.

- **Over half the annelid species** are marine (sea) bristleworms, such as ragworm and lugworms. They are named because they are covered in bristles, which the use to paddle over the seabed or dig into the mud.

▼ *Plants would not grow half as well withou earthworms to aerate the soil as they burrow in it, mix up the layers and make it more fertile with their droppings.*

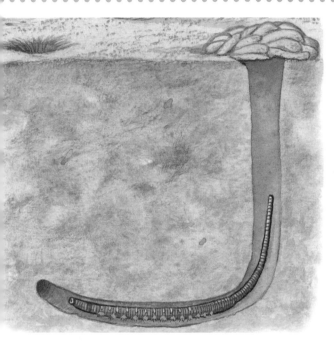

◀ *A lugworm in its U-shaped burrow in the sand. It will stay in its burrow and swallow sand along with bits of dead animal and plant matter. It passes the sand through its body producing a cast – these can be seen on beaches at low tide.*

The sea mouse is a mouse-shaped bristleworm with furry hairs.

Flatworms look like ribbons or as though an annelid worm has been ironed flat. Their bodies donot have proper segments. Of the thousands of flatworm species, many live in the sea or in pond algae.

Flukes are flatworms that live as parasites inside other animals. Diseases like bilharzia are caused by flukes.

Tapeworms are parasitic flatworms that live inside their host's gut and eat their food.

257

Snails and slugs

- **Snails and slugs** are small, squidgy, slimy, soft-bodied crawling creatures. They belong to a huge group of animals called molluscs which have no skeleton. Squid and oysters are also molluscs.

- **Snails and slugs** are gastropods, a group that also includes whelks and winkles.

- **Gastropod** means 'stomach foot', because these animals seem to slide along on their stomachs.

- **Most gastropods** live in the sea. They include limpets which stick firmly to seashore rocks.

- **Most land snails and slugs** ooze a trail of sticky slime to help them move along the ground.

- **Garden snails** are often hermaphrodites, which means they have both male and female sex organs.

▼ *Most slugs, like this great black slug, e*
decaying vegetation. Some slugs like t
underground parts of plants and your
leaves which make them unpopul
with gardene

The great grey slugs of western Europe court by circling each other for over an hour on a branch, then launching themselves into the air to hang from a long trail of mucus. They then mate for 7 to 24 hours.

Among the largest gastropods are the tropical tritons, whose 45–cm shells are sometimes used as warhorns. Conches are another big kind of gastropod.

Some cone snails in the Pacific and Indian oceans have teeth that can inject a poison which can actually kill people.

▶ *Garden snails have a shell which they seal themselves into in dry weather, making a kind of trapdoor to save moisture. They have eyes on their horns.*

...FASCINATING FACT...
Snails are a great delicacy in France, where they are called *escargot.*

Beetles

- **At least 250,000** species of beetle have been identified. They live everywhere on Earth, apart from in the oceans.

- **Unlike other insects**, adult beetles have a pair of thick, hard, front wings called elytra. These form an armour-like casing over the beetle's body.

- **The goliath beetle** of Africa is the heaviest flying insect, weighing over 100 grams and growing to as much as 13 cm long.

- **Dung beetles** roll away the dung of grazing animals to lay their eggs on. Fresh dung from one elephant may contain 7,000 beetles – they will clear the dung away in little more than a day.

▶ *The over-sized mandibles (jaws) of these stag beetles are quite harmless. They show that the males have reached maturity and are ready to breed.*

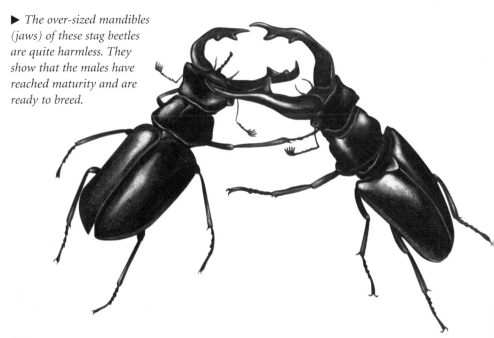

A click beetle can jump 30 cm into the air.

The bombardier beetle shoots attackers with jets of burning chemicals from the tip of its abdomen.

The rove beetle can zoom across water on a liquid given off by glands on its abdomen.

The leaf-eating beetle can clamp on to leaves using the suction of a layer of oil.

Stag beetles have huge jaws which look like a stag's antlers.

The jewel beetles of tropical South America get their name from the brilliant rainbow colours of their elytra (front wings).

Elytra (hard front wings)

...FASCINATING FACT...
The Arctic beetle can survive in temperatures below -60°C.

Butterflies

- **Butterflies** are insects with four large wings that feed either on the nectar of flowers or on fruit.

- **Together with moths,** butterflies make up the scientific order Lepidoptera – the word means 'scaly wings'. There are more than 165,000 species of Lepidoptera – 20,000 butterflies and 145,000 moths.

▲ *Every species of butter has its own wing patte just like humans have th own fingerpri*

- **Many butterflies** are brightly coloured and fly by day. They have slim, hairless bodies and club-shaped antennae (feelers).

- **The biggest butterfly** is the Queen Alexandra's birdwing of New Guinea, with 25 cm-wide wings. The smallest is the Western pygmy blue.

- **Butterflies can only fly** if their wing muscles are warm. To warm up, they bas in the sun so their wings soak up energy like solar panels.

- **The monarch butterfly** is such a strong flier it can cross the Atlantic Ocean (see migration).

- **The shimmering blue wings** of the South American morpho butterfly are ver beautiful – in the 19th century millions of the butterflies were caught and mad into brooches.

- **Most female butterflies** live only a few days, so they have to mate and lay eggs quickly. Most males court them with elaborate flying displays.

- **Butterflies** taste with their tarsi (feet). Females 'stamp' on leaves to see if they are ripe enough for egg laying.

- **Every butterfly's caterpillar** has its own chosen food plants – different from the flowers the adult feeds on.

262

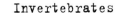

. Egg – eggs
re laid on plants
hat will provide
ood when the
aterpillars hatch

2. Larva – when the
caterpillar hatches, it
begins eating and
growing immediately

3. Pupa – butterfly
caterpillars develop
hard cases and hang
from a stem or leaf

. Imago – the
dult's new wings
re damp and
rumpled, but soon
lry in the sun

4. Metamorphosis – it
takes a few days to a
year for the pupa to
turn into an adult

*Few insects change as much
s butterflies do during their lives.
Butterflies start off as an egg, then
atch into a long, wiggly larva
alled a caterpillar, which eats leaves
reedily and grows rapidly. When it
s big enough, the caterpillar makes
tself a case, which can be either a
ocoon or chrysalis. Inside, it
netamorphoses (changes) into an
dult, then breaks out, dries its new
vings and flies away.*

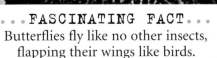

. . . **FASCINATING FACT** . . .
Butterflies fly like no other insects,
flapping their wings like birds.

263

Moths

- **Like butterflies,** moths belong to the insect group Lepidoptera.

- **Most moths** have fat, hairy bodies, and feathery or thread-like antennae.

- **Many moths** fly at dusk or at night. By day, they rest on tree trunks and in leaf litter, where their drab colour makes them hard for predators such as birds to spot. However, there are also many brightly coloured day-flying moths.

  - **Tiger moths** give out high-pitched clicks to warn that they taste bad and so escape being eaten.

    - **The biggest moths** are the Hercules moth and the bent wing ghost moth of Asia, with wingspans of over 25 cm.

      - **Night-flying** moths shiver their wings to warm them up for flight.

▲ *Among the world's largest moths, moon moths are named after their moon-like wing markings. The male's feather antennae can pick up the scent of a female from 2-3 km away.*

Hawk moths are powerful fliers and migrate long distances. The oleander hawk moth flies from tropical Africa to far northern Europe in summer.

The caterpillars of small moths live in seeds, fruit, stems and leaves, eating them from the inside.

The caterpillars of large moths feed on leaves from the outside, chewing chunks out of them.

When threatened, the caterpillar of the puss moth rears up, thrusts its whip-like tail forward, and squirts a jet of formic acid from its head end.

▲ *Hawk moths have very long tongues for sucking nectar from flowers. They often hover like hummingbirds as they feed.*

Every caterpillar spins silk, but the cloth silk comes from the caterpillar of the white Bombyx mori moth, known as the silkworm.

Bees and wasps

- **Bees and wasps** are narrow-waisted insects (usually with hairy bodies). Many suck nectar from flowers.

- **There are 22,000 species of bee.** Some, like leaf-cutter bees, live alone. But most, like honey bees and bumble bees, live in vast colonies.

- **Honey bees** live in hives, either in hollow trees or in man-made beehive boxes. The inside of the hive is a honeycomb made up of hundreds of six-sided cells.

▼ *The main parts of a bee.*

Head

Thorax

Large abdomen

- **A honey bee colony** has a queen (the female bee that lays the eggs), tens of thousands of female worker bees, and a few hundred male drones.

- **Worker bees** collect nectar and pollen from flowers.

- **Each worker bee** makes ten trips a day and visits 1,000 flowers each trip. It takes 65,000 trips to 65 million flowers to make 1 kg of honey.

- **Honey bees** tell others where to find flowers rich in pollen or nectar by flying in a special dance-like pattern.

- **Wasps** do not make honey, but feed on nectar, fruit juice or tiny creatures. Many species have a nasty sting in their tail.

- **Paper wasps build** huge papier maché nests the size of footballs, containing 15,000 or more cells.

- **Paper wasps make** papier maché for their nest by chewing wood and mixing it with their spit.

▶ *Honey bees and bumble bees feed on pollen. They make honey from flower nectar to feed their young*

Ants and termites

- Ants are a vast group of insects related to bees and wasps. Most ants have a tiny waist and are wingless.

- Ants are the main insects in tropical forests, living in colonies of anything from 20 to millions.

- Ant colonies are all female. Most species have one or several queens which lay the eggs. Hundreds of soldier ants guard the queen, while smaller workers build the nest and care for the young.

- Males only enter the nest to mate with young queens, then die.

- Wood ants squirt acid from their abdomen to kill enemies.

- Army ants march in huge swarms, eating most small creatures they meet.

- Groups of army ants cut any large prey they catch into pieces which they carry back to the nest. Army ants can carry 50 times their own weight.

- Ants known as slavemakers raid the nests of other ants and steal their young to raise as slaves.

- Termite colonies are even more complex than ant ones. They have a large king and queen who mate, as well as soldiers to guard them and workers to do all the work.

- Termite nests are mounds built like cities with many chambers – including a garden used for growing fungus. Many are air-conditioned with special chimneys.

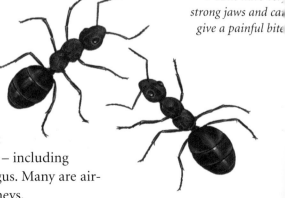

▼ *Ants have very strong jaws and can give a painful bite*

African termites use mud and saliva to build amazing nests more than 12 m high, housing over 5 million termites. Termites (Isoptera) belong to a separate insect group from ants, bees and wasps (Hymenoptera).

269

Flies

▶ *Flies have only one pair of proper wings. The hind wings are small stumps called halteres which help a fly balance in flight.*

- **Flies** are one of the biggest groups of insects, common nearly everywhere – there are over 90,000 species.

- **Unlike other insects,** flies have only one pair of proper wings.

- **Flies** include bluebottles, black flies, gnats, horseflies, midges, mosquitoes and tsetse flies.

- **A house fly** flies at over 7 km/h – equal to flying 350,000 times its own length in an hour. If a jumbo jet flew at the same speed relative to its length for an hour, it would get almost right around the world.

- **Alaskan flies** can stand being frozen at temperatures of -60°C and still survive.

270

Mosquitoes can spread dangerous diseases and their bite is painful. They have a sharp tube (proboscis) with which they pierce their victim's skin. Saliva then mixes with the blood to prevent it clotting.

Flies suck up their food – typically sap from rotting plants and fruit. Houseflies often suck liquids from manure. Blowflies drink from rotting meat.

The larvae (young) of flies are called maggots, and they are tiny, white, wriggling tube-shapes.

Flies resemble or mimic many other kinds of insects. There are wasp flies, beetle flies, ant flies and moth flies.

Many species of fly are carriers of dangerous diseases. When a fly bites or makes contact, it can infect people with some of the germs it carries – especially the flies that suck blood. Mosquitoes spread malaria, and tsetse flies spread sleeping sickness.

...FASCINATING FACT...
The buzzing of a fly is the sound of its wings beating. Midges beat their wings 1,000 times a second.

Dragonflies

- **Dragonflies** are big hunting insects with four large transparent wings, and a long slender body that may be a shimmering red, green or blue.

- **Dragonflies have** 30,000 separate lenses in each of their compound eyes, giving them the sharpest vision of any insect.

- **A dragonfly** can see something that is stationary from almost 2 m away, and something moving two to three times farther away.

- **As it swoops** in on its prey, a dragonfly pulls its legs forwards like a basket to scoop up its victim.

- **Dragonflies** often mate in mid-air, and the male may then stay hanging on to the female until she lays her eggs.

- **Dragonfly eggs** are laid in water or in the stem of a water plant, and hatch in 2 to 3 weeks.

- **Newly-hatched dragonflies** are called nymphs and look like fatter, wingless adults.

- **Dragonfly nymphs** are ferocious hunters, often feeding on young fish and tadpoles.

- **Dragonfly nymphs** grow and moult over a period of several years before they climb on to a reed or rock to emerge as an adult.

◀ *Dragonflies are big insects even today, but hundreds of millions of years ago, there were dragonflies with wings that were well over 70 cm across.*

A blue dragonfly rests on a flower. A stream or pond is sure to be nearby.

...**FASCINATING FACT**...
Dragonflies can reach speeds of almost
100 km/h to escape from birds.

Grasshoppers and crickets

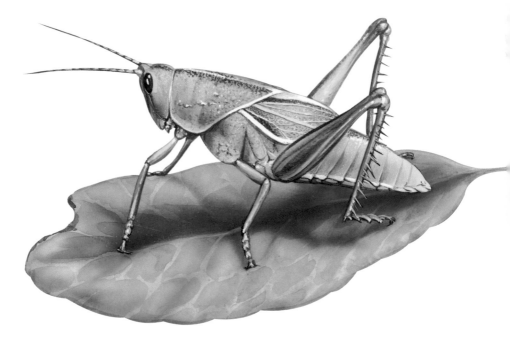

▲ *The spikes on the long-horned grasshopper's back legs are what make the chirruping sound as it rubs them against its forewings.*

- **Grasshoppers** are plant-eating insects related to crickets, locusts and katydids.
- **Grasshoppers** belong to two main families – short-horned, which includes locusts, and long-horned, which includes katydids and crickets.

The mole cricket digs out its tunnel home where it rests and feeds. The male's burrow has a tapering shape like a megaphone to make his mating chirrup louder.

Short-horned grasshoppers have ears on the side of their body. Long-horned grasshoppers have ears in their knees.

Grasshoppers have powerful back legs, which allow them to jump huge distances.

Some grasshoppers can leap more than 3 m.

Grasshoppers sing by rubbing their hind legs across their closed forewings.

A grasshopper's singing is called stridulation.

Crickets chirrup faster the warmer it is.

If you count the number of chirrups a snowy tree cricket gives in 15 seconds, then add 40, you get the temperature in degrees Fahrenheit.

. . . FASCINATING FACT . . .
A frightened lubber grasshopper oozes a horrible-smelling froth from its mouth.

Fleas and lice

- **Fleas and lice** are small wingless insects that live on birds and mammals, including humans. Dogs, cats and rats are especially prone to fleas.

- **Fleas and sucking lice** suck their host's blood.

- **Chewing lice** chew on their host's skin and hair or feathers. Chewing lice do not live on humans.

▼ *The human head louse has a body length of 2-3mm. Once its crab-like legs and hooked claws cling to its victim's hair or skin, it is harder to shift than a limpet on a seaside rock.*

Fleas and lice are often too small to see easily. But adult fleas grow to over 2 mm long.

A flea can jump 30 cm in the air – the equivalent of a human leaping 200 m in the air.

The fleas in flea circuses perform tricks such as jumping through hoops and pulling wagons.

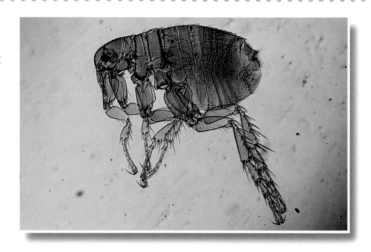

▲ *A much-magnified flea with its powerful back legs for jumping.*

Fleas spread by jumping from one animal to another, to suck their blood.

When fleas lay their eggs, they hatch as larvae and crawl off into the host's bedding, where they spin cocoons and emerge as adults 2 weeks later.

Head lice gum their nits (eggs) to hair and spread from head to head through sharing of combs and hats.

. . . . **FASCINATING FACT** . . . .
Fleas jump with a force of 140 g – over
20 times that required to launch a space rocket.

Poisonous insects

◀ The bold colouring of the ladybird warns birds that it is not for eating. It has a healthy appetite for aphids making it every gardener's friend.

● **Insects are small,** but many have nasty poisons to protect themselves.

● **Most poisonous insects** are brightly coloured – including many caterpillars, wasps and cardinal beetles – to warn off potential enemies.

● **Ants, bees and wasps** have stings in their tails which they use to inject poison to defend themselves or paralyse prey.

● **Bee and wasp stings** have barbed ends to keep the sting in long enough to inject the poison. Honey bees cannot pull the barb out from human skins, and so tear themselves away and die.

▶ The hornet is really a large wasp. Its brightly striped body is a warning to others animals that it stings. When the hornet does sting, it injects a venom that causes a painful swelling.

Velvet ants are not really ants at all, but wingless wasps with such a nasty sting that they are called 'cow killers'.

Ladybirds make nasty chemicals in their knees.

When they are attacked, swallowtail caterpillars whip out a smelly forked gland from a pocket behind their head and hit their attacker with it.

The lubber grasshopper is slow moving, but when attacked it oozes a foul-smelling froth from its mouth and thorax.

The bombardier beetle squirts out a spray of liquid from its rear end, almost like a small spray-gun! This startles and stings the attacker and gives the small beetle time to escape.

▲ *The caterpillar of a swallowtail butterfly. Most swallowtails are tropical.*

279

Spiders

▶ Like all arachnids, spiders have eight legs, plus two 'arms' called pedipalps and a pair of fangs called chelicerae. They also have eight simple eyes.

- **Spiders** are small scurrying creatures which, unlike insects, have eight legs not six, and bodies with two parts not three.

- **Spiders** belong to a group of 70,000 creatures called arachnids, which also includes scorpions, mites and ticks.

- **Spiders** live in nooks and crannies almost everywhere in the world, especially where there is plenty of vegetation to feed tiny creatures.

- **Spiders are hunters** and most of them feed mainly on insects. Despite their name, bird-eating spiders rarely eat birds, preferring lizards and small rodents such as mice.

Spiders have eight eyes, but most have poor eyesight and hunt by feeling vibrations with their legs.

Many spiders catch their prey by weaving silken nets called webs. Some webs are simple tubes in holes. Others, called orb webs, are elaborate and round. Spiders' webs are sticky to trap insects.

The Australian trapdoor spider ambushes its prey from a burrow with a camouflaged entrance flap.

Most spiders have a poisonous bite which they use to stun or kill their prey. Tarantulas and sun spiders crush their victims with their powerful jaws.

The bite of black widow and red-back funnel-web spiders is so poisonous that it can kill humans.

All spiders produce silk. Some turn this silk into inticate webs, first for catching prey and then for trussing them up.

...FASCINATING FACT...
Female black widow spiders eat their mates after mating.

What is a fish?

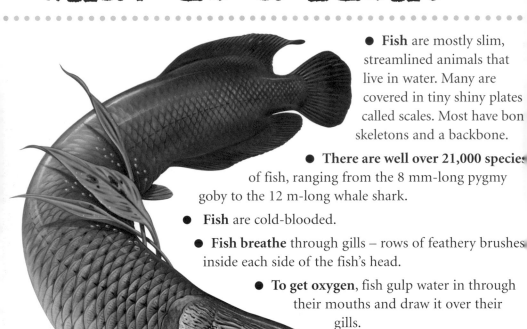

- **Fish** are mostly slim, streamlined animals that live in water. Many are covered in tiny shiny plates called scales. Most have bon skeletons and a backbone.

- **There are well over 21,000 species** of fish, ranging from the 8 mm-long pygmy goby to the 12 m-long whale shark.

- **Fish** are cold-blooded.

- **Fish breathe** through gills – rows of feathery brushes inside each side of the fish's head.

- **To get oxygen**, fish gulp water in through their mouths and draw it over their gills.

- **Fish** have fins for swimming, not limbs.

- **Most fish** have a pectoral fin behind each gill and two pelvic fins below to the rear, as well as a dorsal fin on top o their body, an anal fin beneath, and a caudal (tail) fir

- **Fish let gas in** and out of their swim bladders to float at particular depths.

- **Some fish** communicate by making sounds with their swim bladder. Catfish use them like bagpipes.

▲ *The arapaima lives in the swampy parts of tropical south America. It can breathe in the normal fish way using its gills or gulp down air. It can grow to a vast 3 m in length and weigh up to 200 kg.*

▼ *Angling (catching fish) is a popular pastime all around the world. The fish is hooked as it bites the lure or bait.*

...FASCINATING FACT...
The drum fish makes a drumming sound
with its swim bladder.

Jellyfish

- **Jellyfish** are sea creatures with bell-shaped, jelly-like bodies, and long stinging tentacles.

- **Biologists** call jellyfish medusa, after the mythical Greek goddess Medusa, who had wriggling snakes for hair.

- **Jellyfish** belong to a large group of sea creatures called cnidarians, which also includes corals and anemones.

- **Unlike anemones**, jellyfish float about freely, moving by squeezing water out from beneath their body. When a jellyfish stops squeezing, it slowly sinks.

- **A jellyfish's tentacles** are covered with stinging cells called nematocysts, which are used to catch fish and for protection. The stinging cells explode when touched, driving tiny poisonous threads into the victim.

- **Jellyfish vary in size** from a few millimetres to over 2 m.

- **The bell of one giant jellyfish** measured 2.29 m across. Its tentacles were over 36 m long.

- **The Portuguese man-of-war** is not a true jellyfish, but a collection of hundreds of tiny animals called polyps which live together under a gas-filled float.

- **The purple jellyfish** can be red, yellow or purple.

▼ *Jellyfish are among the world's most ancient animals.*

Corals and anemones

▼ *Sea anemones look like flowers with petals, but they are actually carnivorous animals with their ring of tentacles.*

- **Sea anemones** are tiny, meat-eating animals that look a bit like flowers. They cling to rocks and catch tiny prey with their tentacles (see life on the seashore).
- **Coral reefs** are the undersea equivalent of rainforests, teeming with fish and other sea life. The reefs are built by tiny, sea-anemone-like animals called polyps

Coral polyps feed mainly on the tiny larvae of sea creatures such as shell fish, which they catch with their tentacles.

Coral polyps live all their lives in just one place, either fixed to a rock or to dead polyps.

When coral polyps die, their cup-shaped skeletons become hard coral.

Coral reefs are long ridges, mounds, towers and other shapes made from billions of coral polyps and their skeletons.

Fringing reefs are shallow coral reefs that stretch out from the seashore.

Barrier reefs form a long, underwater wall a little way offshore.

The Great Barrier Reef off eastern Australia is the longest reef in the world, stretching over 2,000 km.

Coral atolls are ring-shaped islands that formed from fringing reefs around an old volcano (which has long since sunk beneath the waves).

Coral reefs take millions of years to form – the Great Barrier Reef is about 18 million years old, for example. By drilling a core into ancient corals, and analysing the minerals and growth rate, scientists can read history back for millions of years.

Cockles and mussels

▲ *There are two main kinds of seashell – univalves like these (which are a single shell), and bivalves (which come in two, hinged halves).*

- **Cockles and mussels** belong to a group of molluscs called bivalves, which includes oysters, clams, scallops and razorshells.

- **Bivalve** means 'having two valves', and all these creatures have two halves to th shells, joined by a hinge that opens rather like that of a locket.

- **Most bivalves feed** by filtering food from the water through a tube called a sip

- **Cockles** burrow in sand and mud on the seashore. Mussels cling to rocks and breakwaters between the high and low tide marks.

Oysters and some other molluscs line their shells with a hard, shiny, silvery white substance called nacre.

When a lump of grit gets into an oyster shell, it is gradually covered in a ball of nacre, making a pearl.

The best pearls come from the Pinctada pearl oysters that live in the Pacific Ocean. The world's biggest pearl was 12 cm across and weighed 6.4 kg. It came from a giant clam.

Scallops can swim away from danger by opening and shutting their shells rapidly to pump out water. But most bivalves escape danger by shutting themselves up inside their shells.

A giant clam found on the Great Barrier Reef was over 1 m across and weighed more than 0.25 tonnes.

There are colonies of giant clams living many thousands of metres down under the oceans, near hot volcanic vents.

▼ *The swan mussel is a bivalve – a mollusc type of shellfish similar to clams and oysters on the seashore. It lives in lakes and slow, deep rivers. It draws a currrent of water into its shell, both for breathing and to filter out tiny particles of food.*

Octopuses and squid

- **Octopuses and squid** belong to a family of molluscs called cephalopods.

- **Octopuses** are sea creatures with a round, soft, boneless body, three hearts and eight long arms called tentacles.

- **An octopus's tentacles** are covered with suckers that allow it to hold on to rocks and prey.

- **Octopuses** have two large eyes, similar to humans, and a beak-like mouth.

- **When in danger** an octopus may send out a cloud of inky black fluid. Sometimes the ink cloud is the same shape as the octopus and may fool a predator into chasing the cloud.

▶ *Most of the hundreds of species of octopus live on the beds of shallow seas around the world. Octopuses are quite intelligent creatures.*

The giant squid is rarely seen and
is usually partly decomposed when
caught. For this reason it is the
subject of many myths. Its eyes
however are truly massive,
the biggest of any animal.

**Some octopuses can
change colour** dramatically
to startle a predator or blend
in with its background.

The smallest octopus is just
2.5 cm across. The biggest
measures 6 m from tentacle tip to
tentacle tip.

A squid has eight arms and two
tentacles and swims by forcing a jet
of water out of its body.

Giant squid in the Pacific can grow to 18 m or more long.

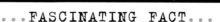

...FASCINATING FACT...
The 30 cm-long blue-ringed octopus's poison is
so deadly that it kills more people than sharks.

Starfish and
sea urchins

▲ *Starfish that live in cooler water tend to be brown or yellow, whereas many tropical starfish can be bright red or even blue.*

- **Despite their name** starfish are not fish, but belong instead to a group of smal sea creatures called echinoderms.

- **Sea urchins** and sea cucumbers are also echinoderms.

- **Starfish** have star-shaped bodies and are predators that prey mostly on shellfis such as scallops and oysters. A starfish uses its five strong arms to prise open it victim, then inserts its stomach into the victim and sucks out its flesh.

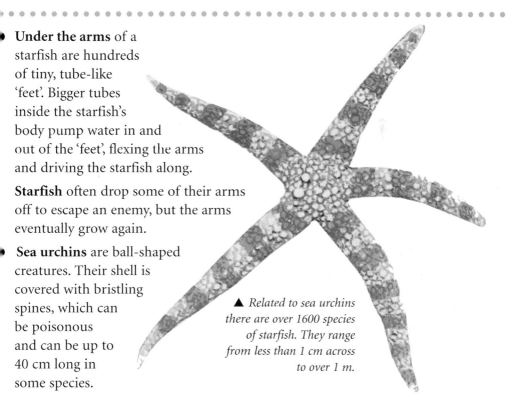

Under the arms of a starfish are hundreds of tiny, tube-like 'feet'. Bigger tubes inside the starfish's body pump water in and out of the 'feet', flexing the arms and driving the starfish along.

Starfish often drop some of their arms off to escape an enemy, but the arms eventually grow again.

Sea urchins are ball-shaped creatures. Their shell is covered with bristling spines, which can be poisonous and can be up to 40 cm long in some species.

▲ *Related to sea urchins there are over 1600 species of starfish. They range from less than 1 cm across to over 1 m.*

A sea urchin's spines are used for protection. Urchins also have sucker-like feet for moving.

A sea urchin's mouth is a hole with five teeth, on the underside of its body.

Sea cucumbers have no shell, but a leathery skin and a covering of chalky plates called spicules.

When threatened, a sea cucumber chucks out pieces of its gut as a decoy and swims away. It grows a new one later.

Crabs and lobsters

- **Crabs and lobsters** are part of an enormous group of creatures called crustaceans.

- **Most crabs and lobsters** have their own shell, but hermit crabs live inside the discarded shells of other creatures.

- **Crabs and lobsters are decapods,** which means they have ten legs – although the first pair are often strong pincers which are used to hold and tear food.

- **For spotting prey**, crabs and lobsters have two pairs of antennae on their head and a pair of eyes on stalks.

- **One of a lobster's claws** usually has blunt knobs for crushing victims. The other has sharp teeth for cutting.

- **Male fiddler crabs** have one giant pincer which they waggle to attract a mate.

- **Robber crabs** have claws on their legs which they use to climb up trees to escape from predators.

▶ *Lobsters are dark green or blue when alive and only turn red when cooked.*

Apart from climbing trees the robber crab is notable for another strange and unfortunate characteristic – it drowns in water!

The giant Japanese spider crab can grow to measure 3 m across between the tips of its outstretched pincers.

When American spiny lobsters migrate, they cling to each others' tails in a long line, marching for hundreds of kilometres along the seabed.

Sponge crabs hide under sponges which they cut to fit. The sponge then grows at the same rate as the crab and keeps it covered.

Sharks

- **Sharks** are the most fearsome predatory fish of the seas. There are 375 species, living mostly in warm seas.

- **Sharks** have a skeleton made of rubbery cartilage – most other kinds of fish have bony skeletons.

- **The world's biggest fish** is the whale shark, which can grow to well over 12 m long. Unlike other sharks, the whale shark and the basking shark (at 9 m long) mostly eat plankton and are completely harmless.

- **A shark's main weapons** are its teeth – they are powerful enough to bite through plate steel.

▼ A shark's torpedo-shaped body makes it a very fast swimmer.

Sharks put so much strain on their teeth that they always have three or four spare rows of teeth in reserve.

Nurse sharks grow a new set of teeth every 8 days.

Up to 20 people die from recorded shark attacks each year.

The killing machine of the shark world is the great white shark, responsible for most attacks on humans.

Hammerhead sharks can also be dangerous . They have T-shaped heads, with eyes and nostrils at the end of the T.

The super-streamlined blue shark lives in arm seas and is 3.7 m in length. It has very ng side fins and eats surface fish like herring d mackerel.

. . . FASCINATING FACT . . .
Great white sharks are the biggest meat-eating sharks, growing to over 7 m long.

Rays

- **Rays** are a huge group of over 300 species of fish, which includes skates, stingrays, electric rays, manta rays, eagle rays and guitar fish.

- **Many rays** have flat, almo diamond-shaped bodies, with pectoral fins elongate into broad wings. Guitar fish have longer, more shark-like bodies.

- **A ray's gills** are slot like openings beneath its fins.

- **Rays have no bones.** Instead, like sharks, they are cartilaginous fish – their body framework is made of rubbery cartilage (you have this in your nose and ears).

- **Rays live mostly** on the ocean floor, feeding on seabed creatures suc as oysters, clams and other shellfish.

▲ *The Atlantic manta ray is shown here with the much smaller spotted eagle ray.*

Manta rays live near the surface and feed on plankton.

The Atlantic manta ray is the biggest ray, often over 7 m wide and 6 m long.

Stingrays get their name from their whip-like tail, with its poisonous barbs. A sting from a stingray can make a human very ill.

Electric rays are tropical rays able to give off a powerful electric charge to defend themselves against attackers.

The black torpedo ray can put out a 220 volt shock – as much as a household electric socket.

◀ *The manta ray is also known as the devil ray because the two fleshy flaps on the head were thought to look like horns. The flaps scoop water into the mouth as the manta swims by powerfully beating its vast 'wings'.*

Eels

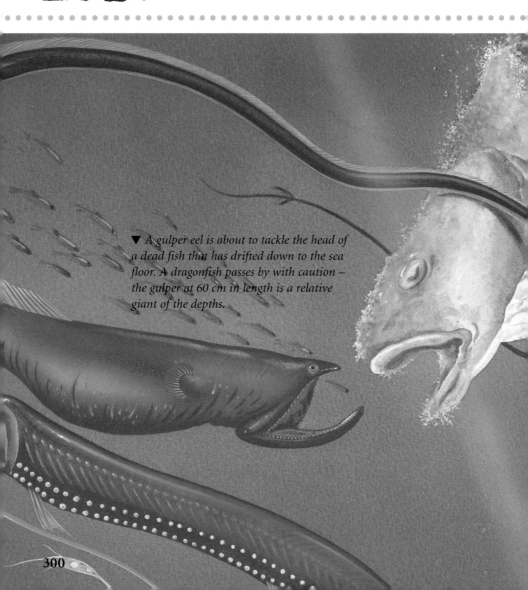

▼ *A gulper eel is about to tackle the head of a dead fish that has drifted down to the sea floor. A dragonfish passes by with caution – the gulper at 60 cm in length is a relative giant of the depths.*

Eels are long, slimy fish that look like snakes.

Baby eels are called elvers.

Some eels live in rivers, but most live in the sea, including moray eels and conger eels.

Moray eels are huge and live in tropical watcrs, where they hunt fish, squid and cuttlefish.

Gulper eels can live more than 7,500 m down in the Atlantic Ocean. Their mouths are huge to help them catch food in the dark, deep water – so big that they can swallow fish larger than themselves whole.

Every autumn, some European common eels migrate more than 7,000 km, from the Baltic Sea in Europe to the Sargasso Sea near the West Indies to lay their eggs.

Migrating eels are thought to find their way partly by detecting weak electric currents created by the movement of the water.

When European eels hatch in the Sargasso Sea they are carried northeast by the ocean current, developing as they go into tiny transparent eels known as glass eels.

The electric eels of South America can produce an electric shock of over 500 volts – enough to knock over an adult human.

Garden eels live in colonies on the seabed, poking out from holes in the sand to catch food drifting by. Their colonies look like gardens of weird plants.

Salmon

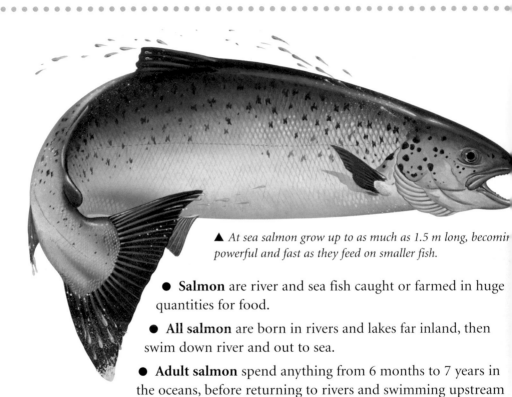

▲ *At sea salmon grow up to as much as 1.5 m long, becoming powerful and fast as they feed on smaller fish.*

● **Salmon** are river and sea fish caught or farmed in huge quantities for food.

● **All salmon** are born in rivers and lakes far inland, then swim down river and out to sea.

● **Adult salmon** spend anything from 6 months to 7 years in the oceans, before returning to rivers and swimming upstream to spawn (lay their eggs).

● **More than five salmon species,** including the sockeye and the chinook, spawn in North American rivers running into the North Pacific.

● **Cherry salmon** spawn in eastern Asian rivers, and amago salmon spawn in Japanese rivers.

Atlantic salmon spawn in rivers in northern Europe and eastern Canada.

Spawning salmon return to the same stream they were born in, up to 3,000 km inland. They are probably sensitive to the chemical and mineral make-up of streams and rivers, helping them to recognise their own stream.

To reach their spawning grounds, salmon have to swim upstream against strong currents, often leaping as high as 5 m to clear waterfalls.

When salmon reach their spawning grounds, they mate. The female lays up to 20,000 eggs.

After spawning, the weakened salmon head down river again, but few make it as far as the sea.

Salmon returning to their spawning ground make mighty leaps up raging torrents. The journey can take months.

Ocean fish

- **Nearly 75%** of all fish live in the seas and oceans.

- **The biggest, fastest swimming fish,** such as swordfish and marlin, live near th surface of the open ocean, far from land. They often migrate vast distances to spawn (lay their eggs) or find food.

- **Many smaller fish** live deeper down, including seabed-dwellers like eels and flatfish (such as plaice, turbot and flounders).

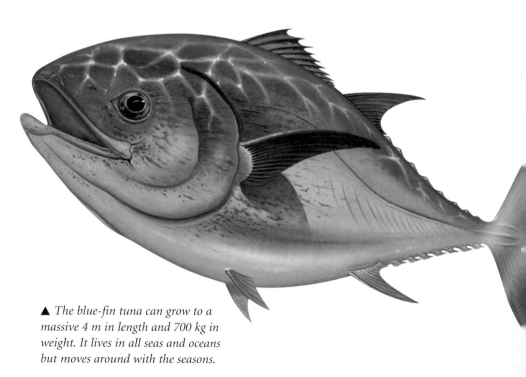

▲ *The blue-fin tuna can grow to a massive 4 m in length and 700 kg in weight. It lives in all seas and oceans but moves around with the seasons.*

◀ *Flying fish beat their tails so fast they are able to 'fly' away from predators.*

● **Flatfish** start life as normal-shaped fish. As they grow older, one eye slowly slides around the head to join the other. The pattern of scales also changes so that one side is the top and one side is the bottom.

● **Plaice** lie on the seabed on their left side, while turbot lie on their right side. Some flounders lie on their left and some on their right.

The upper side of a flatfish is usually camouflaged to help it to blend in with the sea bed.

In the temperate waters of the Atlantic there are rich fishing grounds for fish such as herring.

The swordfish can swim at up to 80 km/h. It uses its long spike to stab squid.

The bluefin tuna can grow to as long as 3 m and weigh more than 500 kg. It is also a fast swimmer – one crossed the Atlantic in 199 days.

... FASCINATING FACT ...
Flying fish can glide over the sea for 400 m and soar up to 6 m above the waves.

Strange deep-sea creatures

- **Deep-sea anglerfish** live deep down in the ocean where it is pitch black. They lure prey into their mouths using a special fishing-rod-like fin spine with a light at its tip.

- **Anglerfish** cannot find each other easily in the dark, so when a male meets a female he stays with her until mating time.

- **Hatchet fish** have giant eyeballs that point upwards so they see prey from belo as silhouettes against the surface.

▼ *The viperfish looks fearsome and is one of the larger predators of the ocean depths. Yet it is only 30 cm long. The general lack of food in the deep means animals are mostly small.*

Viperfish shine in the dark, thousands of metres down, and look like a jet airliner at night, with rows of lights along their bodies.

Siphonophores are colonies of tiny creatures that live in the deep oceans. They string themselves together in lines 20 m long and glow – so they look like fairy lights.

The cirrate octopod looks like a jelly because its skin is 95% water – the water cannot be crushed by the intense pressure of the deep oceans where the octopod lives.

▲ *The porcupine fish inflates like a spiny balloon.*

The weedy seadragon of Australia is a seahorse, but it looks just like a piece of flapping seaweed.

The sleeper shark lives in the freezing depths of the North Atlantic and Arctic Oceans. This shark is 6.5 m long, but very slow and sluggish.

Flashlight fish have light organs made by billions of bacteria which shine like headlights. The fish can suddenly block off these lights and change direction in the dark to confuse predators.

In the Arab-Israeli War of 1967 a shoal of flashlight fish was mistaken for enemy frogmen and blown right out of the water.

Coral-reef fish

- **Many fish species** live in warm seas around coral reefs. They are often very colourful, which makes them instantly recognizable to their own kind.

- **Butterfly fish and angelfish** have slender, oval bodies and are popular as aquarium fish.

- **Male triggerfish** boost their colour to attract females.

- **Cuckoo wrasse** are all born female, but big females change sex when they are between 7 and 13 years old.

- **Cleaner fish** are the health clinics of the oceans. Larger fish such as groupers queue up for cleaner fish to go over them, nibbling away pests and dead skin.

▲ *The long, sharp fin spines of the lionfish are very poisonous.*

- **The banded coral shrimp** cleans up pests in the same way as cleaner fish do, from fish such as moray eels.

- **The sabre-toothed blenny** looks so like a cleaner fish that it can nip in close to big fish but then it takes a bite out of them.

- **Cheilinus** is a carnivorous fish of coral reefs which changes colour to mimic harmless plant-eating fish, such as parrotfish and goatfish. It swims alongside them, camouflaged, until it is close to its prey.

The gaudy underworld of a healthy coral reef.

...**FASCINATING FACT**...
Cleaner fish will go to work inside
a shark's mouth.

Seals and sea lions

- **Seals, sea lions and walruses** are sea mammals that mainly live in water and are agile swimmers, but which waddle awkwardly when they come on land.

- **Most seals** eat fish, squid and shellfish. Crabeater seals eat mainly shrimps, not crabs.

- **Seals and sea lions** have ears, but only sea lions (and fur seals) have ear flaps.

- **Only sea lions** can move their back flippers under their body when travelling about on land.

- **When seals come ashore** to breed, they live for weeks in vast colonies called rookeries.

- **Walruses** are bigger and bulkier than seals, and they have massive tusks and face whiskers.

- **When hunters kill seal pups** for their fur, or to keep numbers down, it is called culling.

- **Elephant seals** spend up to 8 months far out in the ocean continuously diving, with each dive lasting 20 minutes or so.

- **There are freshwater seals** in Lake Baikal in Russia.

Seal pups (babies) like this one grow a thick, furry coat.

....FASCINATING FACT...
The 4 m-long leopard seal of Antarctica
feeds on penguins and even other seals.

Walruses

- **A single walrus tusk** can measure up to 1 m long and weigh 5.4 kg.

- **Walruses swim** by sweeping their huge rear flippers from side to side, each one opening in turn like a 1-m wide fan.

- **The walrus is protected from the cold** by a thick layer of blubber – a third of its total weight.

- **In the summer**, basking walruses turn a deep pink as their blood vessels dilate to radiate heat away from the body.

- **Walruses** excavate shellfish from seabed mud by squirting a high-pressure blast of water from their mouths.

The walrus has 300 whiskers on each side of its moustache, which it uses to help it find food in murky waters.

A walrus uses its long tusks to help it clamber onto ice floes – its scientific name, *Odobenus*, means 'tooth walker'.

In water, a walrus turns a pale grey colour as blood leaves its skin to maintain the temperature of its body core.

A walrus can eat 3000 clams in one day.

◀ *Walruses are very sociable, and like to gather in huge groups on coastal ice or rocks.*

▸ *A walrus's tusks are actually extra-long upper canine teeth. The tusks of the male are longer, and used both for display and for competing with rivals during the breeding season.*

. . . **FASCINATING FACT** . . .
Walrus pups are born 15 months after the parents have mated – 4 to 5 months pass before the egg starts to grow in the mother's womb.

Whales

- **Whales,** dolphins and porpoises are large mammals called cetaceans that live mostly in the seas and oceans. Dolphins and porpoises are small whales.

- **Like all mammals,** whales have lungs – this means they have to come to the surface to breathe every 10 minutes or so, although they can stay down for up to 40 minutes. A sperm whale can hold its breath for 2 hours.

- **Whales breathe** through blowholes on top of their head. When a whale breathes out, it spouts out water vapour and mucus. When it breathes in, it sucks in about 2,000 litres of air within about 2 seconds.

- **Like land mammals,** whales nurse their babies with their own milk. Whale milk is so rich that babies grow incredibly fast. Blue whale babies are over 7 m long when they are born and gain an extra 100 kg or so a day for about 7 months.

Dorsal fin

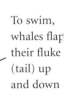

To swim, whales flap their fluke (tail) up and down

▶ *Killer whales or orcas are big deep-sea predators, growing to as long as 9 m and weighing up to 10 tonnes. They feed on fish, seals, penguins and dolphins.*

Humpback whales live together in groups called pods and keep in touch with their own 'dialect' of noises.

Toothed whales, such as the sperm whale and the orca or killer whale, have teeth and prey on large fish and seals. The six groups of toothed whale are sperm whales, beaked whales, belugas and narwhals, dolphins, porpoises, and river dolphins.

Baleen whales, such as the humpback and blue, have a comb of thin plates called baleen in place of teeth. They feed by straining small, shrimp-like creatures called krill through their baleen. There are five baleen whale groups, including right whales, grey whales and rorquals. Rorquals have grooves on their throats and include humpback, minke and blue whales.

The blue whale is the largest creature that ever lived. Blue whales grow to be over 30 m long and weigh more than 150 tonnes. In summer, they eat over 4 tonnes of krill every day – that is 4 million krill.

Whales keep in touch with sounds called phonations. Large baleen whales make sounds which are too low for humans to hear, but they can be heard by other whales at least 80 km away.

Most baleen whales live alone or in small groups, but toothed whales – especially dolphins – often swim in groups called pods or schools.

> **...FASCINATING FACT...**
> Male humpbacks make elaborate 'songs' lasting
> 20 minutes or more – perhaps to woo females.

Dolphins

◀ *The Atlantic hump-backed dolphin inhabits mainly shallower waters, but is also known to swim close to fishing boats where it can feed on the rich shoals.*

- **Groups of common dolphins**, travelling and feeding together, may number up to 2000 individuals.

- **Orcas**, or killer whales, are actually the largest species of dolphin, though they feed on other dolphin species.

- **There are five species** of freshwater dolphin living in Asian and South American rivers. Most catch fish by sound rather than sight.

- **Dolphins** have been known to aid humans by keeping them afloat and driving off attacking sharks.

- **Spinner dolphins** are named for the acrobatic leaps they perform, spinning up to seven times in mid air.

- **The Atlantic hump-backed dolphin** helps fishermen in West Africa by driving shoals of mullet into their nets.

In Mexico's Baja California, bottle-nosed dolphins chase fish up onto the shore, then roll up onto the beach, completely out of the water, to grab them.

Military observers once recorded a group of dolphins swimming at 64 km/h in the bow wave of a warship.

The striped dolphin, seen in ancient Greek paintings, leaps up to 7 m to perform somersaults and spins.

The Yangtse dolphin, or baiji, is one of the world's rarest mammals – probably less than 300 survive.

▼ *Many dolphin species 'spy-hop'. Holding their heads out of the water as they check on their surroundings for predators and potential food.*

Reptiles and amphibians

- **Reptiles** are scaly-skinned animals which live in many different habitats mainly in warm regions . They include crocodiles, lizards, snakes and tortoises.

- **Reptiles are cold-blooded,** but this does not mean that their blood is cold. A reptile body cannot keep its blood warm, and the animal has to control its temperature by moving between hot and cool places.

◀ *Like all reptiles, crocodiles rely on basking in the sun to gain energy for hunting. At night, or when it is cold, they usually sleep.*

◀ Newts are amphibians. The long, fin-like crest on the back of this great crested newt becomes taller and more colourful in spring when the male attracts a female for mating. This large newt measures 17 cm.

● **Reptiles bask in the sun** to gain energy to hunt, and are often less active at cooler times of year.

● **A reptile's skin** looks slimy, but it is quite dry. It keeps in moisture so well that reptiles can survive in deserts. The skin often turns darker to absorb the sun's heat.

● **Although reptiles grow** for most of their lives, their skin does not, so they must slough (shed) it every now and then.

Amphibians are animals that live both on land and in water. They include frogs, toads, newts and salamanders.

Most reptiles lay their eggs on land, but amphibians hatch out in water as tadpoles, from huge clutches of eggs called spawn.

Like fish, tadpoles have gills to breathe in water, but they soon metamorphose (change), growing legs and lungs.

Amphibians never stray far from water.

> ...**FASCINATING FACT**...
> Reptiles were the first large creatures to live
> entirely on land, over 350 million years ago.

Dinosaurs

- **Dinosaurs** were reptiles that dominated life on land from about 220 million to 65 million years ago, when all of them mysteriously became extinct.

- **Although modern reptiles** walk with bent legs splayed out, dinosaurs had straight legs under their bodies – this meant they could run fast or grow heavy.

- **Some dinosaurs** ran on their back two legs, as birds do. Others had four sturdy legs like an elephant's.

- **Dinosaurs** are split into two groups according to their hipbones – saurischians had reptile-like hips and ornithischians had bird-like hips.

▶ Stegosaurus *had a tiny skull relative to its body size, and a brain the size of a walnut. It had rows of plates along its back with four long spines at the end of its tail.*

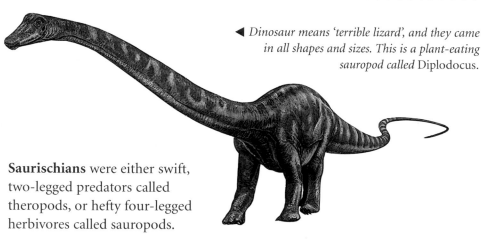

◀ *Dinosaur means 'terrible lizard', and they came in all shapes and sizes. This is a plant-eating sauropod called* Diplodocus.

Saurischians were either swift, two-legged predators called theropods, or hefty four-legged herbivores called sauropods.

Theropods had acute eyesight, fearsome claws and sharp teeth. They included *Tyrannosaurus rex*, one of the biggest hunting animals to ever live on land – over 15 m long, 5 m tall and weighing more than 7 tonnes.

Sauropods had massive bodies, long tails, and long, snake-like necks.

The sauropod *Brachiosaurus* was over 23 m long, weighed 80 tonnes and towered 12 m into the air. It was one of the biggest creatures ever to live on land.

Most dinosaurs are known from fossilized bones, but fossilized eggs, footprints and droppings have also been found. In 1913, mummified hadrosaur skin was found.

Some scientists think the dinosaurs died out after a huge meteor struck Earth off Mexico, creating a cloud that blocked the sun's light and heat.

321

Turtles and tortoises

- **Turtles and tortoises** are reptiles that live inside hard, armoured shells. Together with terrapins, they make up a group called the chelonians.

- **Turtles** live in the sea, freshwater, or on land, tortoises live on land, and terrapins live in streams and lakes.

- **The shield** on the back of a chelonian is called a carapace. Its flat belly armour is called a plastron.

- **Most turtles and tortoises** eat plants and tiny animals. They have no teeth, just jaws with very sharp edges.

▲ *Tortoises are very slow moving and placid.*

322

Tortoises live mostly in hot, dry regions and will hibernate in winter if brought to a cold country.

Turtles and tortoises live to a great age. One giant tortoise found in 1766 in Mauritius lived for 152 years.

The giant tortoise can grow as long as 1.5 m.

The leatherback turtle grows to as long as 2.5 m and weighs more than 800 kg.

Every three years, green turtles gather together to swim thousands of kilometres to Ascension Island in the mid-Atlantic, where they lay their eggs ashore by moonlight at the highest tide. They bury the eggs in the sand, to be incubated by the heat of the sun.

▼ *The spotted turtle largely lives and feeds in water. It will eat fish, water snails and other animals.*

carapace

... FASCINATING FACT ...
Giant tortoises were once kept on ships to provide fresh meat on long voyages.

Lizards

- **Lizards** are a group of 3,800 scaly-skinned reptiles, varying from a few centimetres long to the 3 m-long Komodo dragon.

- **Lizards cannot** control their own body heat, and so rely on sunshine for warmth. This is why they live in warm climates and bask in the sun for hours each day.

- **Lizards move** in many ways – running, scampering and slithering. Some can glide. Unlike mammals, their limbs stick out sideways rather than downwards.

- **Most lizards** lay eggs, although a few give birth to live young. But unlike birds or mammals, a mother lizard does not nurture (look after) her young.

- **Most lizards** are meat-eaters, feeding on insects and other small creatures.

▲ *Lizards have four legs and a long tail. In most lizards, the back legs are much stronger than the front, and are used to drive the animal forwards in a kind of writing motion.*

324

Geckos are small lizards that are mainly active at night. Their toes are covered in hairy pads, which help them to stick to rough surfaces. Some types of gecko can even walk upside down.

The glass lizard has no legs. Its tail may break off and lie wriggling as a decoy if it is attacked. The lizard later grows another one.

The Australian frilled lizard has a ruff around its neck. To put off attackers, it can spread out its ruff to make itself look three or four times bigger.

Horned lizards can squirt a jet of blood from their eyes almost as far as 1 m to put off attackers.

The Komodo dragon of Sumatra is the biggest lizard, weighing up to 150 kg or more. It can catch deer and pigs and swallow them whole.

...FASCINATING FACT...
The Basilisk lizard is also known as the Jesus
Christ lizard because it can walk on water.

Iguanas

- **Iguanas** are large lizards that live in tropical regions around the Pacific and in the Americas.

- **Larger iguanas** are the only vegetarian lizards. Unlike other lizards, most eat fruit, flowers and leaves, rather than insects.

- **The common iguana** lives high up in trees, but comes down to lay its eggs in a hole in the ground.

▼ *Before each dive into water, marine iguanas warm themselves in the sun to gain energy.*

- **Common iguanas** will jump 6 m or more out of the trees to the ground if they are disturbed.

- **The rhinoceros iguana** of the West Indies gets its name from the pointed scales on its snout.

- **The marine iguana** of the Galapagos Islands is the only lizard that spends much of its life in the sea.

- **Marine iguanas** keep their eggs warm ready for hatching in the mouth of volcanoes, risking death to put them there.

- **When in the water,** a marine iguana may dive for 15 minutes or more, pushing itself along with its tail.

- **Although marine iguanas** cannot breathe underwater, their heart rate slows so that they use less oxygen.

- **The chuckwalla** inflates its body with air and wedges itself in a rock crack if it is in danger.

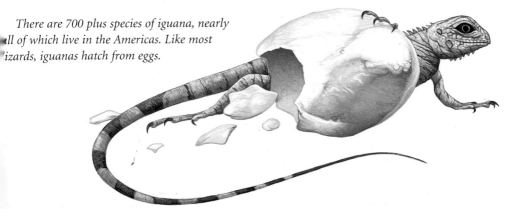

There are 700 plus species of iguana, nearly all of which live in the Americas. Like most lizards, iguanas hatch from eggs.

Chameleons

- **Chameleons** are 85 species of lizard, most of which live on the island of Madagascar and in mainland Africa.

- **The smallest chameleon,** the dwarf Brookesia, could balance on your little finger. The biggest, Oustalet's chameleon, is the size of a small cat.

- **A chameleon** can look forwards and backwards at the same time, as each of its amazing eyes can swivel in all directions independently of the other.

- **Chameleons feed** on insects and spiders, hunting them in trees by day.

- **A chameleon's tongue** is almost as long as its body, but is normally squashed up inside its mouth.

- **The chameleon's tongue** is fired out from a special launching bone that is located on its lower jaw.

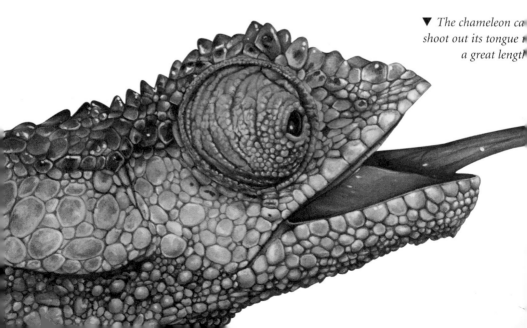

▼ *The chameleon ca*
shoot out its tongue
a great length

Most of a chameleon's bulging eyes are protected by skin.

A chameleon shoots out its tongue in a fraction of a second to trap its victim on a sticky pad at the tip.

Most lizards can change colour, but chameleons are experts, changing quickly to all sorts of colours.

Chameleons change colour when they are angry or frightened, too cold or too hot, or sick – but they change colour less often to match their surroundings.

The colour of the skin is controlled by pigment cells called melanophores, which change colour as they change size.

329

Pythons and boas

- **Constrictors** are snakes that squeeze their victims to death, rather than poisoning them. They include pythons, boas and anacondas.

- **A constrictor** does not crush its victim. Instead, it winds itself around, gradual tightening its coils until the victim suffocates.

- **Constrictors usually swallow** victims whole, then spend days digesting them. They have special jaws that allow their mouths to open very wide. A large mea can be seen as a lump moving down the body.

▼ *Pythons are tropical snakes that live in moist forests in Asia and Africa. They are the world's biggest snakes, rivalled only by giant anacondas. Pythons are one long tube of muscle, well able to squeeze even big victims to death. They usually eat animals about the size of domestic cats, but occasionally they go for really big meals such as wild pigs and deer.*

Pythons are big snakes that live in Asia, Indonesia and Africa. In captivity, reticulated pythons grow to 9 m. Boas and anacondas are the big constrictors of South America.

Boas capture their prey by lying in wait, hiding motionless under trees and waiting for victims to pass by. But like all snakes, they can go for many weeks without eating.

Like many snakes, most constrictors begin life as eggs. Unusually for snakes, female pythons look after their eggs until they hatch by coiling around them. Even more unusually, Indian and green tree pythons actually keep their eggs warm by shivering.

Female boas do not lay eggs, giving birth to live young.

Boas have tiny remnants of back legs, called spurs, which males use to tickle females during mating.

Anacondas spend much of their lives in swampy ground or shallow water, lying in wait for victims to come and drink. One anaconda was seen to swallow a 2 m-long caiman (a kind of crocodile).

When frightened, the royal python of Africa coils itself into a tight ball, which is why it is sometimes called the ball python. Rubber boas do the same, but hide their heads and stick their tails out aggressively to fool attackers.

Cobras and vipers

- **Two kinds of poisonous snake** are dangerous to humans – vipers and elapids such as cobras and mambas.

- **Elapids** have their venom (poison) in short front fangs. A viper's fangs are so long that they usually have to be folded away.

- **The hamadryad cobra** of Southeast Asia is the world's largest poisonous snake, growing to over 5 m.

- **In India, cobras kill** more than 7,000 people every year. The bite of a king cobra can kill an elephant in 4 hours. The marine cobra lives in the sea and its venom is 100 times more deadly than a king cobra's.

- **Snake charmers** use the spectacled cobra playing to it so that it follows the pipe as about to strike – but the snake's fangs have been removed to make it safe.

▶ *When on the defensive, a cobra rears up and spreads the skin of its neck in a hood to make it look bigger. This often gives victims a chance to hit it away.*

- **A spitting cobra** squirts venom into its attacker's eyes, and is accurate at 2 m or more. The venom is not deadly, but it blinds the victim and is very painful.

The black mamba of Africa can race along at 25 km/h with its head raised and its tongue flickering.

A viper's venom kills its victims by causing their blood to clot. Viper venom has been used to treat hacmophiliacs (people whose blood does not clot well).

The pit vipers of the Americas hunt their warm-blooded victims using heat-sensitive pits on the side of their heads (see animal senses).

The wedge-shaped head, narrow ~ck and brown-green scale pattern ' the Gaboon viper make this snake 'most impossible to spot among the ,aves of the forest floor. It has the ·ngest fangs of any viper, up to 5 cm.

. . . .**FASCINATING FACT**. . . .
Fer-de-lance snakes have 60 to 80 babies,
each of which is deadly poisonous.

Crocodiles and alligators

- **Crocodiles, alligators, caimans and gharials** are large reptiles that together form the group known as crocodilians. There are 14 species of crocodile, 7 alligators and caimans, and 1 gharial.

- **Crocodilian species** lived alongside the dinosaurs 200 million years ago, and they are the nearest we have to living dinosaurs today.

- **Crocodilians are hunters** that lie in wait for animals coming to drink at the water's edge. When crocodilians seize a victim they drag it into the water, stun it with a blow from their tail, then drown it.

- **Like all reptiles,** crocodilians get their energy from the sun. Typically, they bask in the sun on a sandbar or the river bank in the morning, then slip into the river at midday to cool off.

▶ *Crocodiles are huge reptiles with powerful bodies, scaly skin and great snapping jaws.*

The crocodile's eyes and nostrils are raised so it can see and breathe while floating under water

crocodile will often kill its
ctims with a swipe from its
ong tail

e skin on
back has
lges formed
dozens of tiny
nes called
teoderms

● **Crocodiles live** in tropical rivers and swamps.
At over 5 m long, saltwater crocodiles are the world's
largest reptiles – one grew to over 8 m long.

● **Crocodiles** are often said to cry after eating their
victims. In fact only saltwater crocodiles cry, and they do
it to get rid of salt.

● **Crocodiles have thinner snouts** than alligators,
and a fourth tooth on the lower jaw which is visible
when the crocodile's mouth is shut.

● **The female Nile crocodile** lays her eggs in
nests which she digs in sandy river banks,
afterwards covering the eggs in sand to keep
them at a steady temperature. When the babies
hatch they make loud piping calls. The mother
then digs them out and carries them one by one
in her mouth to the river.

● **Alligators** are found both in the
Florida Everglades in the United States
and in the Yangtze River in China.

The skin on its belly is
smooth and was once
prized as a material for
shoes and handbags

. . . **FASCINATING FACT** . . .
Crocodilians often swallow stones to help
them stay underwater for long periods.
Without this ballast, they might tip over.

Frogs and toads

- **Frogs** and toads are amphibians – creatures that live both on land and in the water.

- **There are about 3,500 species** of frog and toad. Most live near water, but some live in trees and others live underground.

- **Frogs** are mostly smaller and better jumpers. Toads are bigger, with thicker, wartier skin which holds on to moisture and allows them to live on land longer.

- **Frogs and toads** are meat-eaters. They catch fast-moving insects by darting out their long, sticky tongues.

- **Frogs and toads begin life** as fish-like tadpoles, hatching in the water from huge clutches of eggs called spawn.

- **After 7 to 10 weeks**, tadpoles grow legs and lungs and develop into frogs ready to leave the water.

◀ Frogs are supe jumpers, w long back legs propel them ir the air. M also ha suckers on th fingers to he them land secur on slippery surfac

In midwife toads, the male looks after the eggs, not the female – winding strings of eggs around his back legs and carrying them about until they hatch.

The male Darwin's frog swallows the eggs and keeps them in his throat until they hatch – and pop out of his mouth.

The goliath frog of West Africa is the largest frog – at over 25 cm long. The biggest toad is the cane toad of Queensland, Australia – one weighed 2.6 kg and measured 50 cm in length with its legs outstretched. The cane toad was introduced to Australia from South America to help control pests.

The arrow-poison frogs that live in the tropical rainforests of Central America get their name because natives tip their arrows with deadly poison from glands in the frogs' skin. Many arrow-poison frogs are very colourful.

The natterjack toad is ...ily recognized by a ...tinctive yellow line down ... head and back. It gives ... a smell of burning ...ber when alarmed.

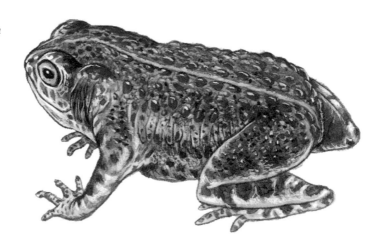

What are birds?

◀ *One of Europe's smallest birds, the wr is found in many habitats from open moor dense marsh. It holds its tail almost upri and builds a domed nest among tree ro*

- **Not all birds** are able to fly, but they have feathers.

- **Feathers** are light, but they are linked by hoo called barbs to make them strong enough for flight.

- **Wrens** have 1,000 feathers, while swans have 20,000.

- **Birds have four kinds** of wing feather – large primaries, smaller secondaries, coverts and contours.

- **Every kind of bird** has its own formation pattern and colour of feathers, calle its plumage.

- **Instead of a teeth,** birds have a hard beak or bill.

- **Unlike humans,** birds do not give birth to babies. Instead they lay eggs, usual sitting on them to keep them warm until they hatch (see birds' nests and eggs

- **Birds fly in two ways** – by gliding with their wings held still, or by flapping their wings up and down.

- **Gliding is less effort** than flapping, and birds that stay in the air a long time tend to be superb gliders – including birds of prey, swifts, gulls and gannets.

- **Albatrosses and petrels** have long narrow wings that help them sail upwards on rising air currents.

Most birds flap their wings to fly. Even birds that spend much of their time gliding have to flap their wings to take off and land.

...FASCINATING FACT...
Birds may be descended from dinosaurs
and took to the air 150 million years ago.

Early birds

- **The earliest known bird** is *Archaeopteryx*, which lived 155–150 million years ago. It had feathers like a modern bird but teeth like a reptile.

- **Ichthyornis** was a seabird with long, toothed jaws. It lived alongside dinosaurs in the Late Cretaceous period.

- **Although it could fly**, *Archaeopteryx* could not take off from the ground, and probably had to climb a tree before launching itself into the air.

- **Scientists believe** that birds evolved from lightly built dinosaurs such as *Compsognathus*, which ran on two legs.

- **The dodo** stood 1 m tall and lived on the island of Mauritiu in the Indian Ocean. It became extinct in the 17th century.

◀ Archaeopteryx h
a wingspan of about
50 cm. Its name mea
'ancient wing'.

Aepyornis (also known as the 'elephant bird'), a 3-m tall ostrich ancestor from Madagascar, probably became extinct in the 17th century.

The eggs of *Aepyornis* may have weighed as much as 10 kg – more than 9 times the weight of an ostrich egg today.

The tallest bird ever was the moa (*Dinornis*) of New Zealand. It was a towering 3.5 m tall.

The great auk first lived 2 million years ago. It became extinct in the mid 19th century after being overhunted for its fat, which was burned in oil lamps.

An early member of the vulture family, *Argentavix* of South America had an amazing 7.3 m wingspan.

▶ *Like today's seabirds,* hthyornis *probably fed on* sh *which it caught in its long* othed *jaws.*

Beaks and feet

- **No bird** has more than four toes, but some have three and the ostrich has only two.

- **Four-toed birds** have different arrangements of toes: in swifts, all four toes point forwards; in most perching birds, three point forwards and one backwards; and in parrots, two point forwards and two backwards.

- **A beak** is made up of a bird's projecting jaw bones, which are covered in a hard horny material.

- **The hyacinth macaw** has one of the most powerful beaks of any bird, strong enough to crack brazil nuts.

- **Webbed feet** make all waterbirds very efficient paddlers.

- **The Australian pelican** has the largest beak of any bird, at up to 50 cm long.

- **Nightjars** have the shortest beaks, at 8–10 mm long.

◄ *The sword-billed hummingbird has an extremely long beak and a long tongue for extracting nectar from flowers.*

342

The crossbill is so-called because the upper and lower portions of its beak cross over one another.

Below is the foot of a bird of prey. Its long, curving talons make deadly weapons.

> ...FASCINATING FACT...
> A baby bird has a spike called an
> 'egg-tooth' on its beak for
> breaking its way out of its egg.

● **A bird stands** on the tips of its toes –
  the backward bending joint halfway
  down its leg is the ankle joint.

● **A bird's beak** is extremely sensitive to
  touch. Birds that probe in the ground
  for food have extra sensory organs at
  the beak tip.

Feathers

- **Feathers** are made of a protein called keratin. Human hair and nails are also made of keratin.

- **Feathers grow** at a rate of 1–13 mm a day.

- **The ruby-throated hummingbird** has only 940 feathers, while the whistling swan has 25,216.

- **A bird's feathers** are replaced once or twice a year in a process that is known as 'moulting'.

- **Feathers** keep a bird warm, protect its skin, provide a flight surface, and may also attract mates.

- **In most birds**, a third of the feathers are on the head.

- **The longest feathers ever known** were 10.59 m long, and belonged to an ornamental chicken.

- **The feathers** that cover a bird's body are called contour feathers. Down feather underneath provide extra warmth.

- **The 7182 feathers** of a bald eagle weighed 677 g, more than twice as much as the bird's skeleton.

- **Birds** spend time every day 'preening' – cleaning and rearranging their feathers with their beaks.

▶ *The peacock has the most ornate feathers of any bird.*

Bird song and calls

- **Birds** make two sorts of sounds – simple calls, giving a warning or a threat, and the more complicated songs sung by some males at breeding time.

- **Birds' songs** have a definite dialect. The songs of a group of chaffinches in one area, will sound slightly different from those of a group somewhere else.

- **A songbird** reared in captivity away from its family produces a weak version of its parents' song, but cannot perform the whole repertoire.

- **Gulls and parrots** do not sing, but they do make various calls to attract mates or warn off enemies.

- **A bird sings** by vibrating the thin muscles in its syrinx – a special organ located in its throat.

- **A sedge warbler** may use at least 50 different sounds in its songs.

▶ *The chaffinch is the commonest of Europe's finches and has a cheerful, attractive song.*

◄ *Skylarks make special, fluttering flights accompanied by a distinctive song.*

● **Male and female boubou shrikes** sing a duet together, performing alternate parts of the song.

● **Songbirds** may make as many as 20 calls; gulls make only about 10.

● **Birds** make other sounds, too. During courtship flights, male woodpigeons make a loud clapping with their wings.

...FASCINATING FACT...
A baby songbird starts to learn to sing about 10 days after it hatches, and continues to learn for about 40 days.

Migration

- **Migration** is the journey made twice a year between a summer breeding area, where food is plentiful, and a wintering area with a good climate.

- **Many migrating birds** have to build up fat stores to allow them to fly non-stop for many days without food.

- **A migrating bird** can fly across the Sahara Desert in 50–60 hours without stopping to 'refuel'.

- **Birds find their way** by observing landmarks, the patterns of stars and the position of the setting sun. They also use their sense of smell and monitor the Earth's magnetic field.

- **Most birds** that migrate long distances fly at night.

- **The snow goose** migrates nearly 5000 km south from Arctic Canada at an altitude of 9000 m.

- **Before migration was studied**, some people thought swallows simply spent the winter asleep in mud.

- **Even flightless birds migrate.** Emus make journeys on foot of 500 km or more, and penguins migrate in water.

- **Every year** at least 5 billion birds migrate from North to Central and South America.

- **The Arctic tern** spends the northern summer in the Arctic and migrates to the Antarctic for the southern summer, enjoying 24 hours of daylight in both places.

▶ *Geese migrate in huge flocks,* *pairs stay together within the flo*

Birds

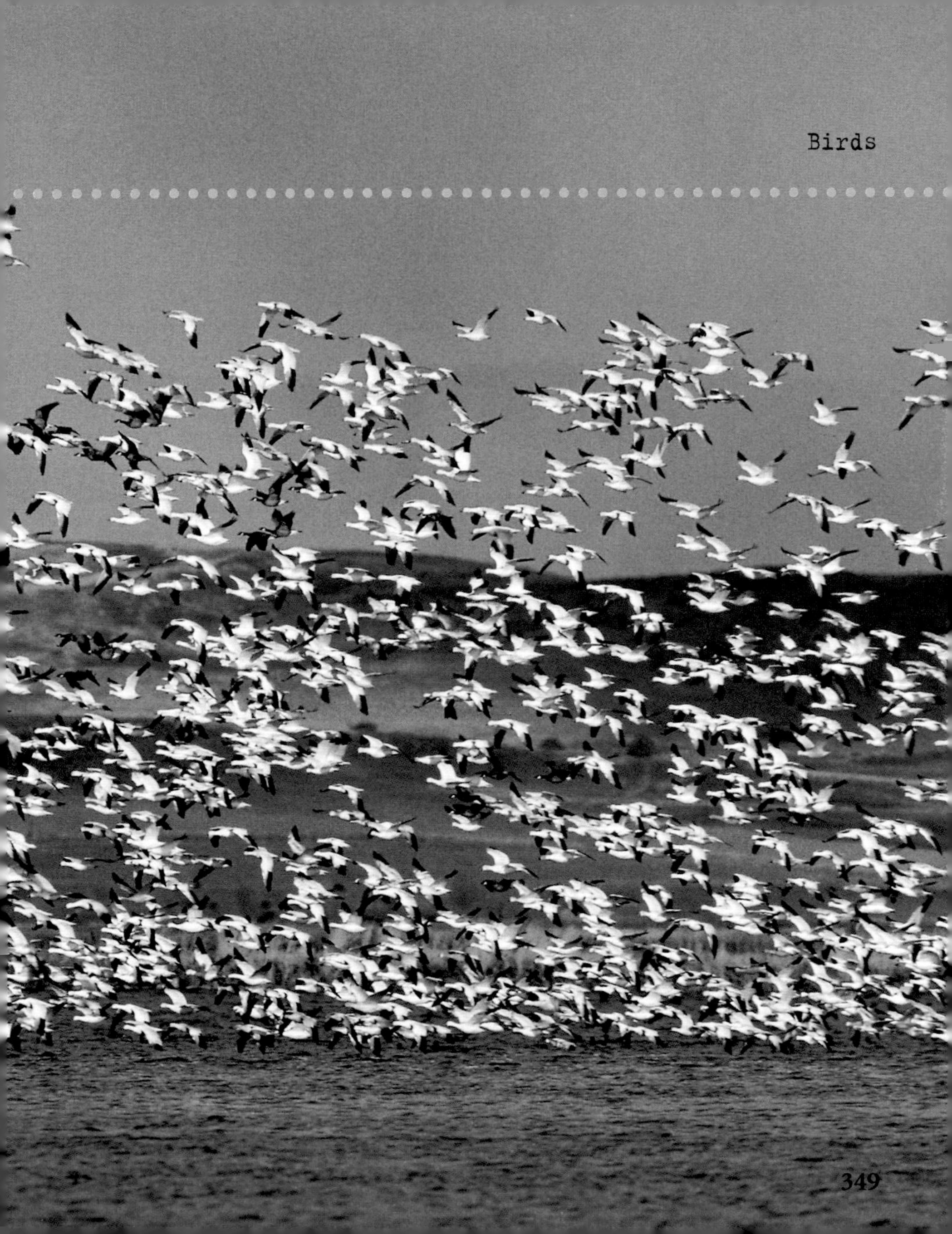

Birds' eggs and nests

◀ After they lay their eggs, most birds sit on them to keep their eggs warm until they are ready to hatch. This is called incubating the eggs.

- **All birds** begin life as eggs. Each species' egg is a slightly different colour.

- **The plover's egg** is pear-shaped. The owl's is round.

- **Hornbills** lay just one egg a year. Partridges lay up to 20 eggs. Hens and some ducks can lay around 350 a year.

- **Most birds build nests** to lay their eggs in – usually bowl-shaped and made from twigs, grasses and leaves.

- **The biggest nest** is that of the Australian mallee fowl, which builds a mound of soil 5 m across, with egg-chambers filled with rotting vegetation to keep it warm.

- **The weaverbirds** of Africa and Asia are very sociable. Some work together to weave huge, hanging nests out of straw, with scores of chambers. Each chamber is for a pair of birds and has its own entrance.

- **Ovenbirds** of Central and South America get their name because their nests look like the clay ovens made by local people. Some ovenbirds' nests can be as much as 3 m high.

Flamingos nest on lakes, building mud nests that look like upturned sandcastles poking out of the water. They lay one or two eggs on top.

The great treeswift lays its single egg in a nest the size of an eggcup.

▼ *The bittern, famous for its bull-like booming call, feeds on animals living in reed beds. This is where it makes its nest.*

....FASCINATING FACT....
Great auks' eggs are pointed at one end to stop them rolling off their cliff-edge nests.

351

Sparrows

- **More than 70%** of all bird species – over 5,000 species altogether – are perching birds, or Passerines. They have feet with three toes pointing forwards and one backwards, to help them cling to a perch.

- **Perching birds build** neat, small, cup-shaped nests.

- **Perching birds sing** – this means that their call is not a single sound, but a sequence of musical notes.

- **Songbirds**, such as thrushes, warblers and nightingales, are perching birds with especially attractive songs.

- Usually only male songbirds sing – and mainly in the mating season, to warn off rivals and attract females.

◀ *Sparrows are sma perching birds found many parts of the worl Sparrows are seed-eate with the house sparro specializing in grai Changes in farmir practices are thought account for this bird dramatic decline numbers in Britai*

Starlings often gather on overhead cables ready to migrate.

Sparrows are small, plump birds, whose chirruping song is familiar almost everywhere.

Starlings are very common perching birds which often gather in huge flocks, either to feed or to roost.

All the millions of European starlings in North America are descended from 100 set free in New York's Central Park in the 1890s.

Many perching birds, including mynahs, are talented mimics. The lyre bird of southeastern Australia can imitate car sirens and chainsaws, as well as other birds.

The red-billed quelea of Africa is the world's most abundant bird. There are over 1.5 billion of them.

Swallows and martins

- **There are about 80 species of swallows and martins** found all over the world. Most migrate between breeding grounds and wintering areas.

- **The sand martin** digs a 120 cm long nesting burrow in riverbanks.

- **Only discovered in 1968**, the white-eyed river martin spends the winter in reedbeds on Lake Boraphet in Thailand.

- **Purple martins** often nest in old woodpecker holes or in nest-boxes. The female incubates the 4–5 eggs alone, but the male helps feed the young.

- **There is an old saying** that the weather will be good when swallows fly high, but bad when swallows fly low. This is based on fact – in wet weather, insects stay nearer the ground, so their predators – the swallows – do the same.

- **Adult swallows** will carry a mass of crushed insects, squashed in a ball in the throat, back to their young. A barn swallow may take 400 meals a day to its chicks.

◀ *The house martin often lives near people, making its nest under the eaves of buildings or under bridges or other structures.*

Sand martins breed in the northern hemisphere, migrating south in the winter in flocks of thousands.

In most swallow species, males and females are alike, but in the rare blue swallow, the female has a short tail, while the male's is long and forked.

Swallows catch their insect food in the air as they fly.

▲ *Swallows may lay up to eight eggs at a time, often in 'mud cups' attached to buildings.*

. . . FASCINATING FACT . . .
The ancient Romans used swallows as messengers to carry news of the winners of chariot races to neighbouring towns.

Thrushes and dippers

- **The wheatear breeds** in the Arctic, but in autumn flies some 3200 km to Africa where it spends the winter.

- **The dipper** is the only type of songbird to live in and around water – it can swim underwater and even walk along streambeds as it searches for insect prey.

▼ *Dippers make their homes near water. When they walk on the stream bed, they hold onto stones to keep themselves from surfacing.*

The familiar orange-red breast of a robin indicates that the bird is at least 2 months old.

More than 300 species of thrush are found nearly all over the world.

Best known for its beautiful song, the nightingale sings during the day as well as at night.

The female blackbird makes a cup-shaped nest of plant stems, grass, twigs and roots. The 4–5 eggs hatch after 11–17 days.

The five species of dipper live in Europe, Asia and parts of North and South America.

The dome-shaped nests of dippers usually have an entrance over running water.

The American robin – the largest of the North American thrushes – lives both in cities and mountains.

Blackbirds were taken to Australia and New Zealand in the 19th century. Their songs are now clearly different to blackbirds living in Europe.

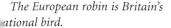

The European robin is Britain's national bird.

Warblers

▶ *The willow warbler (left) and the chiffchaff (right) look extremely similar. They can be told apart, however, by their different song patterns.*

- **The willow warbler** is only 11 cm long, but flies all the way from northern Europe and Siberia to Africa to spend the winter – a distance of some 12,000 km.

- **The rarely seen grasshopper warbler** has an extraordinary whirring song and can 'throw its voice' like a ventriloquist.

- **The warbler family** has more than 380 species. Most live in Europe, Africa, Asia and Australasia, but there are a few species in North and South America.

- **Most warblers** are 9–16 cm long, but the two largest – the South African grassbird and the Australian songlarks – are up to 23 cm long.

The Aldabra warbler, discovered in 1967, lives only on a small part of Aldabra Island in the Indian Ocean. It has not been seen since 1983, so may well be extinct.

Insects are the main food of most warblers, but they also eat some fruits, berries and seeds.

The marsh warbler can mimic about 80 other species.

Chiffchaffs and willow warblers look almost exactly alike, but their songs are quite different.

The blackcap lays 4–6 eggs in a neat, cup-shaped nest. Both parents incubate them for 10–15 days.

The tailorbird makes a cradle like nest from two leaves which it sews together with plant fibres or spiders' webs.

▶ *At 19 cm long, the great reed warbler is larger than most European warblers.*

Parrots and budgerigars

▲ *The blue-and-yellow macaw of the Amazon rainforest has been trapped so much for the pet trade, it is now quite rare.*

- **Parrots** are colourful birds with curved bills for eating fruits and seeds and for cracking nuts. They are very noisy birds and they live mostly in tropical rainforests.

- **Parrots** have feet with two toes pointing forwards and two backwards, allowing them to grip branches and hold food.

- **There are 330 or so parrot species** divided into three main groups – true parrots, cockatoos and lories.

- **Half of all parrot species,** including macaws, green Amazon parrots and parakeets, live in Latin America.

- **Australia and New Guinea** are home to parrots called cockatoos (which are white with feathered crests on their heads), as well as to lories and lorikeets.

- **The budgerigar** is a small parakeet from central Australia which is very popular as a pet.

The hanging parrots of Southeast Asia get their name because they sleep upside down like bats.

The kea of New Zealand is a parrot that eats meat as well as fruit. It was once wrongly thought to be a sheep killer.

Parrots are well known for their mimicry of human voices. Some have a repertoire of 300 words or more.

An African grey parrot called Alex was trained by scientist Irene Pepperberg to identify at least 50 different objects. Alex could ask for each of these objects in English – and also refuse them.

The pink cockatoo's headcrest displays bands of scarlet and yellow when spread

▶ *The white plumage of the pink cockatoo is shot through with a soft pink flush.*

361

Birds of paradise

- **Birds of paradise**, of which there are about 44 species, are found only in New Guinea and northeastern Australia.

- **The king of Saxony bird of paradise** has two 50 cm head plumes decorated with small, sky-blue squares, so unusual-looking they were first thought to be fake.

- **The magnificent riflebird** gets its name from its loud whistling call, which sounds like a passing bullet.

- **Most female birds of paradise** make a cup or dome-shaped nest and lay 1–2 eggs.

▲ *The blue bird of paradise is a rare member of this exotic family*

The male king bird of paradise uses his long, wirelike tail feathers in his courtship display.

During courtship, the blue bird of paradise hangs upside-down from a branch with his splendid blue feathers and tail plumes spread over his head.

Fruit and insects are the main foods of the birds of paradise. Some also eat leaves and buds.

New Guinea tribesmen traditionally wear bird of paradise feathers in their head-dresses.

During the early 19th century, 100,000 bird of paradise skins were sold each year in Europe for hat and dress decorations.

The first bird of paradise skins brought to Europe from New Guinea did not have feet, so some people thought the birds never landed.

Swifts and hummingbirds

- **Swifts and hummingbirds** are on the wing so much that their feet have become weak – which is why they are called Apodiformes, meaning 'footless ones'.

- **Swifts** are among the fastest flying birds. Spine-tailed swifts of eastern Asia have been recorded at 240 km/h.

- **Swifts use** their short, gaping bills to catch insects on the wing.

- **Swifts may fly** through the night without landing. They may even sleep on the wing. European swifts fly all the way to Africa and back without stopping.

- **When swifts land,** they cling to vertical surfaces such as walls, cliffs and trees.

- **Great dusky swifts** nest and roost behind waterfalls, and have to fly through the water to get in and out.

- **Hummingbirds** are 325 species of tiny, colourful, tropical birds which sip nectar from flowers.

- **Hummingbirds** are the most amazing aerial acrobats, hovering and twisting in front of flowers.

- **The bee hummingbird** is the world's smallest bird – including its long bill, it measures just 5 cm.

▲ *Swifts winter in Afric then fly north and east Europe and Asia to bree Their feet are so sm and weak that they c hardly perch on twi*

Hummingbirds have long bills
suck nectar from flowers.

...FASCINATING FACT...
To hover, horned sungem
hummingbirds beat their
wings 90 times per second.

Kingfishers

- **The common kingfisher** nests at the end of a 60-cm long tunnel that it excavates in a riverbank. The female lays 4–8 eggs.

- **The tiny African pygmy kingfisher** dives not into water, like the common kingfisher, but into grass, where it snatches grasshoppers and beetles.

- **The 86 or so species of kingfisher** are found all over the world, except parts of the far north.

- **The giant kingfisher** of Africa and the Australian laughing kookaburra are the largest of the family, at about 45 cm long.

- **Common kingfishers** incubate their eggs for 19–21 days, and feed the young for up to 4 weeks.

- **The shovel-billed kingfisher** is armed with its own spade for digging in mud – it uses its large, heavy bill to dig up worms, shellfish and small reptiles.

- **A flash of iridescent** turquoise feathers streaking at high speed along a quiet riverbank indicates the presence of a common or European kingfisher.

◀ *The kingfisher fiercely defends the stretch of riverbank where it feeds and nests.*

In the forests of New Guinea, the male paradise kingfisher shows off its very long tail feathers to females as part of its courtship display.

The laughing kookaburra is named for its call, which sounds like noisy laughter. It makes its call to claim territory. Once one starts, others tend to join in!

In northern Australia, termite mounds are adopted as nest sites by the buff-breasted kingfisher.

The long, pointed beak of most ngfishers is ideally suited to striking d catching fish.

Cuckoos and hoatzin

- **The greater roadrunner**, which is a type of cuckoo, can move at a speed of 20 km/h or more on land.

- **The Eurasian cuckoo** is a 'brood parasite' – it lays its eggs in the nests of other birds.

- **Most birds** take several minutes to lay an egg, but the cuckoo lays one in just nine seconds, so it can quickly take advantage of any brief absence of the host bird.

- **Of the 129 or so species of cuckoo**, only about 50 lay their eggs in other birds' nests.

- **The 60-cm long hoatzin** (there is only one species) lives deep in South America's rainforest.

- **Hoatzin chicks** leave the nest soon after hatching. Two little claws on each wing help them clamber about.

- **The 22 species of turaco** live only in Africa. Largest is the 90-cm long great blue turaco, weighing 1 kg.

▲ *The hoatzin, from northern South America, has a large plume on its head and, unlike other birds, feeds almost entirely on leaves.*

These flycatchers are busy feeding a cuckoo chick in their nest.

Turacos feed mostly on fruit, leaves and flowers, but also catch some insects in the breeding season.

Amazingly, the eggs of brood parasite cuckoos vary in colour and markings according to the host they use. A Eurasian cuckoo's eggs may resemble those of reed warblers, garden warblers or redstarts.

The Australian koel prefers fruit to the caterpillars and other creatures eaten by other cuckoos.

Woodpeckers and toucans

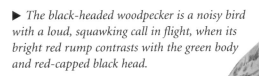

▶ *The black-headed woodpecker is a noisy bird with a loud, squawking call in flight, when its bright red rump contrasts with the green body and red-capped black head.*

- **Woodpeckers** are closely related to the colourful toucans and jacamars that live in tropical rainforests.

- **Woodpeckers,** toucans, barbets, jacamars and honeyguides all have two toes on each foot pointing forwards and two pointing backwards. Their toes help them cling to trees and branches.

- **Woodpeckers** use their powerful bills to bore into tree trunks to get at insects. They spear the insects with their incredibly long tongues.

- **Gila woodpeckers** escape the desert heat by nesting inside giant saguaro cacti (where it can be 30°C cooler).

- **Redhead woodpeckers** drill holes in trees and use them to store acorns for winter – wedging them in very tightly so that squirrels cannot steal them.

- **Woodpeckers** claim their territory not by singing, but by hammering their bill against trees.

Honeyguides lead honey badgers to bees' nests. The badger opens them to get the honey and the bird gets beeswax.

When toucans sleep, they turn their heads around and lay their bills down their backs.

The toucan's giant beak is full of air holes, so it is not heavy enough to overbalance the bird. Toucans eat mainly small fruit.

...FASCINATING FACT...
At 23 cm, the toucan's bill is much
longer than its body.

Turkeys and hens

- **Turkeys,** chickens, geese and ducks are all kinds of poultry – farm birds bred to provide meat, eggs and feathers.

  - **Chickens** were first tamed 5,000 years ago, and there are now over 200 breeds, including bantams and Rhode Island reds.

    - **Female chickens** and turkeys are called hens. Male chickens are called roosters or cockerels. Male turkeys are toms. Baby turkeys are poults.

◀ *The wild turkey North America li in forest and scru where it feeds on t ground eating see nuts and berries. night it flaps branches to re*

*Roosters are renowned for their noisy cries
very morning as the sun comes up. This harsh
ry is called a crow.*

To keep hens laying, their eggs must
be collected every day. If not, the hens
will wait until they have a small clutch
of eggs, then try to sit on them to
hatch them.

Battery hens spend their lives crowded
into rows of cages called batteries inside
buildings.

Free-range hens are allowed to scratch
outdoors for insects and seeds.

Chickens raised only for eating are
called broilers.

Turkeys are a kind of pheasant. There are several species, but all are descended
from the native wild turkey of North America, first tamed by Native Americans
1,000 years ago.

Male turkeys have a loose fold of bare, floppy skin called a wattle hanging
down from their head and neck.

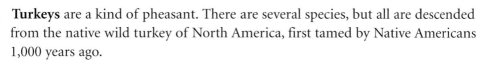

. . . **FASCINATING FACT**. . .
All domestic chickens are descended from
the wild red jungle fowl of India.

Pheasants and peafowl

- **A game bird** is a bird that is hunted for sport.

- **Game birds** spend most of the time strutting along the ground looking for seeds. They fly only in emergencies.

- **There are 250 species** of game bird, including pheasants, grouse, partridges, quails, wild turkeys and peafowl.

- **Most of the 48 species** of pheasant originated in China and central Asia.

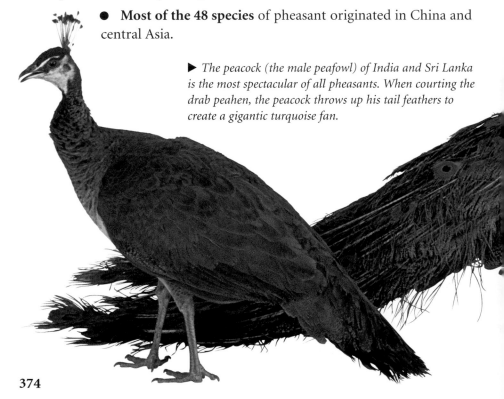

▶ *The peacock (the male peafowl) of India and Sri Lanka is the most spectacular of all pheasants. When courting the drab peahen, the peacock throws up his tail feathers to create a gigantic turquoise fan.*

▶ *The common partridge is familiar as a game bird on farm land in Europe and south-western Asia. Partridges eat seeds and young shoots which they find on the ground.*

● **Many hen (female) game birds** have dull brown plumage that provides good camouflage in their woodland and moorland homes.

● **Many cock (male) game birds** have very colourful plumage to attract mates.

● **In the breeding season,** cocks strut and puff up their plumage to attract a mate. They also draw attention to themselves by cackling, whistling and screaming.

● **Pheasant cocks** often fight each other violently to win a particular mating area.

● **The jungle fowl** of Southeast Asia is the wild ancestor of the domestic chicken.

● **Peacocks** were carried as treasure from India throughout the ancient world.

375

Cassowaries and kiwis

- **There are three species of kiwi**, found only in New Zealand. All are flightless birds that live in burrows.

- **The female dwarf cassowary**, or moruk, is an extremely dangerous bird and will attack anything that comes near its nest with its 10-cm long claws.

- **The three species of cassowary** live in rainforests in New Zealand and northeastern Australia.

- **Largest of its family is the brown kiwi**, which is about 55 cm long and weighs up to 3.5 kg.

- **Only the kiwi** has nostrils at the end of its beak.

- **The kiwi** is the national symbol of New Zealand, appearing on stamps, coins and banknotes.

> **...FASCINATING FACT...**
> A kiwi lays the largest eggs for its size of any bird – each egg weighs 25% of its body weight. Females lay up to 100 in a lifetime.

- **Cassowaries** in Australia are known to eat the fruits of at least 75 different types of tree.

- **The female cassowary** mates with several males, laying 6–8 eggs each time. The males care for the young.

- **About 1200 years ago** there were probably 12 million kiwis in New Zealand. Today there are only 70,000.

The nocturnal kiwi's good sense of smell helps it to find worms, insects and spiders on the ground at night.

Ostriches and emus

- **Ratites are big, flightless birds** like the ostrich, emu, cassowary, rhea and kiwi. Ratites always walk or run everywhere, only using their small wings for balance and for show.

- **The ostrich** is the biggest living bird, towering up to 2.75 m in height and weighing over 150 kg.

- **To escape a lion,** the ostrich can hurtle over the African savannah grasslands, where it lives, at speeds of 60 km/h – faster than a racehorse. Even when the ostrich tires, its strong legs can still deliver a massive kick.

- **Ostriches** have only two toes on each foot – unlike the rhea of South America which has three.

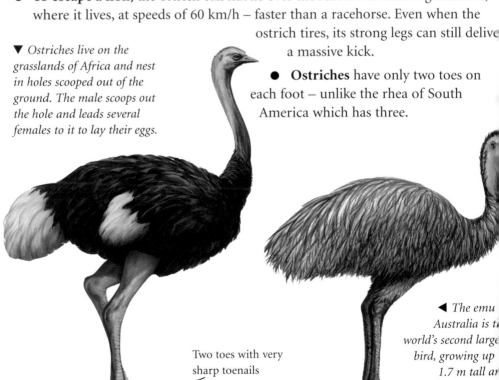

▼ *Ostriches live on the grasslands of Africa and nest in holes scooped out of the ground. The male scoops out the hole and leads several females to it to lay their eggs.*

◄ *The emu Australia is t world's second large bird, growing up 1.7 m tall an weighing upto 45 k*

Two toes with very sharp toenails

The ostrich lays the largest egg – almost as big as a football.

The kiwi of New Zealand is the smallest ratite, no bigger than a chicken. It has fur-like feathers and is the only bird with nostrils at the tip of its bill, which it uses to sniff out worms and grubs.

The rare kakapo parrot of New Zealand could fly once, but it lost the power of flight because it had no natural predators – until Europeans introduced dogs and cats to New Zealand.

The dodo was a flightless bird that once lived on islands such as Mauritius in the Indian Ocean. It was wiped out in the 17th century when its eggs were eaten by pigs and monkeys imported by Europeans.

The emu of Australia is the best swimmer of any flightless bird. Ostriches can swim well, too.

Bony crest

◀ *The cassowary lives in the forests of tropical Australia and New Guinea. It has a crest which it uses like a crash helmet as it charges through the undergrowth.*

... FASCINATING FACT ...
The biggest bird ever is now extinct – the flightless elephant bird of Madagascar grew up to 4.5 m tall (taller than two grown men).

Ducks and geese

- **Ducks, geese and swans** are known as waterfowl, and they all live on or near freshwater.

- **Waterfowl** can float for hours and have webbed feet for paddling along. On water they are graceful, but on land they waddle awkwardly, since their legs are set far back under their body for swimming.

- **Ducks** have shorter necks and wings, and flatter bills than swans. Male ducks are called drakes, and females, ducks. Babies are called ducklings.

▼ *The ruddy duck has a stiff tail held up at an angle. The male's courtship display involves rapid paddling as he holds his head against his chest.*

Canada geese breed in the far north of Canada and Alaska, and migrate south to warmer regions in the autumn.

Diving ducks (such as the pochard, tufted duck and the scoter) dive for food such as roots, shellfish and insects on the river bed.

Dabbling ducks (such as the mallard, widgeon, gadwall and the teal) dabble – they sift water through their beaks for food.

Some dabblers lap water at the surface. Others up-end – sticking their heads into the water to sift out water weeds and snails from muddy water.

Swans are the largest waterfowl. They have long elegant necks and pure white plumage – apart from the black-neck swan of South America and the Australian black swan.

Baby swans are called cygnets and are mottled grey.

Geese mostly graze on grass. Unlike ducks, which quack and swans which hiss, geese honk.

Baby geese are called goslings.

Seagulls and albatrosses

▲ *Seagulls catch small fish, steal eggs and young from other birds,*
scavenge on waste – and sometimes fly inland to find worms.

The wandering albatross can glide for hours without a single flap of its huge wings. It glides quite low, usually less than 20 m above the waves, where rising winds keep it aloft.

● **Gulls are big sea birds** that live on coasts all around the world, nesting on cliffs, islands or beaches.

● **Gulls are related** to skuas and terns.

● **Skuas** have hooked claws and sharp bills, which they use to attack other birds and force them to disgorge (throw up) their food – which the skua then eats.

● **Skuas are such good acrobats** that they can catch the disgorged meal of another bird in mid-air.

● **The great skua** often pounces on seagulls, drowns them, and then steals their chicks.

● **Wandering albatrosses** are the biggest of all sea birds, with white bodies and dark wings.

● **The wandering albatross** has the biggest wingspan of any bird – 3.7 m across.

● **An albatross** will often follow a ship for days without stopping to rest.

● **Wild albatrosses** may live for more than 50 years.

> ... FASCINATING FACT ...
> Herring gulls watch ducks diving for fish
> and then steal it when the ducks resurface.

Penguins

- **There are around 17 different species** of penguin, most of them living in colonies called rookeries along the coast of Antarctica and nearby islands.

- **Penguins** are superb swimmers, using their wings as flippers to push them through the water, and steering with their webbed feet.

- **Penguins have coats** waterproofed with oil and thick fat so they can survive in temperatures as low as -60°C.

- **The smallest** is the fairy penguin, at 40 cm high.

- **The emperor penguin** is the biggest swimming bird, at up to 1.2 m tall and weighing over 40 kg – twice the weight of any flying bird.

▼ *Penguins are sociable birds that live in large colonies.*

Emperor penguins can dive briefly to depths of 250 m or more chasing fish, their main diet.

Penguins can leap high out of the water to land on an ice bank, but on land they can only waddle clumsily or toboggan along on their bellies.

Adélie penguins waddle more than 320 km across the ice every year to reach their breeding ground.

When crossing the ice, Adélie penguins use the sun to navigate by. When the sun goes down they lose their way.

The largest penguin at 1.2 m tall, the emperor *nguin also weighs in as the heaviest seabird. Each* *ale holds his partner's single egg on his feet for* *ne 60 days until the chick hatches.*

Storks

- **In tropical regions**, storks' nests that are perched high on buildings can get very warm, so parent birds cool their young by regurgitating a shower of water over them.

- **The huge beak** of the whale-billed stork, or shoebill, is 23 cm long and 10 cm wide. It uses it to catch lungfish, young crocodiles and turtles.

▲ *Like other wading birds, storks have long, spindly legs, plump bodies and long bills for catching fish.*

The white stork has long been a symbol of fertility in Europe. Parents used to tell their children that new babies were brought by a stork.

The 17 species of stork live in North and South America, Europe, Africa, Asia and Australia.

Marabou storks often scavenge on rubbish tips.

The openbill stork's beak meets only at the tip. This enables it to hold its favourite food – large snails.

The tail feathers of marabou storks were once used to trim hats and dresses.

When the wood stork's partly open beak touches a fish under water, it snaps shut in 25 milliseconds – this is one of the fastest reactions of any animal.

▲ *The saddlebill stork of southern Africa is easily recognized by its large red, yellow and black bill.*

Male and female white storks take turns to incubate their clutch of 3–5 eggs. When the partners change shifts, they perform a special bill-clattering display.

The adjutant stork is named after the adjutant army officer, because of its stiff, military-style walk.

Pelicans

- **The great white pelican** catches about 1.2 kg of fish a day in its large throat pouch.

- **The brown pelican** dives from a height of 15 m above the water to catch fish below the surface.

- **Great white pelican breeding colonies** may number as many as 30,000 pairs of birds.

- **There are seven species of pelican**. Most live and feed around fresh water, but the brown pelican is a seabird.

▲ *A great white pelican comes in to land on the water.*

- **One of the largest pelicans** is the Australian pelican, which is up to 180 cm long and weighs about 15 kg.

- **The white pelican** lays 1–2 eggs in a nest mound on the ground. Both parents help to incubate the eggs and care for the young.

- **Pelican chicks** are able to stand at 3 weeks old and can fly at 7–10 weeks old.

- **In heraldry**, a pelican is shown pecking its breast to feed its young on its blood. This may stem from the bird's habit of resting its beak on its breast.

- **White pelicans** work as a group to herd fish into a shoal by swimming around them in a horseshoe formation. Then they scoop up pouchfuls of fish with their large beaks.

- **In flight**, a pelican flaps its wings 1.3 times a second. This is one of the slowest wingbeat speeds, when actively flying, of any bird.

▼ *Pelicans are often found in large colonies, particularly during the breeding season.*

Owls

▲ *An owl's big eyes face straight forward to focus on an object. However, owls cannot move their eyes and have to swivel their whole head to look to the side or rear.*

- **Owls** are nocturnal and hunt by night, unlike most other hunting birds.

- **There are two big families of owl** – barn owls and typical owls.

- **There are 135 species** of typical owl, including the great horned owl.

- **There are about 10 species** of barn owl. The common barn owl is the most widespread – found on every continent except Antarctica.

- **Small owls** eat mostly insects. Bigger owls eat mice and shrews. Eagle owls can catch young deer.

- **In the country,** the tawny owl's diet is 90% small mammals, but many now live in towns where they eat mainly small birds such as sparrows and starlings.

390

▼ *Most owls roost by day in holes inside tree trunks. There are few trees in the desert where the elf owl lives, so it roosts inside a giant saguaro cactus. Elf owls live in the dry regions of southwest North America.*

- **Owls have huge eyes** that allow them to see in almost pitch darkness.

- **An owl's hearing** is four times as sharp as a cat's.

- **Owls can pinpoint** sounds with astonishing accuracy from the slight difference in the sound levels it receives in each of its ears.

Most bird's eyes look out to the sides, but an owl's look straight forward like a human's. This is probably why the owl has been a symbol of wisdom since ancient times.

The flight feathers on an owl's wing muffle the sound of the bird's wingbeat so that it can swoop almost silently down on to its prey.

Eagles and hawks

- **Eagles and hawks** are among 280 species of raptor (bird of prey). The group also includes kestrels, falcons, goshawks, buzzards and vultures.

- **Most birds of prey are hunters** that feed on other birds, fish and small mammals.

- **Most birds of prey** are strong fliers, with sharp eyes, powerful talons (claws) and a hooked beak.

- **Birds of prey lay** only one or two eggs at a time. This makes them vulnerable to human egg collectors – one reason why many are endangered species.

- **Eagles** are the biggest of the hunting birds, with wing spans of up to 2.5 m. The harpy eagle of the Amazon region catches monkeys and sloths.

◀ *Stellar's sea eagle is one of the most powerful of all birds. It has a wingspan of 2.4 m and a massive beak.*

▲ *The bald eagle eats fish, snatching them from rivers.*

The American bald eagle is not really bald, but has white feathers on its head.

There are two kinds of hawks. Accipiters, like the goshawk, catch their prey by lying in wait on perches. Buteos, like the kestrel, hover in the air.

Buzzards are buteo hawks.

In the Middle Ages, merlins and falcons were trained to fly from a falconer's wrist to catch birds and animals.

. . . FASCINATING FACT . . .
The peregrine falcon can reach speeds of
350 km/h when stooping (diving) on prey.

393

Vultures

- **Vultures and condors** are the biggest birds of prey. They do not hunt, but feed on carrion (dead animals).

- **The palmnut vulture** is the only vegetarian bird of prey, and it feeds on oil nuts.

- **Many vultures are bald,** with no head feathers to mat with blood when digging into corpses.

- **The seven species** of New World vulture (those that live in the Americas) have a nostril hole right through their beak.

▼ *A vulture closes in to feed on a dead animal.*

The Californian condor is very rare. All the wild ones were captured in the mid 1980s, but some have since been bred in captivity and returned to the wild.

Vultures are great fliers and spend hours soaring, scanning the ground for corpses with sharp eyes.

Condors have such a sharp sense of smell that they can pinpoint a corpse under a thick forest canopy.

Vultures have such weak bills that flesh must be rotten before they can eat it.

The lammergeier is known as the bearded vulture because it has a beard of black bristles on its chin.

▼ *The Andean condor holds the bird world record for wingspan. And it can spot a dead sheep from 5 km away.*

...FASCINATING FACT...
The Andean condor is the world's biggest flying bird, with a wingspan of 3 m or more.

395

What are mammals?

- **Humans** feel close to mammals because they, too, are mammals, with hairy bodies, a large brain and special mammary glands for feeding milk to their young.

- **There are about 4500 species** of mammals in the world (and at least 1 million insect species!).

- **All mammals** except the duckbilled platypus and spiny anteater give birth to live young.

- **Mammals** evolved from reptiles, but are warm blooded.

- **The two main mammal groups** are the marsupials (whose young develop in the mother's pouch) and placentals.

- **All mammals have three little bones** in their ears that transfer sound vibrations to the inner ear from the eardrum.

- **Mammals** have a variety of teeth shapes: chisels for gnawing, long fangs for fighting and killing prey, sharp-edged slicers and flat-topped crushers.

▲ *Some mammals are very vulnerable because of human influences such as hunting or loss of habitat. The tiger is in the 'critically endangered' category on the Red List of Threatened Species.*

The platypus and spiny anteater are egg-laying mammals called monotremes.

Mammals have a palate that enables them to breathe through their noses while chewing.

Mammals give a level of maternal care beyond that of other animals.

Young mammals mature more slowly than other animal young, so they are looked after for longer.

Mammals' senses

- **Cheetahs have a band of light-sensitive nerve cells** across their retinas that give clear vision ahead and to the sides.
- **Desert mammals** such as the long-eared kit fox find sharp hearing more useful than a keen sense of smell in the dry air.
- **Polar bears** can smell seals up to 60 km away across the ice.
- **Cats have glands** between their toes that leave an identifying scent when they scratch trees.
- **Blue whales** and fin whales communicate by means of the loudest sounds produced by any living creature (up to 188 dB).

▼ *Large cats have eyes on the front of their heads rather than at the sides, helping them to focus on their prey as they hunt.*

▲ *Both whales and dolphins communicate using echolocation.*

● **Baby wood-mice** emit ultrasonic distress calls in their first 10 days to summon their mother.

Many nocturnal mammals have reflective areas in their eyes that help night vision.

Migrating whales can sense the Earth's magnetic field, due to particles of the mineral magnetite in their bodies.

The exceptionally large ears of fennec foxes can detect the sound of termites chewing beneath the ground.

Skunks use a powerful scent weapon to deter their enemies.

Heat regulation

◀ *The coat of a bighorn sheep comprises a double layer of hairs to protect it from harsh winds and snow.*

- **Fruit bats** are susceptible to heat stroke, so to keep themselves cool, some lick themselves all over and fan cool air at their bodies with their wings.

- **The oryx** has special blood vessels in its nose to keep its blood temperature low in the desert heat.

- **Large-eared desert species** such as fennec foxes use their ears as radiators to get rid of body heat.

- **The desert bighorn sheep** draws air over a thickly veined area of its throat to cool its blood.

- **Wallowing in mud** keeps pigs cool and protects their skin from the sun.

- **A hippos' skin** exudes a red, lacquer-like substance to protect it from sunburn.

During hot spells, kangaroos lick their wrists a lot, so that the evaporation of the saliva causes cooling.

Indian zebu cattle have more sweat glands than western cattle, and can maintain a lower body temperature, making them common in warm countries, such as China, Africa and South America.

The eland's temperature can rise several degrees without causing sweating, allowing it to conserve 5 litres of water daily.

After feeding their young, mother bats often leave them in the heat of the cave and perch near the cooler entrance.

Hippopotamuses spend much
their time submerged in water
their skin quickly dries out and
acks in the hot African sun.

Camouflage

- **Stripes** benefit both predators and prey by breaking up the body shape, for example in tigers and zebras.

- **The simplest camouflage** makes an animal a similar colour to its surroundings, such as the white of a polar bear in snow.

- **Some dolphins** and whales are dark on top and light underneath, camouflaging them against the dark of deep water or the light of sky.

- **Some camouflage** mimics the broken shapes of light shining through trees, as in the dappled markings of giraffes.

▶ *The pattern of a giraffe's coat varies according to area and is an important camouflage tool.*

The young of many mammal species, such as lions and pigs, have early camouflage markings that disappear as the animals grow older.

The coats of Arctic foxes and hares change from dark in summer to white in winter.

Bold markings, such as the contrasting shapes of the oryx, camouflage by breaking up body outline.

The bobcat's spots camouflage it in rocks, while the similar-shaped plain lynx merges with its forest home.

The elephant's huge grey form disappears as it stands still in the shadows.

▲ *The orca's light underparts make it less visible against the water's surface in daytime.*

. . . **FASCINATING FACT** . . .
Not all camouflage is visual –
some mammals roll in dung to disguise
their own scents.

Migration

- **Florida manatees** usually migrate south in winter, but recently they have moved instead into the warm water outlets of hydroelectric generating plants.

- **Hooded seals** usually migrate south from Greenland in the Atlantic Ocean, but in 1990 one seal ended up off California in the Pacific, having taken a wrong turn.

- **Migrating noctule bats** established themselves in Hawaii, after being blown 3000 km off course.

- **Migrating whales** travel immense distances with the aid of their internal magnetic navigation.

▼ *Reindeer and caribou (North American reindeer) may make short, daily journeys to find food or longer, seasonal migrations of up to 1200 km.*

◀ It is thought that the blue whale migrates to warmer climates for the winter, when the female will give birth.

Oil pipe-lines are serious obstacles to caribou, which follow traditional migratory routes every year.

Migrating European noctule bats fly at high altitude, emitting loud, low-frequency sounds at one second intervals to keep in ground contact.

American grey squirrels sometimes travel in their thousands, crossing roads, rivers and towns in their search for food.

Beluga whales return to the estuaries where they were born to give birth.

Over 1 million wildebeest take part in a circular seasonal migration in east Africa's Serengeti region.

> ...FASCINATING FACT...
> Each year, grey whales migrate
> 20,000 km in all, going to and from their
> breeding grounds.

405

Parental care in mammals

- **Many mammals carry their young** around with them. Some bats even go hunting with a youngster aboard.

- **Mother whales** have to nudge and encourage newly born young up to the surface to take their first breath, often aided by 'aunts' from the same pod.

- **In wild dog packs**, several females may take turns to suckle and guard all the young in the group.

- **Sperm whale** offspring may suckle for up to 15 years.

- **Elephant young** are born after 22 months. Several of the herd cows help the new baby to stand.

- **Mother cheetahs** teach their young how to hunt by bringing small live prey back for them to practise on.

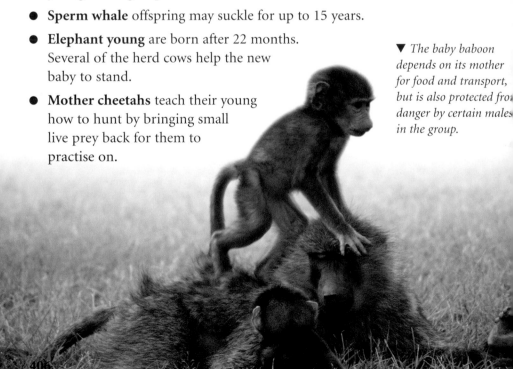

▼ *The baby baboon depends on its mother for food and transport, but is also protected from danger by certain males in the group.*

Elephants live in family groups of females and their young, led by a dominant female.

A female big cat carries her young by holding the entire head in her mouth, in a gap behind her teeth.

Young kangaroos leave the pouch at 5–11 months, but continue to stick their head in to suckle for 6 months.

Many cats, large and small, start to train their young by allowing them to attack their twitching tails.

...FASCINATING FACT...
Baby gorillas may only climb on the silverback while they still have a white rump tuft.

Kangaroos and koalas

- **Kangaroos** are big Australian mammals that hop around on their hind (back) legs.

- **A kangaroo's tail** can be over 1.5 m long. It is used for balance when hopping, and to hold the kangaroo up when walking.

- **Red kangaroos** can hop at 55 km/h for short distances.

- **Red kangaroos** can leap forwards 9 m in one huge bound.

▲ *Koalas drink very little water, and their name comes from an Aboriginal word for 'no drink'.*

- **There are two kinds of kangaroo** – red kangaroos and grey kangaroos. Red kangaroos live in the dry grasslands of central Australia. Grey kangaroos live in the southeast, in woods and grassland

- **Kangaroos are marsupials** – animals whose babies are born before they are ready to survive in the outside word and so live for a while protected in a pouch on their mother's belly.

- **Koalas** are Australian mammals that look like teddy bears, but which are not related to any kind of bear.

- **Like kangaroos,** koalas are marsupials. A koala baby spends 6 months in its mother's pouch and another 6 months riding on her back.

- **Koalas** spend 18 hours a day sleeping. The rest of the time they feed on the leaves of eucalyptus trees.

- **Other Australian marsupials** include the wombat, several kinds of wallaby (which look like small kangaroos) and bandicoots (which looks like rats).

▼ *When they are first born, kangaroos are naked and look like tiny jellybabies – just a few centimetres long, with two tiny arms. But straight away they have to haul themselves up through the fur on their mother's belly and into her pouch. Here the baby kangaroo (called a joey) lives and grows for 6 to 8 months, sucking on teats inside the pouch. Only when it is quite large and covered in fur will it pop out of the pouch to live by itself.*

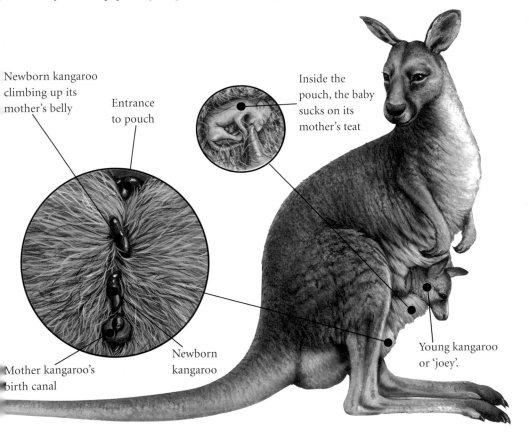

Newborn kangaroo climbing up its mother's belly

Entrance to pouch

Inside the pouch, the baby sucks on its mother's teat

Mother kangaroo's birth canal

Newborn kangaroo

Young kangaroo or 'joey'.

409

Rabbits and rats

- **Mice and rats** belong to a group of 1,800 species of small mammals called rodents. The group also includes squirrels, voles, lemmings beavers, porcupines and guinea pigs.

- **All rodents** have two pairs of razor-sharp front teeth for gnawing nuts and berries, and a set of ridged teeth in their cheeks for chewing.

- **A rodent's front teeth,** called incisors, grow all the time. Only gnawing keeps them the same length.

- **Rats and mice** are by far the most common rodents – they have adapted well to living alongside humans.

- **Brown and black rats** carry germs for diseases such as food poisoning, plague and typhus.

▶ *Rabbits and hares look like rodents but they belong to another group of mammals called lagomorphs or 'leaping shapes'.*

▶ Rats and mice have long thin tails, pointed noses, beady black eyes and four very sharp front teeth.

- **Hares** live above ground and escape enemies through sheer speed. Rabbits live in burrows underground.

- **Baby hares** are born above ground, covered in fur and with their eyes open. Rabbits are born naked and blind in burrows.

- **Rabbits breed quickly** – a female can have 20 babies every month during the breeding season, and her babies will have their own families after 6 months.

- **One single rabbit** could have more than 33 million offspring in just 3 years, if they all survived to breed.

- **A single mouse** can produce up to 34 young in one litter.

Hedgehogs

- **The Eurasian hedgehog** has between 5000 and 7000 spines on its back and sides, each erected by its own muscle, creating a defence difficult for predators to penetrate.

- **When a hedgehog rolls into a ball** at the approach of danger, a special muscle draws its loose skin together (like a drawstring on a bag) over its head and rump.

- **From Roman** to medieval times in Europe, it was believed that hedgehogs often carried a supply of fruit with them, impaled on their spines.

- **Over 150,000 hedgehogs** are killed every year on the roads of France alone.

- **The moonrats** of Southeast Asia and China are closely related to hedgehogs, but have no spines.

- **The long-eared** and desert hedgehogs of Asia and North Africa dig their own individual, short burrows.

- **Hedgehogs** can go without water for long periods, and if dehydrated will drink half their bodyweight in one go.

▶ Scent is important to hedgehogs, as they communicate and track food by smell.

412

▲ *The hedgehog gets its name from its piglike habit of foraging in the hedgerows in search of food.*

- **A male western European hedgehog** has a foraging territory of up to 35 hectares.

- **Lack of food** rather than cooling temperatures causes a hedgehog to hibernate.

...FASCINATING FACT...
The hedgehog keeps up a ceaseless whistling sound while hunting for food.

413

Squirrels

- **Grey squirrels** have been known to kill and eat rabbits, rats, cockerels and stoats.

- **Flying squirrels** are nocturnal, and when gliding may emit high-pitched squeaks that help them to locate a landing place.

- **North American red squirrels** tap birch and maple trees for their sweet sap in spring.

- **Many squirrel species** spread woodland trees by burying nuts and then forgetting where they put them.

- **The North American red squirrel**, or chicaree, buries green pine cones in damp soil to delay their ripening until they are needed.

- **The largest member of the squirrel family** is the alpine marmot, at 73 cm long not including the tail.

- **Southeast Asian giant squirrels** prefer to hang upside down by their hind feet while eating.

- **Chipmunks,** or ground squirrels, store huge quantities of nuts in a single cache.

- **To prevent it slipping backwards** down a tree trunk, the scaly-tailed flying squirrel presses the horny scales of its tail against the trunk.

- **An adult red squirrel** can sniff out a pine cone buried 30 cm deep.

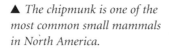

▲ *The chipmunk is one of the most common small mammals in North America.*

▼ *The squirrel's bushy tail is a good balancing aid and rudder when climbing and leaping.*

Mice

- **In the early 1940s**, a huge population of house mice in California had a density of about 200,000 per hectare.

- **The Andes fishing mouse** – only discovered in 1994 – fishes in streams at an altitude of at least 3,600 m.

- **The Australian pebble mound mouse** builds large piles of rounded stones, and then takes up residence in them.

- **The Oldfield mouse** has an escape tunnel leading from its nest near to the surface, so it can escape intruders by breaking through the apparent 'dead end'.

- **The water mice** of Central America have webbed, hairy feet that help them dive for water snails and fish.

- **American grasshopper mice** defend their territory by standing on their hind legs, shrieking at rival mice.

- **Grasshopper mice** are sometimes kept as pets to clear a house of insect pests such as cockroaches.

- **An ancient Greek legend** tells how a Cretan army owed its success to divine mice, which gnawed through the shield straps of the enemy.

- **The Old World harvest mouse** climbs through tall grasses using its grasping tail and flexible feet.

- **American kangaroo mice** have long, hairy hind feet and a long tail, and often travel in a series of leaps.

▶ *Though mice have small appetites they ruin vast amounts of food especially stores of grain.*

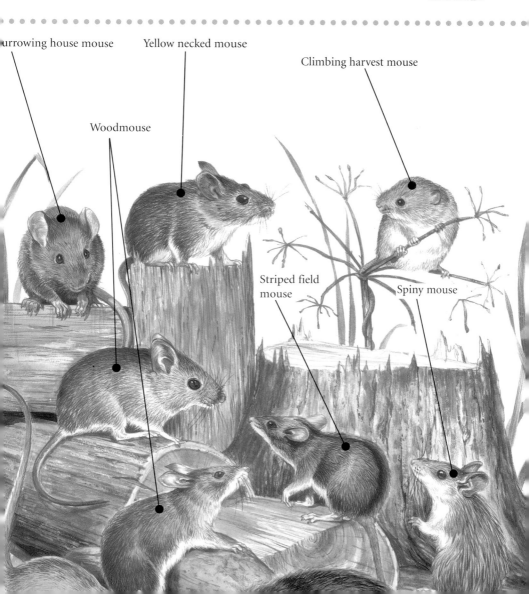

urrowing house mouse

Yellow necked mouse

Climbing harvest mouse

Woodmouse

Striped field mouse

Spiny mouse

Beavers

- **Beavers** are born with innate dam-building instincts. In zoos, they regularly 'repair' concrete dams with twigs.

- **It takes two adult beavers** about 15 minutes to gnaw their way through a tree-trunk with a 10 cm diameter.

- **Mother beavers** push tired youngsters ahead of them through the water, like swimming floats.

- **Storing extra oxygen** in its lungs and body tissues, a beaver can remain under water for up to 15 minutes.

- **Beavers use the split claws** on their hind feet for grooming and spreading waterproof oil.

- **A beaver signals danger** by smacking the water with its tail. The noise carries over 1 km.

▼ *The secretion glands in the base of this Eurasian beavers tail produce an oily waterproofing substance that is spread through the coat when grooming.*

- **The territory-marking secretion** of the beaver contains the main ingredient in the painkiller aspirin.

- **Beavers' dams** and lodges can help create environments for fish.

- **In some parts of the USA,** beavers are parachute-dropped into areas where remote rivers need damming to reduce erosion.

▲ *The beaver uses its huge incisor teeth to gnaw through branches and tree trunks.*

. . . **FASCINATING FACT** . . .
European beavers took to living in burrows
to avoid hunters. They are now
protected by law.

Foxes

- **The larder of one Arctic fox** was found to contain 50 lemmings and 40 little auks, all lined up with tails pointing the same way and their heads bitten off.

- **African bat-eared foxes** have huge ears for radiating heat away from the body.

- **Arctic foxes** live only 480 km from the North Pole.

▲ *Fox cubs stay with their parents for up to a year, and will often go out with their mothers foraging for food.*

- **The grey fox** of North and Central America is the oldest surviving member of the dog family, first appearing 9 million years ago.

- **The African fennec fox's** 15-cm long ears are the largest of any carnivore.

- **The American grey fox** leaps with ease between tree branches.

- **Some foxes roll about** and chase their tails to 'charm' rabbits, which seem fascinated and come closer, allowing the fox to make a grab.

- **The red fox** has adapted with great success to urban life, even moving into houses via cat flaps.

- **When locating insects** beneath the ground, the bat-eared fox cups its large ears, gradually pinpointing the exact position of the prey before digging.

- **In early autumn**, up to 90% of the red fox's diet may consist of apples, blackberries and other fruits.

▲ *Basically a night hunter, the red fox is often seen during the day, and shows up sharply against winter snow.*

Lemurs and lorises

▶ *India and Sri Lanka are home to the slender loris. It eats many insects including caterpillars.*

- **Lemurs** are small furry creatures with long tails and big eyes. They are primates, like monkeys and humans.
- **Lemurs** live only on the islands of Madagascar and Comoros, off the east coast of Africa.
- **Most lemurs** are active at night and live in trees, but the ring-tailed lemur lives mostly on the ground and is active by day.
- **Lemurs** eat fruit, leaves, insects and small birds.

The ring-tailed lemur rubs its rear on trees to leave a scent trail for other lemurs to follow.

In the mating season, ring-tailed lemurs have stink fights for females, rubbing their wrists and tails in stink glands under their arms and rear – then waving them at rivals to drive them off.

Lorises and pottos are furry, big-eyed primates of the forests of Asia and Africa. All are brilliant climbers.

Bushbabies are the acrobats of the loris family. They get their name because their cries sound like a human baby crying.

Bushbabies are nocturnal animals and their big eyes help them see in the dark. Their hearing is so sensitive they have to block their ears to sleep during the day.

▲ *Ring-tailed lemurs get their name from their black-ringed tail which they raise to show where they are.*

Tarsiers of the Philippines are tiny, huge-eyed primates which look like cuddly goblins. They have very long fingers and can turn their heads halfway round to look backwards.

Skunks

- **The skunk squirts a sticky spray** at its enemy from glands under its tail. It can reach a target up to 6 m away, and is accurate up to 2 m.

- **The skunk's spray**, which consists of 7 different chemical components, can cause temporary blindness.

- **Before spraying**, a skunk warns its enemy by stamping its feet. The spotted skunk does a handstand and walks with its hind legs in the air.

- **Skunks** belong to the same family as weasels and polecats, all of which have smelly sprays, but the skunk's spray is the smelliest of all.

- **Vets** recommend that dogs which have been sprayed by a skunk should be given a bath in tomato juice.

- **Most predators avoid skunks**, but it is a favourite prey of the great horned owl, which has a poor sense of smell and catches it at night!

- **Skunks have little fear of humans** and are often sold as pets – after a de-scenting operation.

◄ *The skunk is a mainly solitary animal though it will group for the winter in communal dens made among rocks, crevices and outbuildings.*

- **Skunks are great diggers**. They use their long, straight claws to rip apart rotten logs for grubs, and to dig in sand and mud for turtle eggs.

- **Skunks sleep in communal dens** when temperatures reach freezing, with up to 20 skunks in a den.

> ...FASCINATING FACT...
> In the USA, skunks are major carriers
> of rabies.

▼ *Skunks eat mainly live prey, such as insects and small mammals, and also enjoy fruit and birds' eggs.*

Bats

- **Bats** are the only flying mammals. Their wings are made of leathery skin.

- **Most types of bat sleep** during the day, hanging upside down in caves, attics and other dark places. They come out at night to hunt.

- **Bats find things** in the dark by giving out a series of high-pitched clicks – the bats tell where they are and locate (find) prey from the echoes (sounds that bounce back to them). This is called echo location.

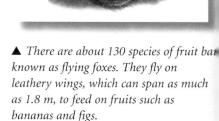

- **Bats are not blind** – their eyesight is as good as that of most humans.

- **There are 900 species** of bat, living on all continents except Antarctica.

- **Most bats feed** on insects, but fruit bats feed on fruit.

- **Many tropical flowers** rely on fruit bats to spread their pollen.

▲ *There are about 130 species of fruit bat known as flying foxes. They fly on leathery wings, which can span as much as 1.8 m, to feed on fruits such as bananas and figs.*

- **Frog-eating bats** can tell edible frogs from poisonous ones by the frogs' mating calls.

- **The vampire bats** of tropical Latin America feed on blood, sucking it from animals such as cattle and horses. A colony of 100 vampire bats can feed from the blood of 25 cows or 14,000 chickens in one night.

- **False vampire bats** are bats that do not suck on blood, but feed on other small creatures such as bats and rats. The greater false vampire bat of Southeast Asia is one of the biggest of all bats.

*Bats spend their lives in
darkness, finding their way
with sounds so high-
pitched only a
young child can
hear them.*

Sloths

- **The sloths of South America** have a variable body temperature, and each morning need to bask in the sun above the forest canopy.

- **The sloth** has the most neck vertebrae of any mammal, and can look forwards when it is upside down.

- **Sloths even mate** and give birth while hanging upside down, holding on with their powerful, curved claws.

- **Sloths' fur** grows in the opposite direction to that of most mammals, pointing towards the ground so the rain runs off the body.

- **A sloth's large stomach** is divided into many compartments; the food inside can account for up to a third of the animal's body weight.

- **A meal of leaves** may be retained in a sloth's digestive system for over a month.

▲ *The mother sloth carries her infant for up to 9 months on her belly, where it feeds on the leaves it can reach.*

428

This Lime's two toed [s]loth has two extremely [l]ong clawed toes on each [o]f its front feet but three [o]n each rear foot.

- **The main predator** of the sloth is the harpy eagle.

Algae grows in the grooves on a sloth's fur, helping to camouflage it in the forest greenery.

Sloths have an amazing ability to heal themselves, and their wounds rarely become infected.

On land, sloths can only move in an awkward, spread-eagled crawl, impeded by their long claws.

Gliders

- **Gliding mammals** include the flying squirrels of America and Asia, the scaly-tailed squirrels of Africa, and the marsupial gliding possums of Australia.

- **The Australian feather-tailed glider** is the smallest gliding mammal, weighing just 12 g.

- **Gliding mammals** achieve their glides by means of a hairy membrane called a patagium that joins the fore and hind limbs, and acts like a parachute.

- **The Southeast Asian colugo's** glide membrane stretches from the neck to fingers, toes and tail-tip.

- **When flying squirrels** come in to land on a tree trunk, they brake by turning their tail and body under, like the landing flaps on an aircraft's wing.

- **Africa's scaly-tailed flying squirrels** live in colonies of up to 100, and glide from tree to tree after dark.

▶ *The colugo (also known as a flying lemur) is about the size of a domestic cat. It has sharp claws for climbing and mottled fur for camouflage.*

- **Australia's gliders** feed on sap and gum, biting through tree bark and lapping up the sweet liquids.

- **Some flying squirrels**, when they land, quickly move to the opposite side of the tree trunk to avoid predators.

- **The colugo** is virtually helpless on the ground.

▶ *The southern flying squirrel fluffs out its tail and uses it as a rudder in mid-air.*

...FASCINATING FACT...
The longest glide by a gliding mammal ever recorded was 450 m by a giant flying squirrel.

431

Orang-utans

▲ *Orang-utans are slow breeders, and may only give birth to three or four babies in a lifetime.*

- **Orang-utans** spend much more time in trees than the other great apes, and are the largest tree-dwelling mammals in the world.

- **Insatiable eaters**, orang-utans can spend an entire day feasting in one heavily laden fruit tree.

- **The name 'orang-utan'** means 'man of the forest' in the language of the local tribespeople of Southeast Asia.

A mature male orang-utan makes his presence known to other orang-utans by breaking branches, bellowing and groaning. Local legends explain this as a sign of the ape's grief over losing a human bride.

In Sumatra, the major predators of orang-utans are tigers at ground level, and clouded leopards in trees.

Once found all over Southeast Asia, orang-utans now live only in tropical Borneo and Sumatra.

Like chimpanzees, orang-utans use sticks as tools to retrieve food from crevices and to scratch themselves.

▲ *Young orang-utans stay with their mothers until they are about eight years old.*

Male orang-utans have large air sacs that extend from their throats, under their arms and over their shoulders, and increase the loudness and range of their calls.

To help her young move from tree to tree, a mother orang-utan pulls the branches of two trees closer together and makes a bridge with her body.

Orang-utans make a nest at night, building a roof to keep off the rain.

Gorillas

- **Male gorillas walk on four limbs** most of the time, but will run on two legs for short distances, beating their chests, when showing off.

- **Adult gorillas** sleep in a new nest every night.

- **The mature male leader** of a gorilla group is called a 'silverback', after the saddle of white hair on its back.

- **Young male gorillas** form their own groups by kidnapping females from other groups.

- **Mountain gorillas** spend almost all their lives at 2800 to 3400 m above sea level, in damp, cloudy conditions.

▼ *The male gorilla is far larger than the female, and is the largest of all the primates – big silverbacks can weigh as much as 200 kg.*

◀ *The bond between a mother gorilla and her young is very strong. Babies are not properly weaned until they are three years old, but may stay with the mother for another year, or until another baby has been born.*

● **Some gorillas supplement their plant diet** by eating handfuls of potassium- and calcium-rich soil.

● **If a gorilla cannot keep up** with the group because of a wound, the silverback slows down so it is not left behind.

● **When aggressive male gorillas** beat their chests and mock-charge one another, they give off an armpit odour powerful enough to be detected 25 m away by humans.

● **Despite their huge strength**, silverbacks are gentle with their offspring, allowing them to play on their backs.

...FASCINATING FACT...
The 'nose-prints' of gorillas are as distinctive as human fingerprints – no two are identical.

Chimpanzees

▲ *Chimpanzees have a repertoire of up to 30 distinct noises for communicating with other members of their social group.*

● **Chimps have a strict social ladder**, with dominant males at the top. These top males recognize property rights, and never steal food from their inferiors.

● **Observers** have noted chimpanzees carefully lifting a fellow chimp's eyelid to remove a speck of grit.

● **Chimps are the best tool-users** after humans. They use grass stems to fish for termites in their mounds, stones and anvils to crack nuts, and chewed leaves as sponges for gathering water.

● **Chimpanzees** actively hunt for meat, especially when plant food is scarce, and collaborate to catch colobus monkeys, young baboons, birds and rodents.

● **If a chimpanzee** finds a tree laden with fruit, it drums on a tree trunk and makes loud panting cries to summon other chimps from many kilometres away for a share of the feast.

● **Bands of male chimpanzees** have been observed attacking and killing all the males in a neighbouring band. Up to a third of adult male chimp deaths result from territorial disputes.

● **Bonobos**, or pygmy chimpanzees, are found in the dense forests along the Congo River. They are darker than other chimps, with longer legs and smaller heads, and walk upright more often.

436

- **A bonobo named Kanzi,** a very successful participant in language experiments, also learned how to light a barbecue and cook his own sausages.

- **Chimps eat** a range of plants as medicines, to combat problems such as stomach aches and parasitic worms.

◀ *Grooming is a very important activity amongst chimps. It helps to create strong bonds between individuals, and to establish the group's pecking order.*

...FASCINATING FACT...
Chimpanzees reach puberty at about
10 years, give birth every 4 or 5 years, and
may live into their 50s.

Gibbons

- **The gibbons of Southeast Asia** are the smallest and most agile of the apes. They pair for life, and each couple has its own song of whoops and wails.

- **Swinging by their long arms**, gibbons hurtle through the forest, flying up to 15 m between hand-holds.

- **Gibbons have the longest arms,** relative to body size, of all the primates. They often hang by just one arm.

- **No-one** has been able to keep up with gibbons to time how fast they swing arm over arm (brachiation).

- **Siamangs** are the largest gibbons, at up to 15 kg.

- **About 2 million years ago** there was only one gibbon species, but Ice Age changes in sea levels created forest islands, where separate species developed.

- **A gibbon sleeps** sitting up on a branch with its head between its bent knees, not in a nest like great apes.

- **Gibbons** are more closely related to orang-utans than to the chimps and gorillas of Africa.

- **Gibbons have extremely flexible** shoulder joints, and can rotate through 360° while hanging from one arm.

▲ *Lar gibbons often produce loud calls known as 'duets' in order to reinforce pair-bond relationship between male and female.*

. . . **FASCINATING FACT** . . .
In the black gibbon species, the male is all black, the female light cream with a black face.

439

Baboons

- **Baboons' feet** are more suited to walking than grabbing branches.

- **Some East African baboons** cooperate in hunting and killing small antelopes, but are unwilling to share the catch.

- **Male Hamadryas baboons** herd their females all the time to keep them from other males.

- **The olive baboons** of the East African highlands live in troops of up to 140 individuals.

- **When old male Hamadryas baboons** are defeated by younger males, they lose weight, and their distinctive grey mantle changes to the colour of the females' hair.

◀ *Olive baboons are group dwellers, but male young are driven off to join other troops when they reach maturity.*

▶ *The male mandrill has a bright blue and red face for attracting females.*

- **Chacma baboons**, which are found in the far south of Africa, often enter water to feed on water plants or shellfish.

- **For their first few weeks**, baby baboons hang upside down from their mother's chest, but by 4 or 5 months they are riding on her back, like jockeys.

- **The ancient Egyptians** sometimes trained Hamadryas baboons to harvest figs.

- **Baboons** in South Africa's Kruger National Park will risk electric fence shocks to steal food from tourists.

... FASCINATING FACT ...
Olive baboon males fighting over females will enlist the help of a third male.

441

Polar bears

◀ Apart from pregnant females, which spend the winter in dens where they give birth, polar bears are active all through the winter months, often travelling great distances in search of food.

● **The polar bear** is the only bear which is almost exclusively a meat-eater, other bears eat plants too.

● **While stalking a seal**, a polar bear will sometimes lie on its chest with its front legs trailing at its sides and its rump in the air, pushing itself forward with its rear legs.

● **Polar bears** can detect the scent of seal pups that are in dens buried 1 m deep in snow.

● **Lying in ambush** for a seal, a polar bear will sometimes cover its black nose with its paws to remain unseen against the snow and ice.

● **Polar bears** have a number of tiny protrusions and suction pads on the soles of their feet to give them a firm grip on the ice.

● **The most southerly place** that polar bears regularly visit is James Bay in Canada, which is on the same line of latitude as London.

● **Female polar bears** can put on as much as 400 kg in weight in the course of their summer feeding binge on seal cubs.

442

- **The polar bear** is a powerful swimmer, even though it uses only its front paws as paddles, letting its rear legs trail behind.

- **Beneath its thick white fur,** a polar bear's skin is black. Translucent (semi-transparent) hairs channel heat from the sun to the animal's skin, which absorbs the heat.

▼ *Outside the breeding season, polar bears are normally solitary animals.*

...FASCINATING FACT...
Female polar bears may go without eating
for up to 8 months – existing solely on
their body fat – while overwintering and
feeding their newly born young.

Grizzly bears

- **The great hump** behind a grizzly's head is solid muscle, enabling it to overturn 50-kg rocks with its front paws, or kill an elk with a single blow.

- **During its winter sleep** the grizzly loses about 1 kg of bodyweight each day. Some grizzlies emerge from their sleep 50% lighter.

- **Grizzlies** once ranged across the USA, with numbers as high as 50,000–100,000; but as their terrain has been taken over by humans, their numbers have fallen to 6000–8000.

- **Most grizzlies are dark brown** in colour, but regional colouring ranges from black to very pale yellow.

- **Despite their great size**, grizzlies are nimble enough to catch squirrels and mice, and can reach a speed of over 55 km/h when charging.

- **Native Americans** had great respect for the grizzly, and apologized before killing it, sometimes laying out ceremonial clothes for it to wear when it entered the spirit world.

◄ *Grizzly mothers give birth to their cubs in their dens in winter, and go on to look after them for anything up to a further 4–5 years. During these early years their mothers teach them to forage and hunt and protect them from predators.*

● **Grizzlies** are immensely strong. They have been known to bite through cast iron, bend rifle barrels, and open up cars like sardine cans in search of food.

Originating in China, the ancestors of the modern grizzly crossed land bridges from Asia to North America some 40,000 years ago.

● **Grizzlies** often enter their winter dens just ahead of a snowstorm, so that the snow covers up their fresh tracks and seals them in for their long winter sleep.

▼ *Alaskan grizzlies feed heavily on migrating salmon.*

> ...FASCINATING FACT...
> The huge Kodiak grizzly bear of the Alaskan coastal islands can reach a height of 3 m on its hind legs, and weigh up to 1 tonne.

Black bears

- **American black bears** vary in colour from black, through brown, cinnamon, honey and ice-grey, to white, according to regional races.

- **Beavers** are a favourite food of some black bears, because of their high fat content.

- **In autumn**, when they are feeding up for the winter sleep, black bears put on up to 1.5 kg per day.

- **Black bears** mate in the summer, but the fertilized egg does not begin to develop until the autumn, and the cubs are born in January or February.

▼ *Black bears occasionally raid people's beehives and orchards, as well as city dumps.*

► *Black bears are excellent climbers and in autumn will climb trees and gorge themselves on fruit, nuts and berries.*

● **'Nuisance' bears** that have learned to beg and scavenge garbage in US national parks have to be tranquillized and moved to new areas some distance away.

● **The most northerly Canadian black bears** have a varied diet ranging from caribou and seals to birds' eggs and tiny shrimp.

● **The sun bear** of Southeast Asia is the world's smallest bear, at 27–65 kg. It specializes in gathering honey and insects with its long tongue.

● **South America's only bear** is the spectacled bear, which builds feeding and sleeping platforms in the branches of fruit trees.

● **The black sloth bear of India** has a mobile snout and closable nostrils for dealing with ants.

...FASCINATING FACT...
Asiatic black bears are constipated when they awake from their winter hibernation, and in Russia they drink birch tree sap as a laxative.

Pandas

- **In the late 1900s**, many pandas starved to death because the fountain bamboo they ate came to the end of its 100-year growth cycle and died back.

- **Giant pandas** often give birth to twins, but in the wild one cub is always left to die.

- **Pandas** have an inefficient digestive system – up to 50% of the plant material they eat passes out of their body intact within 10 hours.

- **Although bamboo** forms the bulk of its diet, the giant panda also eats fish, small birds and rodents.

◀ *The giant panda eats sitting up, pushing bamboo canes into its mouth for 16 hours a day.*

- **In ancient China**, pandas were believed to have magical powers, and people wore panda masks to ward off evil spirits.

- **Reduced in number** by hunting and deforestation, there are probably fewer than 1000 giant pandas left in the wild, in forest reserves in southeast China.

- **The giant panda** has an unsuccessful zoo breeding record, with about 20 successes in the last 50 years.

- **Much livelier** than the giant panda, the red panda is a nimble climber. It uses its long tail for balance, and when threatened rears up and hisses.

- **Giant pandas** reach up to 150 kg in weight, but when new-born weigh only 100–150 g.

> **...FASCINATING FACT...**
> Giant and red pandas have an extra 'thumb'
> that enables them to grasp their food.

◄ *The panda's diet is almost 99% bamboo. Eating fresh shoots in spring, mature leaves in summer and stems in winter. Bamboo thickets also provide shelter for sleeping.*

449

Otters

◀ *Otters are naturally playful creatures and are most active at night.*

- **Otters** enjoy playing games, such as dropping pebbles into water and catching them on their heads!

- **The African clawless otter** can move its thumb across the other fingers to hold onto objects.

- **Clawless otters** gather tough-shelled freshwater mussels with their hands, and take them ashore to smash them on rocks.

- **When hunted by hounds**, otters have been known to drag their pursuers under water and drown them.

- **Otters** have special whiskers on their muzzles and elbows that are sensitive to water disturbances and help them to locate prey.

- **Giant otters** clear a series of 7 m wide areas around their territories before scent-marking them.

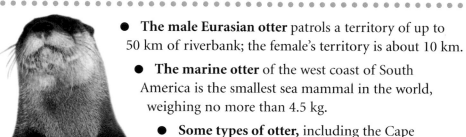

● **The male Eurasian otter** patrols a territory of up to 50 km of riverbank; the female's territory is about 10 km.

● **The marine otter** of the west coast of South America is the smallest sea mammal in the world, weighing no more than 4.5 kg.

● **Some types of otter,** including the Cape clawless otter and the Oriental short-clawed otter, catch their prey in their paws rather than in their mouths.

◄ *The otter's coat is made up of a dense layer of underfur, with an outer layer of long guard hairs.*

...**FASCINATING FACT**...
The giant otter of Brazil is the longest of the otter family, at almost 2 m long.

451

Tigers

- **At over 3 m long** and weighing up to 360 kg, the rare Siberian tiger is the largest living member of the cat family. Tigers originated in Siberia.

- **Tigers need a very large hunting area**, and males in northern India often patrol an area of 130 sq km or more.

- **After feeding**, tigers sometimes save the remains of a kill for a later meal, burying it under branches to hide it from scavengers or other tigers.

- **In 1945 there were only 50 Siberian tigers** left in the wild; now there are 300 to 400 surviving in reserves.

- **Aggressive tigers** flash the distinctive white spots on their ears as a warning.

- **In India and Bangaladesh**, in the Sunderbans mangrove swamps, tigers keep cool in the water and ambush pigs, deer and monkeys.

- **In the early 1900s** there were probably at least 50,000 tigers; now numbers have fallen to 6000 or less, half of them living in India.

▼ *To keep out the cold, the Siberian tiger has an outer coat of long, pale fur over a thick undercoat*

▲ *The tiger uses its long canine teeth to bite the throat or neck of its prey as it brings it to the ground. Its sharp-edged rear teeth cut through the meat by sliding against each other like scissors.*

● **A tiger's stripes** provide it with camouflage as it hunts in the tall grasses by day. But tigers also hunt at night – their night vision is at least 6 times more acute than a human's.

● **Tiger cubs** depend entirely on their mothers for food until they are about 18 months old, when they begin to make their own first kills.

...FASCINATING FACT...
Tigers eat a variety of foods, ranging from fish and turtles during times of flood to locusts during locust swarms.

Lions

- **Lions** (along with tigers) are the biggest members of the cat family, weighing up to 230 kg. Male lions may be 3 m long.

- **Lions used to live** through much of Europe and Asia. Now they are restricted to East and Southern Africa. Around 200 lions also live in the Gir forest in India.

- **Lions usually live** in grassland or scrubland, in families known as prides.

- **Lions are hunters** and they prey on antelopes, zebras and even young giraffes. The lionesses (females) do most of the hunting.

- **Male lions** are easily recognizable because of their huge manes. There is usually more than one adult male in each pride and they usually eat before the lionesses and cubs.

- **Lions usually catch** something to eat every four days or so. They can eat up to 40 kg in a single meal. Afterwards they rest for 24 hours.

The mane can be blonde, but gets darker with age

▲ *To other lions, a male lion's shaggy mane makes him look even bigger and stronger, and protects him when fighting. A male lion is born without a mane. It starts growing when he is about two or three and is fully grown by the time he is five*

- **The lions in a pride** usually spend about 20 hours a day sleeping and resting, and they walk no farther than 10 km or so a day.

- **Lionesses catch their prey** not by speed, but by stealth and strength. They stalk their prey quietly, creeping close to the ground. Then, when it is about 15 m away, the lionesses make a sudden dash and pull the victim down with their strong forepaws.

- **Lionesses usually hunt** at dusk or dawn, but they have very good night vision, and so will often hunt in the dark.

- **Male lion cubs** are driven out of the pride when they are two years old. When a young male is fully grown, he has to fight an older male to join another pride.

◀ *Female lions, or lionesses, are slightly smaller than males but usually do most of the hunting, often in pairs. There are five to ten lionesses in each pride, and each one mates with the male when she is about three years old.*

...FASCINATING FACT...
A male lion can drag along a 300 kg zebra
– it would take at least six men to do this.

Leopards and jaguars

- **A leopard can carry** a prey animal three times its own weight up a tree, out of reach of scavengers.

- **Black panthers** are leopards with black pigmentation. Any leopard litter may include a black cub.

- **The South American jaguar** is America's only big cat.

- **A frozen leopard carcase** was found on Mount Kilimanjaro, Africa, at an altitude of 5692 m.

- **The jaguar catches** not only fish, but also otters, turtles, alligators and frogs.

- **Snow leopards**, which inhabit the mountains of Central Asia, have never been known to roar.

- **The snow leopard** has paws cushioned with hair to act as snow shoes. In the Himalayas it seldom goes below 2000 m, and sometimes goes as high as 5500 m.

◀ *The snow leopard, also known as the ounce, is a solitary animal, active mainly in the early morning and late afternoon.*

- **Leopards** have survived successfully partly because they will eat almost anything, from crabs to baboons.

- **By far the best** climber of the big cats, the leopard sometimes drops straight out of a tree onto its victim.

- **The jaguar** was worshipped as a god by early South American cultures.

▲ *The leopard is by far the best climber of the big cats, and often sleeps in the branches, as well as storing food there.*

457

Cheetahs

▲ *The cheetah's tail helps with balance during high-speed sprints.*

- **Unlike most cats**, cheetahs can hardly retract their claws at all. The claws grip the ground as they run, like the spikes on a sprinter's shoes.

- **A cheetah** can accelerate from 0 to 72 km/h in 2 seconds, and can reach a top speed of 120 km/h.

- **A silver vase** (c.2300 BC), found in the Caucasus, shows a cheetah in a collar, which suggests people used cheetahs then as hunting animals.

- **The 16th-century Mogul emperor** Akbar kept 1000 cheetahs, which he used to hunt blackbuck.

- **Cheetahs** have the same body length as leopards, but stand a good 35 cm taller on their long legs.

- **In the Kalahari Desert,** cheetahs can survive for 10 days without water by eating wild melons.
- **Young male cheetahs** often hunt in small groups (coalitions), and are healthier than solitary males.
- **A cheetah** will chase a warthog that runs, but will usually leave one that stands its ground.
- **If a cheetah does not catch its prey** in the first 300 to 400 m of the chase, it gives up and allows its heart beat to return to normal.
- **Cheetahs** avoid lions, which will kill them.

▼ *Cheetahs often sit on rocks or termite mounds to get a better all-round view when resting.*

Hyenas

- **After making a successful kill**, the spotted ('laughing') hyena emits a blood-curdling, laugh-like cry.

- **The aardwolf** is a small, insect-eating member of the hyena family. One specimen was found to have over 40,000 termites in its stomach.

- **Often portrayed as a skulking scavenger**, the spotted hyena is in fact an aggressive hunter, and is also capable of driving lions from their kills at times.

- **The hyena's powerful jaws** can crush large bones, which its digestive system dissolves in a few hours.

- **Hyenas** may suckle their young for more than 1 year, compared to 2 months in the dog family.

▶ *The hyenas' victim is often brought down by a bite to the leg or back and then ripped to pieces by the pack while it is still alive.*

◀ *A spotted hyena can chase a wildebeest for 5 km at a speed of 60 km/h.*

- **All hyenas hide surplus food** for later – sometimes even underwater in the case of the spotted hyena.

- **Hyenas** are more closely related to mongooses than to members of the dog family.

- **In South Africa**, brown hyenas, or 'beach wolves', beachcomb for dead crabs, fish and sea mammals.

- **A female brown hyena** was once seen to take a springbok carcase from a leopard, and drive the leopard up a tree.

- **Brown and striped hyenas** erect their long manes to make them look larger when displaying aggression.

Dogs and wolves

- **The dog family** is a large group of four-legged, long-nosed, meat-eating animals. It includes dogs, wolves, foxes, jackals and coyotes.

- **All kinds of dog** have long canine teeth for piercing and tearing their prey. (Canine means 'dog').

- **When they are hunting**, dogs rely mainly on their good sense of smell and their acute hearing.

- **Wolves** are the largest wild dogs. They hunt together in packs to track down animals bigger than themselves, such as moose, deer, caribou and musk oxen.

- **A wolf pack** may have 7 to 20 wolves, led by the eldest male and female.

- **A wolf pack's territory** may be 1,000 square km or more. Wolves can travel vast distances when hunting.

- **Wolves once lived** all over Europe and North America, but are now rare in Europe and are found only in remote areas of North America and Asia.

- **Foxes** are cunning hunters which prowl at night, alone or in pairs. Typical prey includes rats, mice and rabbits.

- **The red fox** has adapted to the growth of towns and cities and may often be seen at night raiding surburban rubbish bins and dumps.

- **The jackals** of Africa look like small wolves, but they hunt alone for small prey and only meet in packs to grab the leftovers from the kill of a lion.

▼ *In Europe and North America the adaptable red fox has taken to living in towns and cities. It will raid dustbins for food.*

▶ *Most wolves are grey wolves – either the timber wolf of cold forest regions, or the tundra wolf of the Arctic plains.*

463

Camels

- **Camels** are the biggest desert mammals and they have adapted in many ways to help them live in extremely dry conditions.

- **Arabian camels** have one hump and live mainly in the Sahara desert and the Middle East. Bactrian camels live in central Asia and have two humps.

- **A camel's hump** is made of fat, but the camel's body can break the fat down into food and water when these are scarce.

- **Camels can go** many days or even months without water. But when water is available, they can drink over 200 litres in a day.

◄ *The Bactrian's thick fur helps to keep out the winter cold of the Mongolian high grasslands. The hump of the camel does not store water. It contains fat, which the camel can use as a food store when plants are scarce. However, the fat can be broken down by the camel's special chemistry to produce water too.*

▶ *The Arabian camel has been the 'ship of the desert', transporting people and baggage, for thousands of years.*

- **Camels sweat** very little, to save moisture. Instead, their body temperature rises by as much as 6°C when it is hot.

- **The camel's feet** have two joined toes to stop them sinking into soft sand (Arabian camels) or soft snow (Bactrians).

- **The camel's nostrils** can close up completely to block out sand.

- **Camels have** a double row of eyelashes to protect their eyes from sand and sun.

- **The camel's stomach** is huge, with three different sections. Like cows, camels are ruminants – this means they partially digest food, then bring it back into their mouths to chew the cud.

... FASCINATING FACT ...
Camels have by far the worst smelling breath in the entire animal kingdom.

Antelopes and deer

- **Antelopes and deer** are four-legged, hooved animals. Along with cows, hippos and pigs, they belong to the huge group called artiodactyls – animals with an even number of toes on each foot.

- **Antelopes and deer** chew the cud like cows – they chew food again, after first partially digesting it in a special stomach.

- **Most antelope species live** in herds in Africa. Many are very graceful, including the impala and Thompson's gazelle. Most are also fast runners.

- **The horns** on an antelope's head last its lifetime.

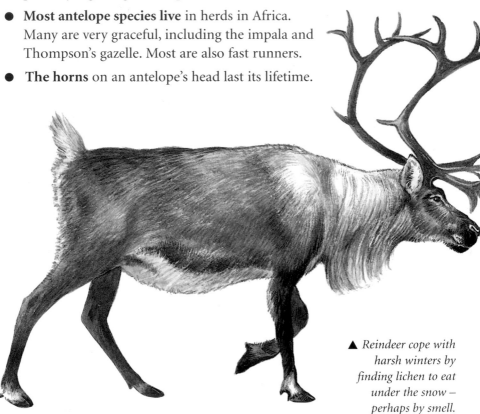

▲ *Reindeer cope with harsh winters by finding lichen to eat under the snow – perhaps by smell.*

- **Deer have branching antlers** of bone (not horn) on their heads, which drop off and grow back again each year.

- **Most deer species live** in woods and grasslands in mild regions such as northern Europe and North America.

- **The moose or elk** grows antlers that are more than 2 m wide.

- **Male deer** are called stags, young males are bucks, females are does and babies are fawns.

- **Usually only stags** have antlers. The only female deer to have them are caribou or reindeer, which are the same species of deer but with different names.

▲ *The dik-dik, named after the sound the female makes when alarmed, is a small antelope living in dry scrub in many parts of Africa.*

... **FASCINATING FACT** ...
Caribou can survive in the icy cold of Spitsbergen Island in the Arctic circle.

467

Giraffes

- **Giraffes** are the tallest mammals, growing to more than 5 m. Their height allows them to reach and eat the leaves, twigs and fruit at the tops of trees.

- **The legs of a giraffe** are almost 2 m long.

- **A giraffe's neck** may be over 2 m long, but it only has seven bones – the same number as humans.

- **Giraffes live** in Africa, south of the Sahara, in bush country.

- **The giraffe's long tongue** is so tough that it can wrap around the thorns of a thorn tree to grab twigs.

- **When drinking,** a giraffe has to spread its forelegs wide or kneel down to reach the water. This position makes it very vulnerable to attack by lions.

▲ *Giraffes are the world's tallest animals – but they are five times as light as elephants.*

468

- **When giraffes walk,** they move the two legs on one side of their body, then the two on the other side. Their long legs mean that when it comes to running they can gallop along faster than the speediest racehorse.

- **A giraffe's coat** is patched in brown on cream, and each giraffe has its own unique pattern. The reticulated giraffes of East Africa have triangular patches, but the South African Cape giraffes have blotchy markings.

- **During the breeding season,** rival male giraffes rub their necks together and swing them from side to side. This is called necking.

- **When it is first born,** a baby giraffe is very wobbly on its legs and so cannot stand up for at least its first half an hour.

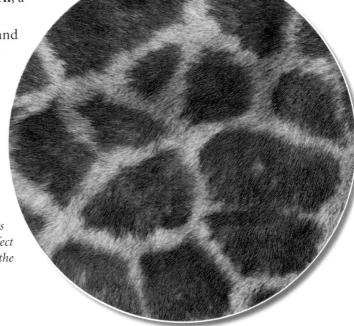

▶ *A close-up of a giraffe's coat. The criss-crossed lines produce a camouflaging effect in the shimmering light of the African grass plains.*

Zebras

◄ *The zebra has a small bristly mane which stands erect, running down the back of its neck. The female gives birth to a single foal, occasionally twins, after a gestation period of up to a year.*

- **A zebra's stripes** are as individual as human fingerprints – no two zebras are exactly the same.

- **The quagga** was a South African zebra that only had stripes on the front part of its body.

- **The home range** of Grevy's zebra, which roams desert and savannah terrains in northeastern Kenya, sometimes exceeds 10,000 sq km.

- **The zebra** can be a formidable foe, driving off lions, and even killing humans to defend its foals.

- **The plains zebra** lived north of the Sahara, in Algeria and Tunisia, up until 10,000 years ago, when it was replaced by the African wild ass.

- **Grevy's zebra** is a large species with narrowly spaced stripes and very large, mule-like ears.

- **A plains zebra herd's stallion** will challenge any potential rival coming within 50–100 m of his herd.

- **The quagga** once existed in very large herds, but became extinct through over-hunting in the 1870s.

- **Mountain zebras** follow ancient trails to mountain springs and pools in the dry season, and dig for subsurface water in stream beds.

- **Chapman's zebra** has shadow stripes – light, greyish stripes that alternate with the dark main stripes.

▼ *Zebras are sociable and like physical contact and mutual grooming.*

Horses

- **Horses** are big, four-legged, hooved animals, now bred mainly for human use.

- **Male horses** are called stallions, females are mares, babies are foals, and young males are colts.

- **The only wild horse** is the Przewalski of central Asia.

- **The mustangs** (wild horses) of the USA are descended from tame horses.

- **Tame horses** are of three main kinds – light horses for riding (such as Morgans and Arabs), heavy horses for pulling ploughs and wagons (such as Percherons and Suffolk Punches), and ponies (such as Shetlands).

▶ *All horses, wild and tame, may be descended from the prehistoric Merychippus (see evolution).*

472

▶ *A domestic horse. The rare Przewalski's horse of the Mongolian steppes is probably similar to the ancestor of today's many domestic horse breeds. Horses are built for grazing on grasses and for galloping at high speed for long distances.*

- **Most racehorses and hunting horses** are thoroughbred (pure) Arab horses descended from just three stallions that lived around 1700 – Darley Arabian, Godolphin Barb and Byerly Turk.

- **Lippizaners** are beautiful white horses, the best-known of which are trained to jump and dance at the Spanish Riding School in Vienna.

- **The shire horse** is probably the largest horse, bred after King Henry VIII had all horses under 1.5 m destroyed.

- **You can tell a horse's age** by counting its teeth – a 1-year-old has six pairs, a 5-year-old has twelve.

- **Quarter horses** are agile horses used by cowhands for cutting out (sorting cows from the herd). They got their name from running quarter-mile races.

Prehistoric elephants

- *Platybelodon*, which lived up to 14 million years ago, had huge, shovel-like lower teeth for scooping up and cutting water plants, and a short, broad trunk.

- **Remains of 91-cm tall elephants** were found on Malta.

- **The last woolly mammoths** were a dwarf species that died out less than 7000 years ago.

- **Two million years ago**, *Deinotherium* may have used its curled tusks for scraping bark from trees.

- **The elephant *Gomphotheres*** had four straight tusks, and lived in Europe, Africa and Pakistan.

- **Forest-dwelling *Anancus*** had straight tusks up to 4 m long, which it used for digging up roots.

- **At one time**, more commercial ivory came from frozen mammoths in Siberia than from modern elephants.

- **Some Stone Age Siberian people** built huts from the tusks and long bones of the mammoths they hunted.

  - **Mastodons** had smaller bodies and tusks than mammoths, and had a different diet.

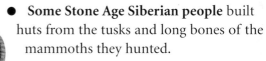

◀ *The* Anancus *was well equipped with long tusks for digging up roots.*

▶ Platybelodon *was a swamp elephant that devoured huge amounts of water plants, scooping them up with its lower jaw.*

···**FASCINATING FACT**···
One of the earliest-known elephant ancestors, *Moeritherium*, lived about 38 million years ago.

Elephants

- **There are three kinds** of elephant – the African forest elephant (Central and West Africa), the African savanna elephant (East and South Africa) and the Asian elephant, which lives in India and Southeast Asia.

- **African elephants** are the largest land animals, growing as tall as 4 m and weighing more than 6,000 kg.

- **Asian elephants** are not as large as African elephants, and have smaller ears and tusks. They also have one 'finger' on the tip of their trunk, while African elephants have two.

- **The scientific word** for an elephant's trunk is a proboscis. It is used like a hand to put food into the elephant's mouth, or to suck up water to squirt into its mouth or over its body to keep cool.

▶ *When the leader of the herd senses danger, she lifts her trunk and sniffs the air – then warns the others by using her trunk to give a loud blast called a trumpet. If an intruder comes too close, she will roll down her trunk, throw back her ears, lower her head and charge at up to 50 km/h.*

▼ *In dry areas, herds may travel vast distances to find food, with the bigger elephants protecting the little ones between their legs.*

● **Elephants** are very intelligent animals, with the biggest brain of all land animals. They also have very good memories.

● **Female elephants,** called cows, live with their calves and younger bulls (males) in herds of 20 to 30 animals. Older bulls usually live alone.

● **Once a year,** bull elephants go into a state called musth (said 'must'), when male hormones make them very wild and dangerous.

● **Elephants** usually live for about 70 years.

● **When an elephant dies,** its companions seem to mourn and cry.

...FASCINATING FACT...
Elephants use their trunks like snorkels
when crossing deep rivers.

Rhinos and hippos

▶ *The African black rhino is almost extinct in the wild. Between 2 to 3 thousand are left on nature reserves. Some gamekeepers have tried cutting off their horns to make them less of a target for poachers.*

- **Rhinoceroses** are big, tough-skinned animals of Africa and southern Asia.

- **African black and white** rhinos and the smaller Sumatran rhino have two horns in the middle of their heads. Indian and Javan rhinos have just one.

- **Powdered rhino horn** is believed by some to be a love potion, so thousands of rhinos have been slaughtered and most kinds are now an endangered.

- **Baluchitherium** lived 20 million years ago and was a type of the rhino. At over 5 m tall, it was much bigger than any elephant.

- **Hippopotamuses** are big, grey, pig-like creatures that live in Africa. They have the biggest mouth of any land animal.

- **When a hippo yawns** its mouth gapes wide enough to swallow a sheep whole, but it only eats grass.

- **Hippos spend their days** wallowing in rivers and swamps, and only come out at night to feed.

- **A hippo's eyes,** ears and nose are all on the top of its head, and so remain above the water when the rest of its body is completely submerged.

- **The word hippopotamus** comes from the Ancient Greek words for horse (hippo) and river (potamos).

▲ *The pygmy hippo is only about 90 cm tall but it is just as tubby as its big cousin and weighs up to 250 kg.*

. . . **FASCINATING FACT** . . .
The African white rhinoceros's horn
can grow to over 1.5 m long.

479

Farm animals

- **Cattle** are descended from a creature called the wild auroch, which was tamed 9,000 years ago. There are now over 200 breeds of domestic cow.

- **Female cows** reared for milk, butter and cheese production are called dairy cows. They give birth to a calf each year, and after it is born they provide milk twice a day.

- **A typical dairy cow** gives 16 litres of milk a day, or almost 6,000 litres a year.

- **Male cattle** are reared mainly for their meat, called beef. Beef breeds are usually heftier than dairy ones.

▼ *Female cattle are called cows and males are called bulls. The young are calves. Female calves are also called heifers*

▶ *Domesticated over 4,000 years ago and at first used for religious sacrifices, the chicken now is probably the most numerous bird in the world.*

- **Sheep were first domesticated** over 10,000 years ago. There are now more than 700 million sheep in the world, and around 800 different breeds.

- **Hairy sheep** are kept for their milk and meat (lamb and mutton). Woolly sheep are kept for their wool.

- **Hens** lay one or two eggs a day – about 350 a year.

- **To keep hens laying,** their eggs must be taken from them every day. Otherwise the hens will try to nest so they can hatch them.

- **Turkeys** may have got their name from the mistaken belief that they came from Turkey.

. . . FASCINATING FACT . . .
When a cow chews the cud, the cud is food regurgitated from one of its four stomachs.

Pets

- **There are over 500 breeds** of domestic dog. All are descended from the wolves first tamed 12,000 years ago to help humans hunt. Dogs have kept some wolf-like traits such as guarding territory and hiding bones.

- **Many pet dogs** were originally working dogs. Collies were sheepdogs. Terriers, setters, pointers and retrievers all get their names from their roles as hunting dogs.

- **The heaviest dog breed** is the St Bernard, which weighs over 90 kg. The lightest is the miniature Yorkshire terrier, under 500 g.

- **Cocker spaniels** were named because they were used by hunters to flush out woodcocks in the 14th century.

- **Chihuahuas** were named after a place in Mexico – the Aztecs thought them sacred.

- **The first domestic cats** were wild African bushcats tamed by the Ancient Egyptians to catch mice 3,500 years ago.

- **Like their wild ancestors**, domestic cats are deadly hunters – agile, with sharp eyes and claws – and often catch mice and birds.

▶ *The domestic cat, of which there are over 30 breeds, is a small member of the cat family measuring 75 cm with tail.*

- **Cats spend** a great deal of time sleeping, in short naps, but can be awake and ready for action in an instant.

- **Tabby cats** get their name from Attab in Baghdad (now in Iraq), where striped silk was made in the Middle Ages.

- **A female cat** is called a queen. A group of cats is called a clowder. A female dog is a bitch. A group of dogs is a kennel.

- **All pet golden hamsters** are descended from a single litter which was discovered in Syria in 1930.

▶ *Powerfully built and strong-jawed, pit bull terriers were first bred from bulldogs and terriers as fighting dogs, by miners in the 18th century.*

Ice age mammals

- **Woolly mammoths** adapted to ice age conditions by developing a thick coat of dark hair, and using their enormous curved tusks to sweep snow off the grasses they ate.

- **The woolly rhinoceros** was up to 5 m long, and roamed the tundras of northern Europe and Asia. Like the mammoth, it featured in the cave drawings of hunters.

- **Several ice age mammals** became giant-sized to help them combat the cold, including aurochs – the giant ancestors of modern cattle.

- **Many mammoths** are so well preserved in the Siberian permafrost that their flesh is still edible, and their last meals remain in their stomachs.

- **On the tundra** at the edge of the ice sheets, some mammals migrated south in winter; others, like the huge European cave bear, hibernated in their lairs.

- *Smilodon*, a large sabre-toothed cat, inhabited ice age North America, dying out along with many of the large animals it preyed on.

- **Many mammal species** died out between 12,000 and 10,000 years ago, as the last ice age ended. But some survived, including musk-oxen, horses, hyenas and saiga antelopes.

- **The ice age bison** were similar to modern bison, but had sweeping 1-m long horns on either side of their heads.

- **The giant short-faced bear**, which inhabited North America until the end of the last ice age, was twice the size of the Kodiak bear, had long legs and weighed up to 1 tonne.

▶ *The woolly mammoth had small ears to prevent heat-loss, and beneath its hairy skin was a thick layer of heat-preserving fat.*

◀ *Sabre-toothed* Smilodon *ranged from Canada to Argentina. It used its huge upper canine teeth to slice through the tough hides of large prey animals and bite out big chunks of flesh.*

...FASCINATING FACT...
Cave bears used the same caves for many generations. One cave in Austria contained the bones of up to 50,000 individual bears.

Strange mammals

- **The duck-billed platypus** and the echidnas live in Australia and are the only monotremes – mammals that lay eggs.

- **Duck-billed platypuses** are strange in other ways, too. They have a snout shaped like a duck's bill and webbed feet, which is why they are so happy in water.

- **Platypuses hatch** from eggs in a river-bank burrow.

- **Platypus babies** lick the milk that oozes out over the fur of their mother's belly.

- **Echidnas** are also known as spiny anteaters because they are covered in spines and eat ants.

- **After a female echidna** lays her single egg, she keeps it in a pouch on her body until it hatches.

- **The Tasmanian devil** is a small, fierce, Australian marsupial (see kangaroos and koalas). It hunts at night and eats almost any meat, dead or alive.

   - **Tasmanian devils** stuff their victims into their mouth with their front feet.

◀ *The duck-billed platypus is one of only three types of egg-laying mammals or monotremes. Its 'duck bill' can sense weak electrical signals in the water made by the moving muscles of its prey.*

▼ *The Tasmanian devil may be small, but can be very fierce.*

● **The sugar glider** is a tiny, mouse-like jungle creature which can glide for 45 m between trees.

● **The aardvark** is a strange South African mammal with a long snout and huge claws. It can shovel as fast as a mechanical digger to make a home or find ants.

Index

A

Asses,
    African wild 470
aster, sea 76
Asteraceae 88, 89
asters 43, 88, 66, 67
athlete's foot 153
Atlantic manta ray 298,
    299
Atlantic salmon 303
Atlantic,
    dolphins 316, 317
    seals 404
atropine 47
atrychnine 47
attar of roses 97
Auks, great 341, 351
auroch 480
aurochs 484
Australasia,
    warblers 358
Australia,
    birds of paradise 362
    blackbirds 357
    cassowaries 376
    gliders 430
    gliding possums 430
    kingfishers 367
    kookaburra 366
    marsupial mouse 224
    pebble mound mouse
        416
    storks 387
Australian koel 369
Australian pelican 342,
    388
Australian songlarks 358
Austria 485
avens 55, 56
avocets 231
azaleas 100

B

baboons **440–441**
    chacma 441
    chimpanzees 436
    Hamadryas 440, 441
    olive 440, 440, 441
    parental care 406
baby animals **246–247**
    giraffes 469
    marsupials 408, 409
    tapirs 222

bacteria 144, 141, 215
Bactrian camels 464, 464,
    465
badgers 450, 235
baiji 317
Baja California 317
bakeberries 195
baked appleberries 195
balance 216
bald cypress 75, 143
bald eagle 393, 393
    feathers 344
balder 46
baleen whales 315
ball python 331
balsa 136
balsam firs 59
Baluchitherium 479
bamboo 82, 83,
    104–105
bananas 161, 192, 194,
    195
banded coral shrimp 308
bandicoot 408
baneberries 59
bantam chickens 372
banyan trees 142, 143
baobab trees 71
barbel 230
barbets 370
barbs 37
barheaded geese 252
bark,
    cork oaks 124
    medicinal plants 207
    oaks 125
    spices 204
    timber 210
    trees 106, 107
    yew 119
barley 105, 172
    crops 166, 167
    farming 169
barn owls 390
barn swallow 354
barnacles 226, 228
barrier reefs 287
basil 202
basilisk lizard 325
basking shark 296
basking,
    butterflies 262

crocodilians 334
    lizards 324
    reptiles 318, 319
basswood 60
bat-eared foxes 420
bathyal zone 228
bats **426–427**, 427, 218
    fruit 400
    hibernation 250
    migration 252
    mother 401
    noctule 404, 405
    parental care 406
    rainforest 236
bay tree 119, 202, 203
beach plants 79
beach wolves 461
beadlet anemones 226
beaked whales 315
beaks 338, 371, 392
beans,
    annuals 40
    cocoa 198
    coffee 200
    crops 167
    fruit 32
    seeds 38
bearded vulture 395
bears 219
    black **446–447**, 446,
        447
    cave 484, 485
    cold climates 244, 245
    grizzly **444–445**, 444
    hibernation 251
    Kodiak 445, 485
    polar **442–443**, 442,
        443, 398, 402
    short-faced 485
    sloth 447
    spectacled 447
    sun 447
    woodland 235
beavers 410, **418–419**,
    418, 419
    black bears 446
    Eurasian 418
    European 419
    hibernation 251
    mating 224
    woodland 235
bee hummingbird 364

bee orchids 93
beech trees 60, 65, 122,
    113
beef cattle 481
beehive 266
bees **266–267**, 268, 278,
    237
    Arctic plants 55
    heathland plants 69
    pollination 30,31
    symbiosis 51
beetles 254, 255,
    260–261
    poisons 278
    woodland 235
beetroots 16, 17, 41
beets,
    sugar 187
    vegetables 184, 185
begonias 43
Beluga whales 405
belugas 315
bent wing ghost moths
    264
benthic animals 228
berries **194–195**
    coffee 200, 201
    fruit 32
    grapes 196
    parasites 53
    poison 46
    rowan 127
    spices 205
biennials **40–41**, 44
big bluestem 66
big cats 238, 243
    jaguar 456
    leopard 457
    lion 454
    parental care 407
bighorn sheep 400, 400
bilberries 195
bilharzia 257
bills 338
    hummingbirds 365
    parrot 360
    platypus 486
    skua 383
    swifts 364
    toucan 371
    vultures 395
birch trees 60, 107, 122,

buff-breasted kingfisher
367
bulbs **44–45**
  biennials 41
  garden 163
  herbs 202
  industry 161
  lilies 95
  tulips 90
bullhead 230
bulls 477, 480
bulrushes 75
bumble bees 266, 267
bunch grasses 71
burdock 88
burrowing anemones 226
burrs 37
bushbabies 423
bushcats 482
bushes 71
buteos 393
butterbur 88
buttercups 40, 87
butterflies 30, 31, 51, 55,
  254, **262–263**, 264
  birdwing 237
  blue morpho 237
  hibernation 250
  monarch 262, 252
  peacock 221, 223
  senses 217
  woodland 235
butterfly fish 308
butterwort 48
button mushrooms 150
buzzards 392, 393
byrsonima 71

C

cabbage 182
  savoy 182
  sea 182
cacao tree 198
cacti 21, **102–103**, 72
caimens 334
California,
  mice 416
  sea-lions 224
  seals 404
Californian condor 395
calls **346–347**
  Canada,

  migration 348
calves 477, 480, 480
  whales 405
calypso orchids 59
calyx 26
cambium,
  dicots 83, 85
  trees 106, 107
camels **464–465**, 239
camouflage 222,
  402–403
  cold climates 245
  defence 220
  flatfish 305
  giraffes 469
  gliders 430
  sloths 429
campion, sea 87, 79
Canada geese 381
Canada,
  black bears 447
  polar bears 442
  sabre-tooth cat 485
candle-snuff fungus 141
cane sugar 187
cane toad 337
canine teeth,
  sabre-tooth cat 485
  walrusses 313
canopy animals 236
canteloupes 193
Cape giraffes 469
caps 150
capsules 157
carapace 322, 323
carbon dioxide,
  leaves 23
  photosynthesis 14, 22,
  24, 25
cardinal beetles 278
caribou 244, 404, 405,
  467,
carnations 41
carnivore 420
carnivores 218, 219, 219,
  286
carnivorous plants **48–49**
carp 230
carpels 15, 26, 27
carrion 394, 218
carrots 17
  biennials 41

  vegetables 184, 185
cartilage 296, 298
cashew family 193
cassava 184, 185
cassowaries **376–377**
  dwarf 376
cassowary 378, 379
castor-oil 47
catawba 100
caterpillars 262, 263, 265,
  278, 279, 279
catfish 282
cats 217
cats,
  big 238, 243
  cheetah 458
  domestic 482, 482, 483
  jaguar 456, 457
  leopard 456, 457
  lion 454
  parental care 407
  sabre-toothed 485, 485
  senses 398
  small 407
cattails 75
cattle 480, 218
  ancestor 484
  Indian zebu 401
  sweat glands 401
Caucasus 458
cauliflory 62
cauliflower 182
cave bear 484, 485
cazabi bread 167
cedars 111, 211
celandines 87
cells,
  algae 144
  carnivorous plants 49
  ferns 159
  growing 83, 85
  leaves 22, 23
  mosses 156, 157
  photosynthesis 24
  phytoplankton 80
  spores 14, 35
  water 18
Central America,
  foxes 420
  migration 348
  mouse 417
Central Asia,

  leopard 456
centuary herb 206
cephalopods 290
cereals **172–173**
  annuals 40
  grain harvest 176
  maize 178
  monocots 82
  rice 180
  wheat 175
cetaceans 314
chacma baboons 441
chaffinches 346, 346
chalkland 60
chameleons **328–329**
chamois 242
chanterelle mushroom
  148
chaparral 69
Chapman's zebra 471
char 230
cheese fungi 148
cheetahs 238, 239,
  458–459, 458, 459,
  398, 406
cheilinus 308
chelicerae 280
chelonians 322
chemicals 23, 25
chernozems 67
cherries 190
  flowers 114, 115
  fruit 33
  poison 46
Cherry Blossom Festival
  115
cherry salmon 302
chestnuts 60, 122, 113,
  143
  horse 112
  sweet 113
  water 167
chewing lice 276
chewing the cud 465,
  466, 481
chicaree 414
chickens 344, 375, 372,
  481
chicle 136
chiffchaffs 358, 359
chihuahuas 482
chimpanzees 433,

lion 454
sloth bear 447
zebu cattle 401
Indian bacco 40
Indian bean tree 112
Indian corn 178
Indian fig tree 142
Indian grass 66
Indian Ocean 359
Indian pythons 331
Indian rhinos 478
Indian rice 180
ink 290
insect-eaters,
    aardwolf 460
insectivores 218
insects 215, **254–255**
    ants 268
    bees 266
    beetles 260, 261
    butterflies 262
    cold climates 244
    communication 248
    deserts 240
    dragonflies 272
    flies 270
    freshwater 231
    Grasshoppers and
    crickets 274
    Moths 264
    poisonous **278–279**
    rainforest 236, 237
    wasps 266
    wingless 276
    woodland 234
intelligence 290, 477
irises 43, 44
iroko 62
ivory 474
ivy, poison 46, 47

J

jacamars 370
jack o' lantern
    mushroom 148
jack pines 59
jackals 462
jaguars **456–457**
James Bay, Canada 442
Japanese cherry 114
Japanese maple 84, 129
jarrah eucalyptus 135

Javan rhinos 478
jaws 261, 281, 322, 334
jaws,
    hyena 460
    prehistoric elephants
    475
jellyfish 215, 228,
    284–285
Jesus Christ lizard 325
jewel beetles 261
jumping 275, 277, 408
jumping cholla 103
June grass 66
jungle fowl 375
jungles 28

K

kakapo parrot 379
Kalahari Desert 458
kale 182
    sea 79
kangaroo grass 71
kangaroo mice 417
kangaroo rats 221, 240
kangaroos 486, 408–409,
    409
    parental care 407
    temperature control
    401
kapok 138
katydids 274
kea 361
kelp 81
    giant 80, 81
Kenya 470
kernels,
    cocoa 198
    maize 178, 179
    wheat 175
kestrels 392, 393
Kew Gardens 160, 161,
    163
keys, maple 128
killer whales 314, 315
king bird 237
king bird of paradise 363
king cobra 332
king of Saxony bird of
    paradise 362
king termites 268
King's Holly 143
kingfishers 231,

366–367, 366
    African pygmy 366
    buff-breasted 367
    common 366
    European 366
    giant 366
    paradise 367
    shovel-billed 366
kino eucalyptus 135
kit foxes 398
kiwi 378, 379
kiwis **376–377**, 377
    brown 376
knots 252
koala 134
koalas **408–409**, 408, 486
Kodiak bear 445, 485
koel, Australian 369
kohlrabi 182
kola nut 117
Komodo dragon 325
kookaburra, laughing
    366, 367
krill 315, 244
Kruger National Park 441

L

labellum 87, 92
lady's slipper orchid 87
ladybirds 222, 278, 279
lakes,
    algae 144
    marshes 76
    plankton 146
    plants 74
lamellae 24
lammergeiers 243, 395
land plants, first 14
land snails and slugs 258
lantern flies 271
lar gibbons 439
larches 119
    boreal forests 59
    deciduous trees 122
    forestry 138
    mountains 65
    timber 211
larvae 263, 271
lateral buds 14
laughing hyena 460
laughing kookaburra
    366, 367

laurels 62, 69, 119
    herbs 202
    spices 204
lavender, sea 76
lawns 66
layers,
    leaves 22
    rainforest 63
leaf pores 19, 23
leaf-cutter ants 50, 51
leaf-cutter bees 266
leaf-eating beetle 261
leaflets 112
leatherback turtle 323
leaves 14, 15, **22–23**
    Arctic 55
    ash trees 127
    biennials 41
    bulbs 45
    carnivorous plants 48
    cereals 172
    conifers 108, 109
    cycads 131
    deciduous trees 122
    desert plants 72
    dicots 84
    eucalyptus 134, 135
    evergreens 118, 119
    ferns 158
    gingko 131
    grassland trees 71
    herbs 202, 203
    lilies 94
    magnolia 99
    maple trees 128
    monocots 82, 83
    oaks 125
    palm 132
    parasites 53
    perennials 42
    photosynthesis 24, 25
    pine trees 120
    rainforest 63
    reeds 76
    river plants 74, 75
    rushes 76
    seeds 38, 39, 116
    symbiosis 50, 51
    tea 201
    trees 106, **112–113**
    vegetables 182, 183
    veins 19

wheat 175
legs,
  dinosaurs 320
  dragonflies 272
  flea 277
  frogs 336
  giraffes 468, 469
  grasshoppers 274, 275
  insects 254
legumes 32
lek 179
lemmings 420
lemons 188, 189
lemurs **422–423**, 423
  flying 430
lenses 254, 272
leopard lilies 95
leopard seals 244, 244, 311
leopard, snow 242, 243
leopards 458, **456–457**
  clouded 433
  snow 456, 456
Lepidoptera 262, 264
lettuces 89, 182, 183
lianas 52, 63
lice **276–277**, 276
lichens **154–155**
light organs 307
light-sensitive nerve cells 398
lilies **94–95**
  water 74, 75
Liliopsidae 82, 94
lily family 183
lily-of-the-valley 95
limba 62
Lime's two-toed sloth 429
limes 112, 188, 189
limpets 226
linchens,
  Arctic 54
  boreal forests 59
  coastal plants 79
  deserts 72
  epiphytes 20
  mountains 64
  Stundra 56
lindens 60, 122
Lindsey Creek Tree 142
linen 167

lingonberries 59
lion, mountain 243
lionfish 308
lions 238, 246, **454–455**, 454, 455
  camouflage 403
Lippizaner horses 473
litters,
  leopard 456
  mating 224
little bluestem 66
live births 324, 331
liverworts 14, 20
lizards 318, **324–325**
  African fringe-toed 241
  armadillo 220
  chameleons 328
  desert 240
  hibernation 250
  iguanas 326
  rainforest 236
  senses 217
lobed leaves 113, 125, 128
lobelias 40
loblolly pine trees 120
lobsters 228, **294–295**, 294
locusts 240, 274
lodgepole pines 59
lodges 419
long-eared hedgehogs 412
long-horned grasshopper 274, 274
lories 360
lorikeets 360
lorises 217, **422–423**, 422
lotus 38
louse 276
louseworts 56
LSD 152
lubber grasshopper 275, 279
lugworms 256, 257, 226, 227
lumber 210, 211
lungs 314
lupins 37, 43, 44
  Arctic 55
lychees 192
lynxes,
  camouflage 403

lyre bird 353

M

macaques 251
macaws 360, 360
  hyacinth 342
mace 75, 204
macroplankton 147
Madagascar periwinkle 207
Madagascar,
  epyornis 341
Madonna lilies 95
maggots 271
magic 53, 204
magnesium fertilizers 171
magnetic senses 399, 404
magnificent riflebird 362
Magnol, Pierre 98
magnolia **98–99**
  broad-leaved 61
  dicots 85
  leaves 113
Magnolia denudata 99
Magnolia liliiflora 99
Magnoliopsida 84
mahogany 62, 136, 139
maidenhair tree 131
maize 172, **178–179**
  annuals 40
  parasites 53
malaria 271
Malayan rainforest 62
male parts,
  ferns 159
  flowers 26, 114
  mosses 156, 157
  pollination 30
malka 195
mallards 381
mallee 69
  blue 135
Mallee fowl 350
malt 172
Malta 474
mambas 332, 333
mammals **396–397**, **486–487**
  babies 246, 247
  defence 220
  desert 464

flying 426
freshwater 231
hibernation 250
hoofed 466, 472
ice age **484–485**
marine 228, 310, 314
marsupials 408
rodents 410
tallest 468
mammary glands 396
mammoths, woolly 474, 484, 485
manatees,
  migration 404
mandibles 260
mandrill 441, 224
man-eating lion 454
mangel-wurzels 185
mangoes 33, 62, 192, 193
mangroves 75, 136
manioc 167
manna 127
manta rays 298, 299, 299
manure 170
maple syrup 128
maple trees **128–129**
  black 128
  broad-leaved trees 60
  deciduous trees 122
  flowers 114
  Japanese 84, 129
  leaves 112
  red 129
  seeds 37
  sugar 128, 129
maquis plants 69
marabou stork 387
mares 472
marine cobra 332
marine iguanas 326, 327
marine plants **80–81**
  plankton 146
marine snails and slugs 258
marine worms 256
marjoram 202
markets 164, 165
markings **222–223**
marlin 304
marmot, alpine 414
marsh warbler 359
marshes 56, 66, **76–77**

504

Acknowledgements

The publishers would like to thank the following artists who have contributed to this book:

Lisa Alderson, Martin Camm, Jim Channell, Kuo Kang Chen, Richard Draper, Wayne Ford, Chris Forsey, Mike Foster, Luigi Galante, Roger Goringe, Alan Hancocks, Alan Harris, Ron Haywood, Mike Hughes, Ian Jackson, Rob Jakeway, Emma Louise Jones, Roger Kent, Steve Kirk, Stuart Lafford, Mick Loates, Kevin Maddison, Alan Male, Janos Marffy, Terry Riley, Steve Roberts, Eric Robson, Peter Sarson, Mike Saunders, Sarah Smith, Rudi Vizi

The publishers would like to thank the following sources for the use of their photographs:
CORBIS: Page 56 Raymond Gehman; 58 Wolfgang Kaehler

All other pictures Corel; Digital STOCK; ILN; PhotoDisc